Systems of
Representation
in Children

WILEY SERIES IN
DEVELOPMENTAL PSYCHOLOGY
AND ITS APPLICATIONS

Series Editor
Professor Kevin Connolly

Morality in the Making: Thought, Action and the Social Context
Edited by Helen Weinreich-Haste and Don Locke

Children's Single-Word Speech
Edited by Martyn Barrett

**The Psychology of Gifted Children:
Perspectives on Development and Education**
Edited by Joan Freeman

Teaching and Talking with Deaf Children
David Wood, Heather Wood, Amanda Griffiths and Ian Howarth

**Culture and the Development of Children's Action:
A Cultural-Historical Theory of Developmental Psychology**
Jaan Valsiner

Computers, Cognition and Development
Edited by Julie Rutkowska and Charles Crook

Psychological Bases for Early Education
Edited by A. D. Pellegrini

**The Child in the Physical Environment:
The Development of Spatial Knowledge and Cognition**
Christopher Spencer, Mark Blades and and Kim Morsley

Children Helping Children
*Edited by Hugh C. Foot, Michelle J. Morgan and
Rosalyn H. Shute*

Systems of Representation in Children: Development and Use
Edited by Chris Pratt and Alison F. Garton

Systems of Representation in Children

Development and Use

Edited by
CHRIS PRATT
Department of Psychology, The University of Western Australia

and

ALISON F. GARTON
Health Department of Western Australia

JOHN WILEY & SONS
Chichester · New York · Brisbane · Toronto · Singapore

Other Wiley Editorial Offices

John Wiley & Sons, Inc., 605 Third Avenue,
New York, NY 10158-0012, USA

Jacaranda Wiley Ltd, G.P.O. Box 859, Brisbane,
Queensland 4001, Australia

John Wiley & Sons (Canada) Ltd, 22 Worcester Road,
Rexdale, Ontario M9W 1L1, Canada

John Wiley & Sons (SEA) Pte Ltd, 37 Jalan Pemimpin #05-04,
Block B, Union Industrial Building, Singapore 2057

Library of Congress Cataloging-in-Publication Data

Systems of representation in children : development and use /
  edited by Chris Pratt and Alison F. Garton.
    p. cm. — (Wiley series in developmental psychology and its
  applications)
    Includes bibliographical references and index.
    ISBN 0-471-92501-2 (ppc.)
    1. Mental representation in children. 2. Symbolism (Psychology)
  in children. I. Pratt, Chris. II. Garton, Alison, 1952– .
  III. Series.
  BF723.M43S96 1993
  155.4'132—dc20   92–25523
                                                             CIP

British Library Cataloguing in Publication Data

A catalogue record for this book is available from the British Library

ISBN 0-471-92501-2

Typeset in 10/12pt Palatino by Mathematical Composition Setters Ltd, Salisbury, Wiltshire
Printed and bound in Great Britain by Bookcraft (Bath) Ltd

Contents

List of Contributors

Ellen Bialystok
Department of Psychology, York University, 4700 Keele Street, Downsview, Ontario M3J 1PA, Canada

J. Gavin Bremner
Department of Psychology, Fylde College, University of Lancaster, Bailrigg, Lancaster, UK

Peter Bryant
Department of Experimental Psychology, University of Oxford, South Parks Road, Oxford OX1 3UD, UK

Nancy M. Burns
Department of Psychology, University of Illinois at Champaign, 603 East Daniel Street, Champaign, IL 61801, USA

Robin Campbell
Department of Psychology, University of Stirling, Stirling FK9 4LA, UK

Judy S. DeLoache
Department of Psychology, University of Illinois at Champaign, 603 East Daniel Street, Champaign, IL 61801, USA

Kevin Durkin
Department of Psychology, The University of Western Australia, Nedlands, Western Australia 6009

Gerard Duveen
Department of Education, 17 Trumpington Street, Cambridge University, Cambridge CB2 1QA, UK

Norman H. Freeman
University of Bristol, Department of Psychology, 8–10 Berkeley Square, Bristol BS8 1HH, UK

Alison F. Garton
Mental Health Policy Unit, Health Department of Western Australia, 189 Royal Street, East Perth, Western Australia 6004

Barbara Lloyd
School of Social Sciences, The University of Sussex, Falmer, Brighton BN1 9QN, UK

Antony S.R. Manstead
Department of Social Psychology, University of Amsterdam, Roetersstraat 15, 1018 WB Amsterdam, The Netherlands

David Olson
Centre for Applied Cognitive Sciences, The Ontario Institute for Studies in Education, 52 Bloor Street West, Toronto, Ontario M5S 1V6, Canada

Chris Pratt
Department of Psychology, The University of Western Australia, Nedlands, Western Australia 6009

Roger Wales
Department of Psychology, The University of Melbourne, Parkville, Victoria 3052, Australia

Series Preface

My dictionary offers three meanings for the word 'represent'. First, to represent is to bring clearly before the mind; second, it is to act the part of and third, it is to symbolize or to stand for. Each of these reflects a regular part of our everyday life. Once we get away from 'reflex' notions it is clear that internal representations are fundamental to even quite simple forms of behaviour. The ability to understand and use representations of objects, events, states, relationships, etc., to varying degrees and in varying ways is an essential feature of humankind. To be sure, it is not exclusive to our species—though it is certainly furthest developed in humans. At one level, psychological development can be seen as a growing capacity to represent objects, events, states, etc., internally and externally and to translate readily and reliably between the two. So, where did these capacities originate? how are they extended and acquired? and what part do they play in developmental processes? The complexity of the notion of representation and the great variety of ways in which the term is used is discussed by Chris Pratt and Alison Garton in their introductory chapter. Wisely, they do not attempt an exact, and consequently limiting, definition at this point. Rather, they let their contributors approach the issue of what representational systems are and how they develop from several different positions. There can be little doubt that the concept of representation is fundamental in psychology and essential to understanding behavioural and mental development. A particularly valuable feature of this book is its emphasis on the variety of phenomena and ideas associated with the notion of representation. It will stimulate a lot more discussion and research.

KEVIN CONNOLLY

Preface

The idea for this book stemmed from conversations and discussions held with many colleagues during a period when we were on study leave, based in Oxford. The conversations and discussions took place during weekly meetings held amongst members of the Department of Experimental Psychology and visitors to the Department in Oxford, as well as during visits made to other institutions in UK and North America. Although at one level the interests of those with whom we spoke differed greatly, there was one theme which arose repeatedly. This theme centred around *representation*. Researchers with interests in such seemingly diverse topics as language, reading, metalinguistics, emotions, theory of mind, problem solving and developing understandings of space all recognised the importance of the development of representational systems and the difficulties that arise in adequately describing and explaining the development of such systems.

Although the book has developed in scope since the idea was conceived, the central theme, representation, remains, as does the recognition of the importance of representation in development. Hence the book examines the development and use of representation in children. The contributors, many of whom were participants in the early discussions that led to the idea of producing this book, bring together expertise from a wide range of backgrounds and areas of interest.

As editors we took a decision not to impose any particular view on what constitutes representation or what mechanisms underlie its development. We have deliberately allowed all contributors to express their own views and to adopt their own interpretations of what constitutes representation. Nevertheless, although the chapters cover a diverse range of views about representation, certain general themes recur.

During development, there is a progressive mastery of systems of representation with the recognition that both internal and external mechanisms may contribute to growing levels of sophistication. Moreover, each system of representation develops according to a progression that culminates in the child's ability to reflect on that system, leading to greater understandings of the system and greater control over its use. There is also the recognition that systems do not develop in isolation from each other, they are interdependent, with many relying on language for their expression.

We would like to offer our sincere thanks to all contributors for the stimulating chapters they have provided. In particular we thank all those who met deadlines for the patience they have shown during the preparation of the book. We would like to thank Stephen Pratt for his general support and for helping with some of the more tedious tasks of detail involved in preparing a book. We also thank Wendy Hudlass, Lewis Derrick and Michael Coombs for their support and patience.

Finally, if this book stimulates further discussion and research, which focuses more specifically on the development of representational systems in children and on children's developing understanding of representations, then it will have served a valuable purpose. In particular, there is a need for research which addresses the mechanisms that stimulate development in children. The explanation of development, including the development of systems of representation, is one of the major challenges in the coming years that faces all researchers with an interest in children.

CHRIS PRATT
ALISON F. GARTON
Perth, Australia

1 Systems of Representation in Children

CHRIS PRATT
The University of Western Australia

ALISON F. GARTON
Health Department of Western Australia

Systems of representation are essential for intelligent behaviour and social interaction. Equally, mastery of these systems forms the very essence of development. Hence, any attempt to document and explain developmental processes must take account of the development of systems of representation. But what exactly are systems of representations, why are they important, and how do children develop mastery over them? These questions, which like so many others are much easier to ask than to answer, form the basis for this book. The chapters that follow address these questions, describing systems of representations and explaining changes that take place in the development and use of these systems of representation. Hence, rather than attempting to answer the questions in full in the first chapter, we intend instead only to draw attention to some of the more significant issues that arise when these questions are addressed.

For a general definition of representation, we draw on the recent writings of Perner (1991) who states that, 'The notion of *representation* ... should cover things as diverse as pictures, models, sentences, and mental states' (p. 16), and that, 'although these things (pictures, models, sentences, and mental states) are used in quite different ways, they all share one essential feature. They are not just objects in themselves but in their representational capacity they evoke something else' (p. 16). We have drawn on these extracts from Perner because we believe they set the scene for this book. The quotes illustrate the diversity of systems covered by the term 'representation' and, of course, to Perner's examples we would add the many other systems covered in the chapters that follow, including space, problems, number, emotions and social representations. The quotes also identify the common feature that brings systems of representations together as representations, namely *the power to evoke something else*. This is the crux of all systems of representation.

Systems of Representation in Children: Development and Use. Edited by C. Pratt and A.F. Garton
© 1993 John Wiley & Sons Ltd

Perner, along with many other authors (e.g. Dennett, 1987; Dretske, 1986, 1988; Leslie, 1987; Wellman, 1990), provides a much more detailed explication of what he takes representation to mean. Rather than enter any (philosophical) debate about the finer points of a definition of represen- tation, however, we will leave it to the individual authors who have contributed to this volume to develop and adopt their own more detailed interpretations of the term.

Nevertheless, there are some important distinctions that should be recognised in any treatise on representations. The first of these is the dis- tinction between external systems of representation such as pictures and spoken or written language, and internal systems, viz mental representa- tions (see, for example, Campbell & Olson, 1990). The existence of these two different kinds of system complicates research in this area, for mastery of external systems of representation clearly must involve developing internal representations of the external representations. We cannot think about pictures, if we cannot represent them mentally. Equally we would not be able to master language and use it for communication if we were unable to represent it mentally. Further intricacies arise because of the close parallels that seem to exist between external and internal representa- tions, that is between pictures and mental images, and between spoken or written language and the language of thought. The resulting temptation to treat these in similar ways can also lead to difficulties. Moreover, there is the additional complication that we must rely on representational systems, mainly language, in order to consider and describe systems of representa- tion. The area is therefore fraught with difficulties and one must proceed with extreme caution.

A second issue is that representation can refer to a system (such as language) or to the application of that system. This duality is basically a distinction between the development of a system for representing objects and events versus the deployment of the system to develop constructs across different domains. Representation can be regarded exclusively as a knowledge base, with the duality being determined by how this is structured and how changes in the knowledge base lead to development (Mandler, 1983a). The relationship, if any, between the development of the system (i.e. how it is structured) and its utilisation to construct ideas about people and things is not entirely clear—an issue explored later. The duality is explored by several authors in this book, where the changes in knowledge base and the uses to which it is put are discussed, for example, in relation to spatial development (Bremner, Chapter 5) and to success in problem solving (Garton, Chapter 13).

Our preference is to regard this duality as a potential strength of the concept. Notwithstanding the existing ambiguity of usage in the devel- opmental literature at present, both aspects ought to be part of its agreed definition. The most commonly agreed on components of representation are the procedural and the declarative aspects of knowledge (e.g. Mandler, 1983b, 1988). This distinction mirrors that made above and further compounds the ambiguity and misinterpretation in the literature. The former, the how of developmental change, is the knowledge component that drives development. The latter, the wherefore of knowledge, is the content of knowledge. Procedural knowledge, it has been argued, is the more abstract component, and can be characterised as knowledge compiled or networked at a level of abstraction that permits flexible and expert problem solving. It is implicit. Declarative knowledge, on the other hand, is accessible to conscious awareness, that is, potentially explicit. It also permits conceptual development (Mandler, 1988), itself dependent on a symbolic, or representational, system.

A third distinction in the literature on representations is that there exist differences in the extent to which representations are related to the objects or events that they represent. Perner (1991) refers to the relationship between an object and its representation as the representing relationship. There are various ways in which these representing relationships have been described by authors when distinguishing types or levels of representation (see, for example, Dretske, 1988; Piaget, 1951; Lloyd & Duveen, Chapter 9). In some systems of representation, including all of those that Dretske (1988) refers to as type one systems of representation, the representing relationships are completely arbitrary. The relationships are normally established in social contexts through shared meaning. Language provides the clearest example of such a system of representation where, by and large, the relationships between words and their referents are completely arbitrary. The arbitrary relationships that obtain between words and whatever they represent are a result of long-standing and well-established conventions. There is nothing about the word *dog*, either in its written or spoken form, that bears any resemblance to the animal. As a result of the arbitrariness, units of language have properties such as length that bear no relationship to the objects to which they refer. In contrast, in other systems of representation the representing relationship is not arbitrary. Models and photographs bear striking resemblances to their referents (see DeLoache & Burns, Chapter 6). Paintings, however, lie somewhere in between photographs and models, and language, varying greatly in the degree to which their contents resemble what is being depicted (see Freeman, Chapter 7).

Although previous authors have classified representations into types according to whether the representing relationship is, or is not, an arbitrary one established solely through convention, it is perhaps of more value to recognise that representations will vary along a dimension of arbitrariness. Some systems, such as language, will be at one end and others, including photographs (taken through lenses that do not distort reality in any major way), will be towards the other end. Certainly, in the course of development children must master systems that vary in the arbitrariness of their relationship to the objects or entities that they represent. This is taken up by Durkin in Chapter 8, concerning the development of number as a representational system.

A further important issue when considering the developing mastery of systems of representation is the status of the representational system for the child. Some systems, particularly spoken language, and mental representations develop without the child initially appreciating that the representations have an existence in their own right. Although there is some dispute about whether children develop an awareness of language as they learn language (see Garton & Pratt, 1989, for further discussion on this point), most researchers accept that the awareness develops after the initial mastery of the language. Even for adults, the structure and form of spoken language is generally transparent in comparison with the meaning it conveys. Similarly, thoughts and beliefs, like language, exist primarily for their content. Nevertheless, during development children gradually become able to focus attention on components of the system in their own right, realising that they have existences, though perhaps not very meaningful ones, in their own right (see Chapters 3 and 11).

In other cases, the representations (e.g. drawings and pictures) have a very obvious physical existence in their own right. Despite this, children appear to develop an understanding of these as serving the primary purpose of representing something else (DeLoache & Burns, Chapter 6) and they interpret them as representations conveying meanings or providing messages, for example about the hidden location of a doll.

Other systems are based on objects that have a primary function of their own, but are used to represent other objects or events. One example of this is when representing relationships are based on temporary, and frequently arbitrary, sets of correspondences. Dretske (1988), for example, describes the use of coins and pieces of popcorn to represent the players in a game, and a glass to represent the basket. (Note that in this case the correspondences may not be totally arbitrary with the glass being selected as the basket.) Similarly DeLoache & Burns (Chapter 6) draw on an extract from *Yes, Prime Minister* in which a saucer is used to represent the men's loo. In these cases the objects that form the basis of the representation have a primary existence and function of their own. Their use as symbols representing other objects, locations or whatever is clearly secondary. Despite precursors of this type of representation being found in the pretend play of very young children (Leslie, 1987; Perner, 1991), such representations may well pose significant problems for the children, who experience trouble mentally representing objects in more than one way. Indeed DeLoache & Burns argue that this is why children experience difficulties with scale models. In contrast to a possible adult conception of a model, as having the primary function of representing whatever it is modelling, children may regard it as having a different primary function (e.g. a collection of toy furniture).

Mastery of some systems will depend on other systems. As Vygotsky (1986) has pointed out, for children, the written form of the language is a second order system of representation, because they gain access to it through spoken language, a first order system of representation. Thus in the early stages of mastery of written language the written word *table* does not represent the object table in the child's mind. Instead, it represents the spoken word 'table' which in turn represents the object. Bryant (Chapter 12) describes in further detail the development of reading, taking account of how children learn correspondences between written and spoken language.

It is evident therefore that the developmental path leading to mastery of systems of representation is not a straightforward one. It could well be a treacherous journey for children, one with plenty of scope to make errors along the way. There is no one set of rules governing representing relationships, such as they will always be arbitrary. There is no guiding principle about what can be used to represent something else and what cannot, or if there is, then the principle would need to be that anything could be used to represent anything else if we so choose. In practice, however, although representations involving temporary correspondences may make use of anything to represent anything else, most correspondences are well-established and reflect longstanding conventions.

Finally, we wish briefly to address in this introductory chapter the sorts of processes which may be involved in development that could account for mastery of such a complex set of systems. Karmiloff-Smith (1990) claims that there are three ways in which knowledge is acquired. Presumably these three ways cover all systems of representation including knowledge about mental representations. The three ways are: 'to have the knowledge innately specified, that is via evolutionary processes, ... to add new representations on the basis of interactions with the external physical and socio-cultural environments ... (and) to exploit the knowledge already represented, that is to engage in a process of internal representational change' (p. 59). An adequate explanation of development must therefore take into account the innate component, the environmental, particularly social, influences on development, and internal processes.

Consequently, one of the challenges that lies ahead is to outline the contributions of each of these processes to the development and use of systems of representation in children. The innate component is important for both the direct and indirect contributions it may make to knowledge. It may make a direct contribution, for example in the area of language acquisition, by setting constraints on the grammatical rules that may be extrapolated from the meanings of language (see Wexler, 1982).

It is likely that there will also be indirect contributions to knowledge acquisition as a result of the infant being innately predisposed to engage in and maintain social interaction. Perhaps the most fundamental assumption of all is that humans are social beings who develop an understanding of mastery over systems of representation in social contexts (although see Olson & Campbell, Chapter 2). In contrast to many other species, human infants remain dependent on more competent others for their care for many years. This dependency relies on infants having innate predispositions which support early interaction and form the basis for growth and the acquisition of culturally transmitted knowledge. In turn, the somewhat lengthy dependency serves as the basis for development, involving mastery of systems of representation, as a social process. Hence the innate contribution is likely to make a direct contribution by constraining the way in which systems of representation may be structured as well as the indirect contribution of providing the mechanisms for the establishment and maintenance of social interaction. The social interactions that take place will then provide the infant with direct input, forming the most significant part of Karmiloff-Smith's second way in which knowledge can be acquired—through interactions with external physical and socio-cultural environments.

Systems of representation are structured. They are structured perhaps as a result of innate constraints on knowledge acquisition, and certainly within those constraints they are structured by those within the culture. But how does the developing child impose this structure on representations? This, we argue, is largely a result of the third of Karmiloff-Smith's ways of acquiring knowledge. It is structured by the child through continuous internal structuring and restructuring of knowledge. We propose that there are two processes, generalisation and specification, governing the way in which systems of representation are structured. These processes are applied to all knowledge acquisition and hence to the development of all systems of representation during development. The processes are complementary though opposing. Generalisation involves forming groupings based on abstractions. Specification involves making distinctions based on differences between members of one grouping and those of another. These processes operate at many different levels and the literature abounds with examples of infants and young children engaging in these processes during development.

For example, Wellman & Gelman (1992) argue that infants and young children acquire framework theories of core domains. The core domains they consider are naive physics, psychology and biology and the majority of the evidence they put forward in support of their claims is based on the ability of infants and young children to make generalisations, based on abstractions, about entities that fall within one domain, and draw distinctions between these and entities in other domains. Moreover, the generalisations and specifications are frequently not based on the more obvious physical attributes of the entities under consideration. Wellman & Gelman point out that even very young children draw a distinction between animate and inanimate and furthermore the groupings within these two categories are not based on a 'simple similarity metric' but involve much more sophisticated abstractions. To illustrate their point, they cite the study by Carey (1985) in which she found that children reported that a mechanical monkey is highly similar to a person. Nevertheless they were aware that it was unlikely to have properties associated with people such as eating and sleeping. Hence, although recognising the similarities between mechanical monkeys and people at one level, these children had already mastered the fundamental distinction between animate and inanimate.

Two further examples of specification and generalisation can be drawn from the literature on language acquisition, the first related more to the development of meaning, the other to the development of rules governing language forms. The phenomenon of over-extension in early language acquisition is well documented, and though researchers may continue to argue about why it occurs, there is no argument about the fact that it does occur. Clark (1973) points out that over-extensions result from generalisations based on characteristics such as size, shape and four-leggedness. These generalisations may initially lead to over-extensions such as calling a cat a dog because it has four legs. However, even at this stage the abstractions that are made also involve making distinctions between, for example, four-leggedness and two-leggedness, between cats and dogs, and people. Through the process of further specification, finer distinctions are also made and the over-extensions disappear.

The other example from the area of language acquisition has been clearly described by Karmiloff-Smith (1979, 1986). In her theory of phases of development involving redescription of knowledge, Karmiloff-Smith states that initially different forms, for example the past tense of verbs, will be learned as individual instances. However, once the child has acquired the different forms of the past tense, both regular (walked, pushed) and irregular (went, took), in phase one, there is a shift to phase two. This phase relies on generalisation and specification. The child groups the regular forms of the past tense, abstracting the general principle and generating the rule. In order to do this an abstraction must occur which identifies the past tense of verbs. Specification also occurs as the past tense is distinguished from present or other tenses. The abstraction is at a level whereby it initially covers all verbs, including the irregular ones. However, further specification, of a different type, leads to the child distinguishing these irregular forms (see Wales, Chapter 4). Hence, we argue that the processes of generalisation and specification are fundamental to mastery of all systems of representation. Examples of these processes coming into play are found in many of the chapters that follow including those by Lloyd & Duveen, and Manstead (Chapters 9 and 10).

There is still a great amount to be determined about the significance of systems of representation for development and the causal factors underlying the development of systems. There is also much to be learned about the relative contributions of innate, environmental and endogenous influences on development. These processes influence the manner in which knowledge is accrued and the concepts learned by children as they develop. The papers in this book reflect the current state of knowledge in this complex area; not only do they reflect, they stimulate and provoke debate and further research.

REFERENCES

Campbell, R. and Olson, D.R. (1990). Children's thinking. In R. Grieve and M. Hughes, (eds), *Understanding Children*. Oxford: Basil Blackwell.

Carey, S. (1985). *Conceptual Change in Childhood*. Cambridge, Massachusetts: MIT Press/Bradford Books.

Clark, E.V. (1973). Non-linguistic strategies and the acquisition of word meanings, *Cognition*, **2**, 161–182.

Dennett, D.C. (1987). *The Intentional Stance*. Cambridge, Massachusetts: MIT Press/Bradford Books.

Dretske, F. (1986). Misrepresentation. In R.J. Bogdan (ed.), *Belief: Form, Content and Function*. Oxford: Clarendon Press.

Dretske, F. (1988). *Explaining Behaviour: Reasons in a World of Causes*. Cambridge, Massachusetts: MIT Press/Bradford Books.

Garton, A.F. and Pratt, C. (1989). *Learning to be Literate: The Development of Spoken and Written Language*. Oxford: Basil Blackwell.

Karmiloff-Smith, A. (1979). Micro- and macro-development changes in language acquisition and other representational systems, *Cognitive Science*, **3**, 91–118.

Karmiloff-Smith, A. (1986). From meta-processes to meta-access: evidence from children's metalinguistic and repair data, *Cognition*, **23**, 95–147.

Karmiloff-Smith, A. (1990). Constraints on representational change: evidence from children's drawings, *Cognition*, **34**, 195–212.

Leslie, A.M. (1987). Pretense and representation: the origins of 'theory of mind', *Psychological Review*, **94**, 412–426.

Mandler, J. (1983a). Structural invariants in development. In L. Liben (ed.), *Piaget and the Foundations of Knowledge*. Hillsdale, New Jersey: Lawrence Erlbaum.

Mandler, J. (1983b). Representation. In P.H. Mussen (ed.), *Handbook of Child Psychology*, Vol. 3, J.H. Flavell and E. Markman (eds), *Cognitive Development*. New York: Wiley.

Mandler, J. (1988). How to build a baby: on the development of an accessible representational system, *Cognitive Development*, **3**, 113–136.

Perner, J. (1991). *Understanding the Representational Mind*. Cambridge, Massachusetts: MIT Press/Bradford Books.

Piaget, J. (1951). *Play, Dreams and Imitation in Childhood*. London: Routledge & Kegan Paul.

Vygotsky, L. (1986). *Thought and Language (new translation)*. Cambridge, Massachusetts: Harvard University Press.

Wellman, H.M. (1990). *The Child's Theory of Mind*. Cambridge, Massachusetts: MIT Press/Bradford Books.

Wellman, H.M. and Gelman, S.A. (1992). Cognitive development: foundational theories of core domains, *Annual Review of Psychology*, **43**, 337–375.

Wexler, K. (1982). A principle theory for language acquisition. In E. Wanner and L.R. Gleitman (eds), *Language Acquisition: The State of the Art*. Cambridge: Cambridge University Press.

2 Constructing Representations

DAVID OLSON
Ontario Institute for Studies in Education

ROBIN CAMPBELL
Stirling University

Any account of the origin of mental representation in children must first confront the perplexing question of just what a representation is. In ordinary discourse, the notion of a representation or symbol is used very broadly, indeed, loosely. We may think of the red dot that a pigeon pecks at as a symbol for food, we may think of children's picture books as containing representations of things even if there is no *thing* they are representations of, we may think of an abstract Moore sculpture as being a representation of a mother and child, and we may call a modernist painting of Churchill a representation of Churchill although it may be adamantly denied by his admirers that it resembles him at all.

A traditional view of a sign or a representation advanced from the time of Aristotle until Saussure (Savan, 1987–88) is that a sign is one element of the pair *signifier–signified*, or *form–meaning* or *designator–designation*. Peirce (Buchler, 1955, p. 99), to whom we owe our modern theory of signs, added to the classical view the idea that signs required a third factor, namely, an *interpretant*: 'A sign ... is something which stands *to somebody* for something in some respect or capacity' [our italics].

Later theorists, including Cassirer (1957), Langer (1942), Rozeboom (1972), Goodman (1978) and Huttenlocher & Higgins (1978) have emphasized one aspect of Peirce's theory, distinguishing signs (smoke is a sign of fire), from symbols, pointing out that symbols are not simply symptoms or indications of an object or event which permit anticipation of that object or event, but rather that they designate, stand for, or represent something other than themselves.

These various semiotic entities—natural signs, pictures, linguistic expressions, etc.—exhibit rather heterogeneous relationships with whatever they signify. Natural signs and some pictures (e.g. landscapes, portraits, photographs, maps) are *caused* by what they designate. Pictures may also *resemble* what they designate. On the other hand, aside from some marginal cases, linguistic expressions neither resemble nor are caused by what they designate. Rather, they are related to it by a *convention* to which users of the language subscribe.

Systems of Representation in Children: Development and Use. Edited by C. Pratt and A.F. Garton
© 1993 John Wiley & Sons Ltd

But what is the relation between the public symbols discussed above and the internal symbols or representations that provide the basis for our thinking about the world? Whereas acting involves some interaction with objects in the world, thinking involves acting not directly on the set of objects themselves but on representations of those objects. This is not, of course, to say that we think *about* these representations; rather, in thinking about, say, Australia, we do so by means of a representation of it. If we do think about some representation, then this is metacognitive activity, not simple cognition. What are mental representations and where do they come from? What relationship binds mental representations to what they represent? A memory may be *caused* by the event it records, an image (or so it was once thought) may *resemble* the thing imaged. But since we can think about the future as well as the past, since—as was demonstrated long ago—thought can proceed without imagery, and since there can scarcely be any *convention* binding mental representations to their designata, either the mind must *construct* its own representational apparatus or the representational powers of the mind must somehow be derived from the 'internalization' of public symbols.

These two possibilities, in fact, bound all current theories of representational development. On the one hand such theorists as Fodor (1986) and Leslie (1987) argue that it is just a particular property of minds that they represent the world in terms of some innate, representational language of thought. This innate, internal language provides the basis for the later acquisition of public symbol systems. On the other hand, others, best exemplified by Vygotsky (e.g. 1981, p. 162), have insisted on the priority of public, external representations in the ontogenesis of internal representations:

> It is necessary that everything internal in higher forms was external, that is, for others it was what it is now for oneself. Any higher mental function necessarily goes through an external stage in its development because it is initially a social function.

Linguistic functions which were initially socially oriented, as in conversation, come to be internalized as an autonomous instrument of thought. This view, we may note in passing, is adopted from Durkheim (1858–1917), who argued that, 'logical life has its first source in society' (Lukes, 1973, p. 441).

Piaget's (1962) account of thought stands in the middle ground. Representations are neither innately given nor are they internalized copies of public symbols. They are constructed by means of a series of internal reorganizations of schemata. By coordinating imitation (massive accommodation) with play (massive assimilation), the children construct their first representations. Thought, for Piaget, proceeds on the basis of *representations* which are the expressions of the symbolic function of which natural language is the most typical example.

The view we shall develop is that the appearance of thought mediated by external representations (public symbols) runs exactly parallel with the development of thought mediated by internal representations. This concurrence is not due to internalization, a concept of doubtful application, but rather is a direct consequence of the fact that the same cognitive structures are required for both. The critical feature in representing an object is not just that such a representation permits one to hold that object in mind, but rather, that holding it in mind permits the construction of representations. But that is to get ahead of our story.

These issues have their clearest theoretical expression in what is known as the *representational theory of mind* (RTM), the view that behavior must ultimately be explained in terms of intentional states including beliefs, desires and intentions. Just what beliefs *are* and how they are to be explained in a materialist ontology, an ontology which eschews the ghost in the machine, is the central question in RTM. It is important to review recent developments in this theory.

Fodor (1981, 1986) has argued that while beliefs are central to a cognitive theory, the content or meaning of a belief may be completely represented by the formal properties of the symbols that constitute it; it is these formal properties which play a causal role in the RTM. Furthermore, if it is these formal properties that play a causal role in cognition, minds share functional properties with computers, for that is clearly what computers operate on. Computers process forms ('symbols' as such writers call them) on the basis of their formal properties without regard to what those forms represent. As with computers, so, by hypothesis, with minds (Pylyshyn, 1984).

However, if meanings are identical with the forms that represent them— if syntax equals semantics—then meanings, the content of the representations, i.e. what the representations stand for or are about, are irrelevant to psychological explanation; such meanings are, as Dretske (1988) points out, predictively useful without being explanatorily relevant. Or, as Dennett (1984) puts it, intentionality is an instrumental stance to cognition, not a causal explanation.

Dretske (1988) and Garfield (1988) both attempt to assign an explanatory role to intentional states such as beliefs by trying to show how internal, mental states could in fact have a content, that is, represent the world. Dretske takes learning to be the decisive indicator. He argues that if an internal state (C) can come to control a movement (M) because of what that state indicates about a fact in the world (F), then C represents F. Dretske (1988, p. 100) writes:

> During this process [learning], C becomes a cause of M. It gets its hand on the steering wheel... *because* of what it indicates about F. C thereby becomes a representation of F. After learning of this sort, the bird pecks the target because it *thinks* (whether rightly or not) that the light is red.

The internal state represents the world.

In a simple creature such as a frog, an internal state may be triggered by a stimulus such as a fly or a dark shadow and that state may in turn cause the tongue-flicking response characteristic of a frog. However, in this case, Dretske argues, the internal state does not represent a fly because it cannot become progressively attuned to the properties of the world, to what distinguishes flies from fly-like shadows, and so that internal state does not represent or mean flies. The pigeon, on the other hand, which learns to adapt its movement to the internal 'representation' of a conditioned stimulus, the red light, has adjusted the internal state to represent or mean the red light and that representation in turn can cause the pigeon to peck the target for food.

Thus the virtue of Dretske's proposal is that it would explain how, by learning, internal states come to be about the world and at the same time cause behavior. It does this without hypostatizing a homunculus (the ghost) to interpret the representation as being about or standing for properties of the world.

But such representations fall some way short of what is required to account for human thinking. Such representations do not serve to represent an object *in its absence*, a primary requirement of any account of human thinking. Furthermore, they could not distinguish the recurrence of the same object from an occurrence of another object of the same kind. Nor could such a representation classify dissimilar objects as members of a kind (see Olson & Campbell, 1990, for discussion). What Dretske has provided is an explanation of what Piaget and others (Head, 1920) called a *schema* (plural *schemata*), a basic building block out of which higher order representations, such as beliefs, may be constructed. Such a schema does provide one critical constituent of a representation. Inasmuch as schemata are activated by events in the world, those schemata are *causally connected* to the world and in that sense are about the world. This is Dretske's central claim. Our purpose is to propose a route from such simple schemata to the more complex mental representations we think of as beliefs.

Representations, to summarize, are artifacts, devices or other means, whether external (public) or internal (mental), for maintaining a relation (an intentional connection) with an object or event *in its absence*. A representation, as we shall use the term, is not necessarily required for responding to an object when it is present. Schemata, as we use the term, are not representations. Representations, to repeat, are required for thinking about objects and events in their absence. Thinking requires that the thinking be about some *particular* thing. A representation is what allows our thinking to be about that object or event and no other. Hence, we say that to think about Madonna, say, we must 'hold her in mind' in her absence, our thought must be 'intentionally connected' to her, and must 'represent' her and no-one else.

The questions we address, then, are the following: What makes representation possible? Can representation develop from no representation? If so, how? We will distinguish three levels of these representational powers, levels that correspond, at least roughly, to observable differences in children's behavior. The first involves the representation of objects to allow the formation of propositions, the second involves the representation of propositions to form beliefs, the third involves the representation of beliefs to form subjective notions of the self. Let us examine these developments in detail.

REPRESENTING OBJECTS TO FORM PROPOSITIONS

Representation, whether externally or internally mediated, becomes possible when the child becomes able to maintain a schema in an active state independently of the stimulating conditions that normally call that schema into play. This resource allows the possibility of simultaneously keeping two schemata active and of forming a relation between them. The product is a proposition. Propositions are the structures required for higher forms of representation. In this section we shall consider how propositions are constructed.

Representations are constructed from schemata. A critical feature of schemata is that they involve only one mental element, regardless of a schema's internal complexity, the activating condition being the object of consciousness. One schema is activated at a time by the present stimulation. Schemata are activated by a present object or event; they are causally connected to that object or event but they do not represent that object or event. Their activity is tied to stimulating conditions; consequently there is no need for the activating condition to be held in mind. It is present, and therefore present to the mind.

The achievement that Piaget describes as object permanence—the ability to hold a particular object in mind when it is no longer present—marks not only the evolution of a means for maintaining an intentional connection with that object, but also, we suggest, it brings with it *the ability to hold that object in mind* in such a way that the mind is free to enter into a relation with a second activating condition (in this case, say, a location) by means of a second schema to form a proposition. A candidate proposition would be *X is under A*. Such propositions are, of course, true or false and could guide actions in the world. An unexpected consequence of representing an object (in its absence), then, is the formation of a proposition. Specifically, representing the absent object by means of the schema for that object allows the child to formulate the proposition, given suitable inducement, that that object is in some location.

Perhaps thinking about some object or event can always be cashed as thinking about that object having some particular property, e.g. that the chocolate is brown or in the cupboard or the like. In that case, we should be led to expect that if the child can search for a displaced object by holding an object in mind while it is transferred through a series of locations, the child could also form propositions relating that object to other properties as well. Two *caveats* are necessary here. It is possible that one can think *of* an object without attributing any property to it, just as (see below) it may be possible to think *of* some proposition without giving it a truth value or adopting any particular attitude to it. Secondly, even if it is argued that such uncommitted thoughts are impossible, it is plain that it is an empirical question whether any particular true property is likely to be attributed. No doubt properties differ in salience and such differences are subject to developmental change, too. So the claim of the present paragraph is certainly not that the 2-year-old is capable of forming any arbitrary proposition warranted by the present state of affairs. Rather it is just that once the capacity for object permanence is established, the possibility of forming other propositions immediately arises (for further discussion, see Olson & Campbell [1990] and, for the case of uncommitted propositional thinking, see Perner [1989]).

Comparable propositions appear to be required for some object sorting tasks in which objects are to be sorted by means of some property: *X is a Y* or *X has property Y*. What is to be held in mind is a schema for the object while a schema for the property in question *is red, is round, is a dog* is activated by the object. In the simplest cases, this is a sort of double perception; the object is first seen as a block and the schema for the block is activated. That schema can serve to hold the object in mind while the perceptual schema for a property of that block is activated. The two schemata, one from memory maintaining the intentional connection to the object, the other from perception identifying a property, are active concurrently. A proposition is formed to link the two schemata: *The block is red*. Such a thought would permit the sorting of objects such as blocks into groups, a form of activity that begins in the two- to four-year age period (Sugarman, 1983). The critical feature of this development is the availability of cognitive resources needed to hold in memory the first schema so that the second is free to be called into play by the stimulating object. These, of course, are internally mediated, or mental, representations.

The acquisition of externally mediated signs or symbols is merely a special case of the formation of such propositions. If representational powers are available to hold an object in mind, thereby freeing up the perceptual mechanism to be activated by a feature of that object to form the proposition *X is red*, the same representational powers can be used to hold the object in mind to form a relation to an arbitrary second stimulus such as a pretence object or a name.

A child's first use of symbols is perhaps the most conspicuous indication of these new representational powers. Pretend play is one of the first clear indications of the understanding of symbols. A child can now sit on a bench while thinking of a horse. This is not a simple achievement. The child may have to be shown how to rock back and forth and say 'Giddy-up' and the like to trigger the horse schema and he has to perceive the bench (by means of the bench schema) in order to form the proposition *The bench is a horse*. But the critical feature is the ability to keep the two schemata active at the same time in order to relate them propositionally.

In learning to call a horse, 'horse', the child has to attend to the sound form while keeping the horse schema active to form a proposition: Horse *is called* 'horse'. Such a proposition could establish either a common or proper name, depending on the nature of the activated horse schema. The critical requirement is again that of keeping both schemata active at once so as to form a relation between them.

However, these first symbols, names for things or pretence objects, are not true symbols in that the symbols do not yet represent any particular thing. At this point, the schema for the horse is what is causally connected to the horse (by means of stimulus conditions); the name is a mere predicate. In pretending that a bench is a horse, the child is not intentionally connected to some particular horse by means of the bench; the bench merely *stands in for a horse*, allowing play to proceed. In the next stage, the symbol may come to represent some particular object. But at this stage, although the bench 'represents' a horse *there is no horse of which it is a representation*. Neither bench nor name stands for any particular object. Representation of this latter sort will come later. A possible way to insist that such representations are true symbols is to say that the bench stands for *a possible particular horse*. But to take that option would be to espouse a theory of development in which very complex forms of representation were mastered before extremely simple ones—a most unlikely and unwarranted theory. To review, in learning properties such as X *is a horse* or X *is green*, or X *is in the cupboard* the child must attend to the property while holding in mind the object bearing the property to form a proposition linking them. And in learning to pretend that a bench is a horse, the horse schema must be kept active while interacting with the bench. These important developments all take place beginning about 18 months but continue to increase in complexity until approximately 4 years of age. At that point the development of representational powers takes another important turn: the child comes to represent propositions.

How is it possible for two schemata to be active at once? Our suggestion is that this achievement exploits the ability of a schema to maintain a connection with an object in its absence. One of the schemata is activated, stored in memory, leaving the perceptual mechanism free to call up a second schema in response to another object or a feature of the same object. Two schemata are thereby active at the same time, one driven by memory and the other driven by the stimulating conditions. The concepts relating them, including *is a*, *is called*, *stands for* and perhaps others are derived from these relations (Olson, 1989).

Some of the propositions formed at this period represent particulars and therefore refer to entities. When the child, holding a banana, says 'banana' he may be either learning a name: *This is called 'banana'*, or he may be expressing the identity: *This banana is a banana*. If the latter, the subject of the proposition would refer to and hence represent the physical object, while the predicate *is a banana* would be the natural kind or property currently picked out from the stimulating object by the perceptual schema. Even if both schemata, the particular banana and the predicated banana, are triggered by the same present stimulus, it is still necessary to have some representational means to keep the first schema active while the second is activated perceptually; both of those schemata must be active simultaneously in order to form a connection between their activating conditions. Thus, representation is involved in that one of the conditions must be held in mind while the second schema is triggered by the stimulating situation. The child has simply added a single recursive loop. This loop accounts for the added representational power.

The defining property of these earliest propositions is that they are built upon the representation of an object by means of a single schema, a schema by means of which an intentional connection is maintained with an object while some feature, name or identity is predicated of that object as in *The baby is dirty* (Nelson, 1976) or *all gone Daddy* (Gopnik & Meltzoff, 1985).

While the ability to represent an object permits the *formation* of a proposition, it does not permit the *representation* of propositions. That is the primary feature of the next stage.

REPRESENTING PROPOSITIONS TO FORM BELIEFS

A limiting feature of the sort of propositional representation described in the preceding section is that only one object has to be represented or held in mind; the other schema implicated is activated by a present stimulus. Indeed, in many of the cases, the object represented is present even if the other schema activated is that triggered by one of its properties. The representing schema serves to maintain the intentional relation with the object while the second schema is activated by the stimulus property. We have not proposed any explanation of why the property is selected for attention; we have argued only that the ability to represent the object by means of the first schema frees up the perceptual mechanism for any potentially relatable second perceptually activated schema. The cultural practices of adults are undoubtedly important for bringing both objects and properties into consciousness; the newly developed ability of the child is that of keeping the first schema active in memory (that is what we mean by representation) while the second schema is called into play by the stimulating situation. The product is a proposition—a thought about some state of affairs.

Pretend play and naming both provide indications of the acquisition of symbols. As we noted earlier, symbols cannot be simply associated with, that is indicate, an object, but must designate something. They must, therefore, involve a fixed functional relation between a symbol type, a sound or mark for example, and a significance or meaning. Such a relation, as Huttenlocher & Higgins (1978, p. 109) point out, allows for processes of decoding and encoding from symbol to meaning: 'A symbol brings to mind something other than itself'. They point out that it is not a simple matter to determine if children's behavior is symbolic. On their view neither play nor imitation necessarily involve symbolic activity but evidence for symbolic activity is strongest when behavior is based on a representation of absent objects or past or future events.

That is precisely what is involved in the next stage. The limiting property of the 'propositional stage' discussed above is that while the child can now construct propositions, some of which are symbolic—the bench stands in for a horse—the child cannot mentally represent the proposition's relation to a perceived state of affairs. To do this, a third mental element is required. This third element allows for the formation of beliefs, that is, for representing propositions as true or false of some state of affairs.

The first use of symbols, say the use of a bench to stand in for a horse, is not fully symbolic in that the symbols do not refer to something other than themselves. As mentioned, when a child pretends that a bench is a horse, *there is no horse of which it is a representation*. Consequently, pretend play is not fully symbolic. Similarly, children's first understanding of pictures may not be fully symbolic. The child may recognize a picture of a horse but again there might well be no horse of which it is a picture. Pictures and utterances as well as internally represented propositions become truly symbolic when the representation refers to some *thing*. Initially, when the child sees a picture of an apple it is seen just as an apple-picture. This expression is due to Goodman (1978). He distinguishes between two pictures which are of the same horse but whereas one depicts it as a black horse, the other picture shows it only as a faint speck of light in the distance. Though both pictures refer to the black horse—represent the black horse—only the first is a black-horse picture. And of course we can have a black-horse picture that represents no particular black horse. Our point is that some pictures are of things, that is, they refer while others do not represent any particular thing. Children's animal picture books are a case in point. They picture, say, a cat, but they are not pictures *of* a cat but merely *cat-pictures*. However, when the child understands an apple-picture as a picture of a particular apple or when the child sees a person-picture as a portrait of a particular individual, the child has mastered some of the equipment needed to form beliefs: if some property of the depicted cat or person activates a second schema, then the resulting thought will be a thought *about* that particular cat or person and may turn out to be true or false.

The distinction just drawn may be illustrated by means of the findings of DeLoache (1987; Chapter 6). DeLoache's task involved presenting children under 3 years of age with a miniature playroom, like a room in a doll's house, which was in fact a model of a real room. For everything in the miniature room there was a corresponding thing in the real room. Of course, 2- and 3-year-old children know how to play with a doll's house —they know that the baby sleeps in the crib, that people sit on the sofa, and so on. This is precisely what is involved in symbolic or pretend play. Children understand symbolic objects: they can form the proposition *This doll's house stands in for a house*. The significance of the DeLoache study is that it indicates that children at this stage remain unable to relate that proposition to an actual house. For them, the miniature room is a real-room-model rather than a model *of* some particular real room. DeLoache found that children under 3 years fail to see that the miniature room can be a model of the real room. They were unable to understand that the miniature room *represented* a real room and that whatever was true of the model should also be true of the real room. For the pre-3-year-old, while the miniature room represents or means a room, there is no room that the miniature room is a representation of. Three-year-olds, DeLoache found, grasp the correspondence.

Beliefs involve the representation of not just an object but a complete thought or proposition, leaving the perceptual mechanism free to activate another schema to which that proposition can be related. The proposition and this third schema are linked through the represented subject of the proposition. The proposition stored in memory can then be compared with the new proposition formed by the represented subject of the stored proposition and the presently active schema. If they should match, then the stored proposition is true; if not, it is false. This is the same kind of recursive process that occurred in earlier stages, but now it is a previous state of affairs that is represented by the stored proposition. It is entirely possible that public symbols, externally mediated representations, are particularly important at this stage, since they may lessen the burden on memory. It is, of course, a matter of much argument currently as to whether any animals other than humans over 4 years old can represent propositions (Premack & Woodruff, 1983; Byrne & Whiten, 1988).

There is now abundant evidence showing that in their fourth year children come to understand how propositional representations relate to the world. Wimmer & Perner (1983) were the first to show that younger children could not understand that someone's behavior could be based on a false belief. They constructed an elaborate but believable scenario in which a story character, Maxi, came to believe that his candy was in container A. Independently, they allowed the child subject, but not Maxi, to discover that the candy was really in B. The critical point was when the child subject was asked where Maxi would look for the candy. Unsurprisingly, 4- and 5-year-olds said he would look in A, and when asked why he'd look there they would reply, *'because that's where he thinks it is'*. But surprisingly, the 3-year-olds said that Maxi would look at B, and when asked why he'd look there they'd reply, *'because that's where it is'*. Younger children apparently cannot represent another's mental state, specifically a false belief.

Parents are familiar with the symptoms of this development. Children suddenly understand games like Hide and Seek which are based on an understanding of a mental state, namely that the seeker does not *know* where the hider is. Similarly they begin to predict surprise as a consequence of the overturning of prior beliefs rather than just as a consequence of the arrival of unearned and valued treats (MacLaren & Olson, in press). And they begin to tell and keep secrets, and to lie and hide their intentions (Peskin, 1992).

The achievement is widely held to depend on *metarepresentational* abilities. Just what is involved in this achievement is subject to some debate centering on the meaning of the term metarepresentation. Leslie (1987) argued that what the child must do is relate the metarepresentational schemata to causal schemata, both of which had been acquired earlier. Forguson & Gopnik (1988) offer a similar view, namely that the child comes to see that metarepresentations also hold in the real world. Wimmer, Hogrefe & Sodian (1988) suggest that what the child has to learn is how beliefs are caused by perception. These three views are similar in granting the presence of metarepresentations to 2-year-olds and argue that what 4-year-olds learn is how such metarepresentations are caused by the stimulating conditions.

Perner (1988, 1991) advances a somewhat different notion of metarepresentation. He argues that only when children are 4 years of age or older can they represent the 'representing relation', namely that there is a relation between the agent or holder and the representational state and the world, a view similar to that advanced in Johnson-Laird (1983). We (cf. Olson, 1989) put a similar point in a somewhat different way, arguing that what is critical is representing a proposition as true or false or as the object of a belief or doubt, etc. If Perner's notion of 'representing the representing relation' is equivalent to our view of representing a proposition as the object of some attitude, then our view is essentially equivalent to Perner's.

The difference between (1) representing an object by means of a schema and so *forming* a proposition by predicating some property of that object, and (2) *representing* a proposition as true or false is the difference between thinking about some state of affairs and thinking about some proposition in relation to that state of affairs. Beliefs arise when the child becomes capable of relating the propositions constructed at the preceding stage to perceived states of affairs. Put simply, we could say that beliefs are symbolic structures with a semantic value.

This is a subtle point and worth laboring. The proposition which is held in mind can be true or false only because the proposition refers to, or as we say, is intentionally connected to, the same object that is currently the object of perception. What earlier accounts of the origins of beliefs have failed to capture is the fact that the content of the belief must be about the object that is currently the object of perception. By introducing the notion of an intentional connection between the object and its representation in the formation of a proposition, we assume that the representation is *about* the very object that is the object of perception. Only then can the proposition be true or false of the perceived situation. A simple depiction of the transitions from schemata to propositions to beliefs is presented in Figure 2.1.

Since propositions have a complex internal structure composed of two related schemata and since beliefs involve the addition of a third schema also intentionally connected to a state of affairs, our tentative account of the fact that beliefs are constructed and ascribed only when children are about 4 years old rests on the premise that the additional representational resources required are added rather slowly in the period from 18 months to 4 years. Indeed, the empirical studies indicate that children come to ascribe beliefs to themselves and others only at about age 4. In relating propositions to perceived situations they construct beliefs. Thus, on this analysis, having beliefs, ascribing beliefs to oneself and ascribing beliefs to others are all manifestations of the same new competence, the ability to represent propositions.

As we noted earlier, since the critical property of this third stage is that children can represent propositions and relate them to perceived states of affairs, it becomes possible to specify that relation either in terms of beliefs (or other propositional attitudes) or in terms of truth/falsity. Indeed, so far as the subject's *own* beliefs are concerned, it may be that these are just propositions represented as true (or false when discarded). There are some indications that the ability to ascribe beliefs is closely associated with the ability to judge truth and falsity (Astington & Olson, 1992).

Younger children have no way of representing a proposition, of holding it in mind so that the perceptual mechanism is free to register a discrepant state of affairs; they can construct either a symbolic proposition or a true proposition but cannot represent one while they construct a second. New propositions simply replace existing ones.

Olson, Graham & Babu (1988), for example, reported that if 3-year-olds hear a protagonist announce his false beliefs the children continue to base their predictions as to the protagonist's action on the true state

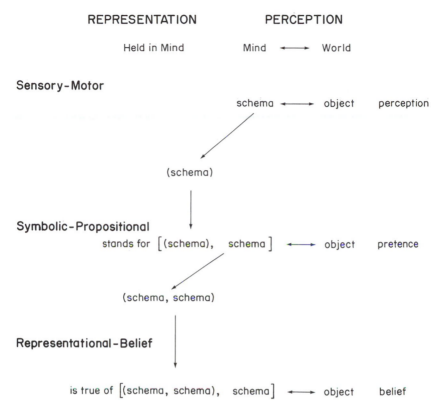

Figure 2.1   The transitions from schemata to propositions to beliefs

of affairs, disregarding that expression of belief (see also Olson, 1989). Most 4-year-olds have the means to represent this relation. Wellman & Bartsch (1988) and Wimmer & Hartl (1991) have reported a similar finding.

It seems that, contrary to the view discussed earlier, public signs or symbols do not make representation possible; the opposite is true. It is possible that a knowledge of such symbols would be useful for holding things in mind—for the management of memory. And certainly one's language provides a ready supply of symbols useful for constructing propositions. But there seems to be no necessary relation between knowing a language and keeping an object in mind or even keeping a proposition in mind.

Nonetheless, it is possible that public symbols are useful for holding a proposition in mind, the condition we have described as necessary for judging a proposition as true or false or for ascribing a belief to self or others. Language does seem to play an important role in reflecting on propositions. Rozeboom (1972) points out why language may play a critical role in forming and reforming beliefs. He writes:

> This... is the technical reality behind the often-voiced intuition that language frees our thinking from the here-and-now, or that signs are symptoms of events while symbols represent them. It is not that propositions with distant reference cannot be thought without words, but that when unverbalized they are likely to be evoked only by stimuli which also control the degree to which they are believed. Language is what makes *contemplative* thought a practical possibility (p. 46).

Cognitivists such as Searle, Fodor, Pylyshyn and Leslie err, we believe, when they take intentional states such as beliefs as the ground level description of mind, assuming that all cognition could be explained in terms of beliefs. People are not born believers, they become believers; beliefs constitute fully intentional, tertiary level representations of the world, a level made possible by an increase in the capacity of the mind to maintain successive schemata in an active state. In the first cycle a single schema maintains intentional connection to the world; in the second cycle, the persistence of this schema allows its activating object to be held in mind while a second schema makes a new intentional connection, permitting the formation of a proposition; finally, in a third cycle the proposition formed is itself held in mind while a third schema, together with the subject of the represented proposition, maintains connection with the present state of affairs, permitting evaluation of the represented proposition. The development leads from schema, to propositions, to beliefs.

We may note that the theory proposed is only incidentally a theory of mind; it is a theory of representations and how they are constructed and used. Hence, it is an analysis of utterances and pictures as much as it is an analysis of people and their actions. Their ascription to oneself and others in the form of beliefs in the attempt to explain talk and action is only one function of representations, though perhaps the most important one.

So what makes representation possible? How does a schema come to be maintained in an active state in the absence of the object? There is no shortage of suggestions. We could turn to Leslie's (1987) de-coupling hypothesis, to Piaget's (1962) theory of play, or to Vygotsky's (1962) theory of the internalization of public symbols. Or to information-processing theories such as Case's (1985) hypothesis that such development simply depends upon increasing attentional resources. Or, at a different level, to hypotheses about brain maturation (e.g. Moscovitch, 1984). These possibilities are, however, only dimly seen. A theory of *what* develops is in any event required before any of these possibilities need be considered seriously. It will be apparent from the many views on offer besides our own that this issue is far from being settled.

ACKNOWLEDGMENTS

The authors gratefully acknowledge the Ontario Ministry of Education for its Block Transfer Grant, and the SSHRCC and NSERC for their financial support.

REFERENCES

Astington, J.W. and Olson, D.R. (1992). Children's understanding of truth and falsity. Paper presented to the Canadian Psychological Association Convention, Quebec City.

Buchler, J. (ed.) (1955). *Philosophical Writings of Peirce*. New York: Dover.

Byrne, R.W. and Whiten, A. (1988). *Machiavellian Intelligence*. Oxford: Clarendon Press.

Case, R. (1985). *Intellectual Development: Birth to Adulthood*. Orlando, Florida: Academic Press.

Cassirer, E. (1957). *The Philosophy of Symbolic Forms, Vol. 3: The Phenomenology of Knowledge*. New Haven: Yale University Press.

DeLoache, J. (1987). Rapid change in the symbolic functioning of very young children, *Science*, **238**, 1556–1557.

Dennett, D. (1984). *Elbow Room: The Varieties of Free Will Worth Wanting*. Cambridge, Massachusetts: MIT Press/Bradford Books.

Dretske, F. (1988). *Explaining Behavior*. Cambridge, Massachusetts: MIT Press.

Fodor, J.A. (1981). *Representations*. Cambridge, Massachusetts: MIT Press.

Fodor, J.A. (1986). Fodor's guide to mental representation: the intelligent auntie's guide to vade-mecum, *Mind*, **94**, 76–100.

Forguson, L. and Gopnik, A. (1988). The ontogeny of common sense. In J.W. Astington, P.L. Harris and D.R. Olson (eds), *Developing Theories of Mind*. Cambridge: Cambridge University Press.

Garfield, J. (1988). *Belief in Psychology: A Study in the Ontology of Mind*. Cambridge, Massachusetts: MIT Press/Bradford Books.

Goodman, N. (1978). *Ways of Worldmaking*. Indianapolis, Indiana: Hackett.

Gopnik, A. and Meltzoff, A.N. (1985). From people to plans to objects, *Journal of Pragmatics*, **9**, 495–512.

Head, H. (1920). *Studies in Neurology*. London: H. Frowde.

Huttenlocher, J. and Higgins, E.T. (1978). Issues in the study of symbolic development. In W. Collins (ed.), *Minnesota Symposia on Child Psychology*. Hillsdale, New Jersey: Lawrence Erlbaum Associates.

Johnson-Laird, P. (1983). *Mental Models*. Cambridge, Massachusetts: Harvard University Press.

Langer, S. (1942). *Philosophy in a New Key*. Cambridge, Massachusetts: Harvard University Press.

Leslie, A.M. (1987). Pretense and representation: the origins of 'theory of mind', *Psychological Review*, **94**, 412–426.

Lukes, S. (1973). *Emile Durkheim: His Life and Works*. Markham, Ontario: Penguin Books.

MacLaren, R. and Olson, D.R. (in press). Trick or treat: children's understanding of surprise. *Cognitive Development*.

Moscovitch, M. (1984). *Infant Memory*. New York: Plenum Press.

Nelson, K. (1976). Some attributes of adjectives used by young children, *Cognition*, **4**, 13–20.

Olson, D.R. (1989). Making up your mind, *Canadian Psychology*, **30**, 617–627.

Olson, D.R. and Campbell, R. (1990). Things which think: on the ascription of mental states to young children and computers. Unpublished manuscript, University of Toronto.

Olson, D.R., Graham, N. and Babu, N. (1988). Young children do not take what one says as an indication of what one thinks. Mimeo, OISE, Toronto.

Perner, J. (1988). Developing semantics for theories of mind: from propositional attitudes to mental representation. In J.W. Astington, P.L. Harris and D.R. Olson (eds), *Developing Theories of Mind*. Cambridge: Cambridge University Press.

Perner, J. (1989). Is 'thinking' belief? (reply to Wellman & Bartsch, 1988). *Cognition*, **33**, 315–319.

Perner, J. (1991). *Understanding the Representational Mind*. Cambridge, Massachusetts: MIT Press.

Peskin, J. (1992). Ruse and representation, *Developmental Psychology*, **28**, 84–89.

Piaget, J. (1962). *Play, Dreams, and Imitation in Childhood* (C. Gattegno & F.M. Hodgson, trans.). New York: Norton.

Premack, D. and Woodruff, G. (1983). *The Mind of an Ape*. New York: Norton.

Pylyshyn, Z. (1984). *Computation and Cognition: Toward a Foundation for Cognitive Science*. Cambridge, Massachusetts: MIT Press.

Rozeboom, J.R. (1972). Problems in the psycho-philosophy of knowing. In J.R. Royce and W.W. Rozeboom (eds), *The Psychology of Knowing*. New York, Paris, London: Gordon & Breach.

Savan, D. (1987–88). *An introduction to C.S. Peirce's full system of semeiotic*. Monograph No. 1 of the Toronto Semiotic Circle, Victoria College in the University of Toronto.

Sugarman, S. (1983). *Children's Early Thought*. Cambridge, Massachusetts: Cambridge University Press.

Vygotsky, L. (1962). *Thought and Language*. Cambridge, Massachusetts: MIT Press.

Vygotsky, L. (1981). The genius of higher mental functions. In J. Wertsch (ed.), *The Concept of Activity in Soviet Psychology*. Armond, New York: M.E. Sharpe.

Wellman, H.M. and Bartsch, K. (1988). Young children's reasoning about beliefs, *Cognition*, **30**, 239–277.

Wimmer, H. and Hartl, M. (1991). Against the Cartesian view on mind: young children's difficulty with own false beliefs, *British Journal of Developmental Psychology*, **9**, 125–138.

Wimmer, H. and Perner, J. (1983). Beliefs about beliefs: representation and constraining function of wrong beliefs in young children's understanding of deception, *Cognition*, **13**, 103–128.

Wimmer, H., Hogrefe, J. and Sodian, B. (1988). A second stage in children's conception of mental life: understanding information accesses as origins of knowledge and belief. In J.W. Astington, P.L. Harris and D.R. Olson (eds), *Developing Theories of Mind*, Cambridge: Cambridge University Press.

3 The Representation of Knowledge and Beliefs

CHRIS PRATT
The University of Western Australia

The domain covered by this chapter is one that has received an enormous amount of attention in the past decade. It concerns the development of the ability to represent knowledge and related entities and how children come to understand these as representations. This area of enquiry is frequently referred to as 'theory of mind' and the developing understanding of the nature of knowledge and associated concepts as the 'development of theory of mind'. During the past decade there have been numerous publications covering the many facets of the topic, including recent edited volumes by Astington, Harris & Olson (1988), Frye & Moore (1991) and Whiten (1991), as well as monographs by Perner (1991) and Wellman (1990). Indeed the proliferation of research on the topic has resulted in Moses & Chandler (1992) producing a *Traveler's Guide to Children's Theories of Mind*.

Rather than attempting to cover all aspects of theory of mind in this chapter, I will focus primarily on the processes involved in the understanding of what knowledge is and how it is obtained. I will consider both children's developing ability to represent knowledge explicitly, so that it may be reflected upon, and their understanding of knowledge and related entities as representations. I begin the chapter by examining the processes involved in the acquisition of knowledge, for without knowledge acquisition there would be nothing on which to reflect. I will then consider the development of the ability to reflect both on knowledge states and on the processes involved in acquiring knowledge, involving a shift to explicit awareness of knowledge. Finally I will examine the understanding of knowledge as representations.

I take as a basic assumption that human infants are social beings who are predisposed to acquire knowledge in social contexts. From their earliest interactions they act in ways that lead to the acquisition of knowledge, even though it may be some considerable time before they develop an appreciation of the processes involved in knowledge acquisition or an appreciation of themselves and others as acquirers and possessors of knowledge.

Systems of Representation in Children: Development and Use. Edited by C. Pratt and A.F. Garton
© 1993 John Wiley & Sons Ltd

DEVELOPING UNDERSTANDING OF KNOWLEDGE AND THE PROCESSES THROUGH WHICH KNOWLEDGE IS ACQUIRED

There would be little disagreement with the claim that from early infancy individuals engage in many activities that result in the acquisition of knowledge. However, it is unlikely that, during the early period of development, these activities are *deliberately* engaged in for the purpose of *deliberately* acquiring knowledge. (For excellent discussions of many of the issues in the early phases of development, the reader is referred to Bretherton, 1991, and Perner, 1991.)

Much of the research into the activities and processes that may underlie knowledge acquisition in early infancy has been concerned either broadly with the infant's predisposition to engage in social interaction or more specifically with the infant's ability to establish and maintain joint visual attention (Garton, 1992). The processes that have been investigated in this research are of great importance because they not only provide the basis for the development of knowledge about persons and objects, they also provide the basis for the developing understanding of persons as possessors of knowledge, desires, intentions and beliefs.

Trevarthen (e.g. Trevarthen, 1980, 1983, Trevarthen & Hubley, 1978), who has carried out intensive studies of early social interaction, emphasises the importance of intersubjectivity, stating, 'I consider it to be of great importance that an intricate mechanism for interpersonal understanding develops precociously, well in advance of the cognitive machinery which will synthesize "ideas" for perceiving, identifying and using physical things' (Trevarthen, 1980, p. 325). He argues that the very young infant engages in social interactions with significant others and that consideration of these interactions leads to the conclusion that the infant is born with 'readiness to know another human' (p. 318). During the course of the first year, this primary interpersonal understanding, or primary intersubjectivity, allows the infant to engage in and understand, at some level, social processes with other humans. However, it is primary in the sense that the abilities the infant brings to the interaction are centred on the interaction *per se*.

Towards the end of the first year there is a shift to another level of intersubjectivity, secondary intersubjectivity. According to Trevarthen, there is a qualitative change in the interactions of infants with others.

> For the first time the infant appears to accept the mother as a teacher of new motives to use objects. Instead of accepting her as an amplifier, extender and facilitator of intended actions ... the baby actively invites her by look, smile and gesture, even by presentation of the object, to take initiative in a joint interaction with some common topic.
>
> (Trevarthen, 1980, p. 330).

As Bretherton (1991) points out, there is a shift from interactions where the topic is the interaction itself to interactions in which both partners are intentionally exchanging messages about a common topic. This common topic will no longer be the interaction but a topic which is the joint focus of attention during the interaction. Hence, according to Trevarthen, during the first year the predisposition of infants to engage in social interaction will lead to a greater understanding and knowledge of others and the contribution others make as interactive partners. It will also lead to forming the basis for the acquisition of knowledge about topics which become the joint focus of attention during interactions.

But how do topics beyond the interaction become the joint focus of attention? Research conducted by Butterworth and his colleagues (Butterworth & Cochran, 1980; Butterworth & Grover, 1988; Butterworth & Jarrett, 1991) has documented in great detail one way in which this may occur. They have studied the mechanisms through which objects and events may become topics that are the joint focus of attention for infants and their interactive partners. Following early work by Scaife & Bruner (1975) on the infant's ability to engage in joint visual attention, Butterworth and colleagues have carried out detailed studies of the way that joint visual attention is established. From at least 6 months of age, infants appear able to follow the head and eye movements of another person in order to locate the object of that person's visual attention. However, as Butterworth & Jarrett have pointed out, establishing joint attention at this early age relies on there being an object within the infant's field of vision. Careful experimentation by Butterworth and his colleagues has shown that joint attention will not be established if there is not a salient, attention-capturing object upon which the infant can fixate. Furthermore, if the mother looks to one side and there is more than one object to that side, the 6-month-old infant cannot reliably determine which object is being fixated and may look towards another object. By 12 months of age the infant is able to determine more precisely which object the mother is looking at, although establishing joint attention still relies on the object being in the infant's visual field. Between 12 months and 18 months, the infant becomes able to follow the mother's direction of gaze to locate objects which are outside the immediate field of vision.

Butterworth & Jarrett (1991, p. 70) argue that the development of the ability to locate objects beyond the immediate field of vision relies on the infant developing '... a representation of space as a *container* of infant, adult and potentially shared objects'. Perhaps of more interest in the context of knowledge acquisition is that the development of the ability to locate an object which another person is looking at, but which is beyond the immediate field of the infant's vision, suggests that the infant has also learned something about other people. The ability to locate such objects may equally rely on a developing understanding that people fixate on something. Normally, unless one is the perpetrator of some spoof, individuals fixate on objects or events of interest. Hence, even if there is nothing within the immediate field of vision, the infant appreciates that it is likely there is something, somewhere, that can be seen. Consequently, it may be necessary to search more persistently in order to locate the object. Certainly, if there was no expectation that there is an object, there would be no need to persist in the search. The infant has learned both that persons look at objects and that objects are looked at by persons.

In all the cases where joint visual attention is established, it is likely that seeing will lead to knowing, in at least some sense of the term *knowing*. It may be that the act of jointly attending simply leads to knowing of the existence of an object in the room. It may be that it leads to further discoveries about the object because the object becomes the focus of ongoing attention. If the topic is a dog, it may lead to knowing that the dog is a member of the class of self-propelled objects (Premack, 1991), and if it is a ball, then the infant may learn more about non self-propelled objects, particularly if the ball is picked up and manipulated by one of the participants in the interaction.

The importance of joint attention in the process of knowledge acquisition and the sophisticated level of understanding of infants is clearly illustrated in recent research by Baldwin (1991, in press). Baldwin (1991) examined the extent to which infants, aged 16–19 months, learned the labels of objects in two conditions. In one of the conditions, *follow-in labelling*, the experimenter, who was the infant's social partner in the study, looked at and named the toy ('It's a *toma*') that was the focus of the infant's attention. In the other condition, *discrepant labelling*, instead of naming the toy that was currently the focus of the infant's attention, the experimenter looked at and named another toy. If infants in the study assumed that there would be joint attention to the toy to which they were attending, without monitoring and checking to see whether the speaker was attending to the same toy, then both conditions would lead to infants learning that the label referred to the toy to which they were attending. Baldwin's findings show that this was not the case and that by 16–19 months infants check the *speaker's* non-verbal cues (focus of visual attention) in order to establish the referent to which the label applies. That is, they act as if they have some appreciation that the object to which they are attending may not be the focus of joint attention.

In a follow-up study, Baldwin (in press) has investigated in more detail the development of gaze checking in infants aged 14–19 months. Using the same experimental procedure, she found that infants of all ages checked the speaker's face when an object was labelled. However, it was not until 18 months that they seemed to be able to use this information systematically to determine which object was being named. It would appear that, for some reason, infants below this age have learned to check the direction of gaze but have not learned the full significance of it. Perhaps the very act of labelling by the speaker triggers gaze checking and this forms the basis for subsequent learning about its importance.

Hence, Baldwin's research illustrates an additional point beyond the importance of joint attention for knowledge acquisition. With the documented shift from primary intersubjectivity to secondary inter-subjectivity, which involves attending to topics other than the interaction, there is a risk that the attention of researchers will be focused on the processes of acquiring knowledge about objects and events in social contexts, while overlooking the fact that infants and young children will continue to acquire much knowledge about the participants in the interaction. It seems that the infants in Baldwin's study, and presumably all infants at similar stages of development, have learned that active participants in interactions will not always focus attention on the same objects. That is, these infants have acquired knowledge about the other participants, and by 18 months they make full use of this knowledge.

Furthermore, it is likely that from the process of establishing joint atten-tion, and most probably because this process is not always successful, infants will develop an awareness of the links between processes involved in acquiring knowledge, in this instance seeing, and knowledge itself. The work of Baldwin illustrates that infants take account of joint attention. There will be times, however, when infants actively seek to attend to objects, but cannot. For example, when an adult is preparing a meal on the counter-top an infant or young child may wish to attend to these activities, but will be unable to do so, because it is not possible to see from a viewing point much closer to the floor than that of the adult's. To take other examples, a child may wish to see what is in a box when the lid is on too tightly to be removed, or what is behind a piece of furniture too heavy to be moved. Episodes such as these may well be as important, if not more important, for the development of further understanding of the acquisition of knowledge and the processes involved in knowing. If all proceeded without any hitches, that is, if joint attention were always established and if there were never any misunderstandings, then children may never have cause to reflect on the processes that lead to knowledge acquisition, or on knowledge acquisition in its own right.

During the course of the first few years young children clearly do learn about the importance of gaining access to information, be this visual access or otherwise, for the acquisition of knowledge. Studies by Pillow (1989) and Pratt & Bryant (1990) have shown that 3-year-old children understand the link between seeing, or not seeing, the contents of a box, and knowing, or not knowing, what is in the box. They can, in fact, correctly assess the status of their own knowledge, or that of another person, depending on whether they or the other person has seen in the box.

These studies are of importance because they reveal a significant development in young children's understanding of knowledge and related processes. In responding correctly to questions about the links between visual access and knowledge, the children are demonstrating some conscious awareness of these processes, linked to the ability to focus deliberately on and assess the knowledge status of self and others. Such an understanding may not be as sophisticated as that possessed by older children or adults, but it certainly exists at an explicit level.

It is of interest to note, however, that the experiments by Pillow (1989) and Pratt & Bryant (1990) do not determine whether 3- and 4-year-old children understand *knowing* as distinguishable from *seeing*. It is possible that children of this age, although appearing to understand the relationship between seeing and knowing, have not separated out the two processes, and hence for them there is no relationship, simply an equivalence. That is, when asked to state whether an individual knows what is in a box, they may be answering the question, 'Has the individual seen what is in the box?'. If this is the case, that is, if for young children seeing equals knowing, then it would be necessary to predict that children would distinguish between different types of knowing.

Fortunately, research by Wimmer, Hogrefe & Perner (1988) and by Gopnik and her colleagues (Gopnik & Graf, 1988; O'Neill & Gopnik, 1991) on children's understanding of informational access provides some evidence on this issue. These authors point out that there are different ways in which we can come to know something or know about something. We can, for example, learn about things by seeing, hearing or making inferences. Consequently, if children assume that seeing is equivalent to knowing, this would have to be regarded as one type of knowing which was distinct from other types of knowing, arising from hearing and making inferences. That is, they would be expected to distinguish between each of the following three processes: (1) seeing/knowing, (2) hearing/knowing and (3) inference/knowing.

The results of the studies by Wimmer *et al.* and by Gopnik & Graf, in which children were given access to knowledge through different sources (seeing, being told and making inferences), revealed that 3-year-old children often did not distinguish between the sources of information even though they had acquired the knowledge. In contrast, 4-year-old children do remember the source of the knowledge and therefore do seem to have explicitly linked sources with the knowledge they have obtained (Astington & Gopnik, 1991). Perner (1991), in reviewing the evidence for children's understanding of the importance of sources of knowledge, recognises that younger children may not show an appreciation of the importance of the source because they have difficulty with the 'how' and 'why' question forms (e.g. 'How did you know?') used in some studies. However, as he points out, children of this age can and do answer 'why' questions when they relate to other domains.

The research that has been considered to this point in the chapter, though focusing largely on gaining knowledge through visual attention, has indicated that children will gain knowledge from other sources as well. For example, from a very early age infants will hear the sounds of rattles, bells, dogs barking, etc. They will also develop knowledge through integrating information accessed simultaneously through different sources. For example, they *see* the dog while *hearing* it barking and learn about the relationship between dogs and the noise they make.

Hence the establishment of joint visual attention serves not only as the source of knowledge that can be obtained by seeing, it provides the basis for much other knowledge. This is especially clear in the development of language. Infants learn about the relationships between the sounds of language and the referents through hearing and seeing, as described by Baldwin. An infant *sees* the dog and *hears* the label 'dog'. Moreover, developing mastery of language and other systems of representation will lead to the acquisition of knowledge in a less direct way than seeing and hearing things first hand. It will, for example, lead to knowing about things through looking at pictures and listening to others talking about objects, people and events. Certainly once the child has learned the basics of language, there seems to be a constant drive to use language to increase the knowledge base. In part, particularly early in development, this drive will be directly linked to developing language further, for example when a child holds up an object and requests, verbally or non-verbally, that it be given a label. In part the drive will lead to book reading, an activity that is often demanded by children, and to the everyday conversations children have with older siblings, parents and (preschool) teachers (Tizard & Hughes, 1984) as well as in more formal teaching sessions (Garton & Pratt, 1989; Wells, 1985). In short, there is a significant shift from learning to talk to talking to learn.

It is probably because of the range of sources of knowledge that young children do become aware of knowing as being distinguishable from the processes such as hearing and seeing that are involved in the act of knowing. If the only way in which we could come to know things were to see them, then it would be much more difficult to distinguish seeing from knowing. However, because we do come to know through different sources, the processes of generalisation and specification described by Pratt & Garton (Chapter 1) will come into play, separating out acts of knowing from sources of knowing and other processes that may be closely related to, or even an integral part of, knowing.

Once children are able to focus attention on the act of knowing, and associated processes, then there is the opportunity to develop a much greater understanding of the importance of social and other sources of knowledge, of themselves and others as individuals who possess knowledge, and of the extent to which the content of one's knowledge is accurate. These developments, which are examined in the next section, rely on an understanding of knowledge as representations.

KNOWLEDGE AS REPRESENTATION: BEYOND KNOWING AND NOT KNOWING

The research that has focused directly on the relationship between access to knowledge and assessing whether an individual does or does not know something, deals only with very straightforward cases of knowing. If an individual sees what is in a box, and the object in the box is easily identifiable, then it is highly likely that visual access will lead to accurate knowledge of the contents. Consequently, 3- to 4-year-old children may be representing knowledge in a way that allows them to reflect on knowledge and ignorance as it relates to sources such as seeing or not seeing.

It would be misleading to assume that the processes involved in knowing are that straightforward. If they were, then it would clearly be possible to reflect on knowledge and make judgements about knowledge without showing any appreciation of the representational characteristics of such knowledge. If knowledge always equated to reality, if all individuals either had each piece of knowledge or did not have it (e.g. knowledge of the contents of a box), and if all individuals who had access to any particular knowledge (e.g. contents of a box) had the same knowledge (of the contents), then it would be much more difficult to develop a full understanding of knowledge as representations. Furthermore, if children do not appreciate the representational qualities of knowledge then it would not be possible for them to consider knowledge as anything other than directly equating to reality nor to entertain notions of anything other than 'correct' knowing.

But knowledge is not always correct knowledge and sources of knowledge will not always lead to correct knowing. In order to continue to function efficiently in social contexts, children must develop an understanding that knowledge is not always correct and that individuals may hold inaccurate or misleading beliefs based on their state of knowledge. It is generally agreed that such understandings play an integral part in the ability of individuals to interpret the behaviours of self and others in meaningful ways and that without such understandings it would not be possible to engage in and maintain social discourse with others.

Related to the understanding that knowledge may not always be correct is the understanding that the source of knowledge may be important in determining its veracity. There are many different sources of information, and though at times consideration of the source may not be important as long as it is reliable, there are other times when the source may be important in assessing the veracity of the knowledge obtained.

Take a specific example which illustrates both the importance of the understanding that one cannot always assume that the knowledge possessed by an individual, in this case another individual, is correct and the importance of taking account of the source of the information for knowledge, in this case one's own knowledge. If I am deciding whether to go out and buy some more beer before the off-licence closes and my wife tells me that there is no need to go because there is some beer in the fridge, then I may not be as confident that there is actually some beer in the fridge as I would be if I had seen it with my own eyes. It may well be that my wife is correct in her assertion. Alternatively it may be that she is incorrect because she is unaware that I have drunk all the cans of beer that *were* in the fridge the last time she looked. It may even be, hypothetically of course for the sake of illustration, that she may be deliberately misleading me into thinking that there is plenty of beer, even though she knows there is not, because she does not want me to go out and buy some more.

It is because we have an appreciation that an individual's assumed knowledge may not always be correct, and that different sources of knowledge can be accepted with differing degrees of confidence, that we are able to assess the veracity of it. (It is also because we are able to make distinctions between sources of knowledge and the reliability of different sources that my wife calls me a 'bloody empiricist', asserting that I do not believe anything unless I have seen or tested it out myself.)

Furthermore, not only is it important to distinguish between different sources of knowledge such as seeing, being told and making inferences, and the certainty that can be attached to such knowledge, it is also important to learn about characteristics of other sources of knowledge and how these characteristics relate to the veracity of the information. It is likely that we will draw conclusions both about the reliability of groupings of sources of information and about individual sources of information. For example, we may draw our own conclusions about the reliability of television news bulletins versus newspapers as sources of information, or politicians versus scientists as sources of information. For children, particularly school-age children, there may well be parallels between them drawing conclusions about the reliability of information provided by teachers and parents, or between children their age and much younger children.

In addition, for both children and adults, conclusions will be drawn about the reliability of information provided by an individual based on the knowledge one has of that individual's knowledge or traits. For example, you may be unlikely to accept information from an individual about, say, how to fix your bike, because you *know* that person *knows* nothing about fixing bikes, or you may be reluctant to accept an individual's claims about his or her achievements because you *know* that particular individual is prone to exaggeration, or worse, deliberate deceit.

Unfortunately there is a dearth of research into children's developing understanding of the links between sources of knowledge, the reliability of different sources, and hence the veracity of the knowledge that results from the different sources. Hence, little can be said with certainty about these issues other than to state that there is an obvious need for research in this area.

In contrast, children's understanding that the knowledge possessed by individuals may not always be veracious, and that consequently individuals may hold false beliefs, has received a staggering amount of research attention in the past decade. As is well documented, the great interest in research in this area over the past 10 years has stemmed largely, though not entirely, from work by Premack & Woodruff (1978) with chimpanzees, and the peer commentary associated with their article in *The Behavioral and Brain Sciences*. Recognising the importance of this area of research, Wimmer & Perner (1983) developed an experimental procedure which they used to investigate children's understanding of beliefs, and particularly false beliefs.

Briefly, the procedure they used in their study involved presenting children with a short scenario in which a protagonist (Maxi) places an object (chocolate) in location *a* (a blue cupboard), and then without the protagonist seeing (and hence knowing), the object is moved to location *b* (a green cupboard). The logic underlying the task is seemingly straightforward. If, when asked, the child answers that Maxi thinks the chocolate is in the blue cupboard, then the child is able to reflect on the knowledge states of others and appreciate that knowledge does not equate with reality but is a representation of it, in this case a false representation.

Interestingly, this research preceded the research reviewed above which examined children's understanding of the importance of informational access for knowledge. Logically, however, understanding informational access must precede, or at least coincide with, the developing understanding of false beliefs. Children certainly would not understand that Maxi has a false belief if they did not realise that because Maxi had not seen the chocolate being shifted, he would not know it was in a different location. Indeed, evidence which suggests that children develop an understanding of knowledge and ignorance before they develop the understanding of a false belief, based on ignorance of the real situation, has been found by Hogrefe, Wimmer & Perner (1986). Although there is some support for Wimmer & Perner's evidence (Pratt & Maiolo, in preparation), Sullivan & Winner (1991) claim on the basis of their research that the two abilities—understanding of knowledge and ignorance and understanding of false beliefs—develop simultaneously. Regardless of whether the two abilities develop simultaneously or not, it is certainly the case that an understanding of false belief relies on more fundamental understandings of the relevance of informational access.

In their original study Wimmer & Perner examined children's under-standing of false beliefs and of deliberate deception, when this deception was premised on the pre-existence of a false belief. Thus they compared two conditions, one in which Maxi told his grandpa where the chocolate was, because he wanted his grandpa to help him get the chocolate, and one in which he told his brother where it was, when he did not want his brother to find it. In both cases, however, Maxi already had a false belief about the location of the chocolate. Thus in the *deception* condition, the intention to mislead his brother would actually lead to Maxi providing his brother with the correct information! Wimmer & Perner found that once children could understand the formation of a false belief they could also construct a deceitful utterance for the protagonist to tell his brother.

Since the original study by Wimmer & Perner (1983), there have been many studies which have examined the developing understanding of false beliefs in children. These studies (e.g. Gopnik & Astington, 1988; Lewis & Osborne, 1990; Moses & Flavell, 1990; Perner, Leekam & Wimmer, 1987; Wellman & Bartsch, 1988), by and large, have adopted or adapted the procedure developed by Wimmer & Perner, and have all contributed to our understanding of the development of false beliefs. They have also produced debates in the literature amongst researchers regarding the actual age at which children demonstrate an understanding of false beliefs and hence an awareness that knowledge is based on representations which are not always accurate representations of current reality. Although there is broad agreement that there are significant developments taking place between the ages of 3 and 5 years, there is certainly a lack of agreement about the specific age at which children develop an understanding of beliefs as representations.

It is clear that the debate about the age at which children develop an understanding of false beliefs is likely to continue for a number of years, as recent developments in the area of false belief and deception illustrate. Chandler and colleagues (Chandler, Fritz & Hala, 1989; Hala, Chandler & Fritz, 1991), in recent studies on deception and theory of mind, have put forward new evidence that children understand false beliefs from an early age. Their task involved children assisting a puppet, which left clear foot-prints on a whiteboard, to hide a treasure in one of five plastic bins so that someone could not find it. The children were taken through the procedure step by step so that they understood that the footprints left by the puppet provided a clear indication of the location of the treasure. When it was their turn to hide it they were encouraged to make sure the other person would not find it. On subsequent trials the children were encouraged to explore other ways of misleading the person who wanted to find the treasure. The results reveal that children have an awareness of a range of strategies including destroying evidence by removing the tell-tale footprints, and laying false trails.

Chandler and colleagues claim from this research that children show an understanding of deception, which relies on an understanding of false beliefs from $2\frac{1}{2}$ to 3 years of age. However, Sodian *et al.* (1991), in applying more stringent tests of young children's understanding of deceptive acts, claim that a full understanding of deception, involving a demonstrated understanding of false beliefs, does not develop until 4 years of age. Consequently there continues to be disagreement about the actual age at which children develop an understanding of false beliefs.

Most of the research to date, whether it has been concerned with the unintentional creation of false beliefs, or the intentional creation for the purposes of deception, has followed procedures in which the beliefs held by protagonists were either right or wrong. Typically, children are faced with a situation where they have a correct belief and the protagonist in a story has a different belief, which is false. It is not clear therefore if the difficulty is solely because the belief is false or because the belief is a different one. In order to obtain information on this, we have been conducting research to examine whether children's difficulties result from the beliefs being false, that is not based on reality, or with the fact that they do not realise individuals may hold different beliefs. In the first of the studies, Chong (1990) examined young children's understanding of alternative beliefs. In addition to presenting 3- to 6-year-old children with two false belief tasks, they were given two alternative belief tasks. Each of the alternative belief tasks involved two dolls, a set of props to illustrate two contexts and a substance that could have more than one identity, such that visual access to the substance was insufficient to ascertain its identity with any certainty. In one task, children were shown a white powder and through a series of questions the experimenter established with each child that the substance could either be baking flour or talcum powder. Once this had been established, the child was introduced to each of the dolls. Each doll was in a different context illustrated by a set of appropriate props. One doll, Sandra, was in a bedroom and children were told that she had just taken a shower. The other doll, Tom, was in the kitchen helping to make cakes. Samples of the white powder were placed in both the bedroom and the kitchen settings. The child was then asked two test questions: 'When Sandra sees this (pointing to the white powder in a container on the dressing table in the bedroom), what will she think it is—powder or flour?' and 'When Tom sees this (pointing to the white powder in a baking bowl on the kitchen table), what will he think it is—powder or flour?'. The other task had a parallel form, illustrating a bathroom and a home workshop, and a tube of white paste that could be either toothpaste or glue.

The performance of the children on the false belief and alternative belief tasks indicated that there was no difference in performance between these two task types. Initially this seemed to suggest that children are not restricted to difficulties with false beliefs, but have as much problem coping with different beliefs regardless of their veracity. However, the nature of the alternative belief task used in the study meant that at least one if not both of the alternative beliefs could not be based on reality. In reality, although the white substance might look like flour and powder, it could not actually be both. At best, it could be one, and therefore at best only one of the protagonists could hold a correct belief. Indeed the ambiguous identity of the substance posed considerable difficulty for many of the younger children, who only accepted that it might be more than one thing with great reluctance. They seemed determined to give it one identity and have it form the basis of one belief for both protagonists. Thus the most frequent error was to claim that both protagonists thought it was flour or both thought it was powder.

In another experiment, conducted by Pratt & Maiolo (1991) with 4- and 5-year-old children, a different alternative belief task was presented which avoided the use of ambiguous stimuli that could not really support two different beliefs without at least one being false. In the task the two alternative beliefs were both based on reality. Children were presented with two modified false belief tasks and two alternative belief tasks. Again, dolls and props were used so that the scenarios were acted out in front of the child. The modified false belief task involved two protagonists, one of whom ended up with a correct belief, the other with a false belief. For example, in one of the tasks Cheryl puts a toy car in the toy box while Kevin is asleep. Cheryl then goes out to play, Kevin wakes up, sees a doll on the floor and puts it in the toy box. He sees the toy car in the toy box and takes it out of the box to play with. Once the child had watched the dolls act out the story, two memory questions, 'What did Kevin put in the box?' and 'What did Cheryl put in the box?', and two test questions, 'What does Kevin think is in the box?' and 'What does Cheryl think is in the box?', were asked.

The alternative belief tasks followed a similar format. In one example Tom is playing in the sandpit outside while Sally is inside eating her breakfast. Tom buries a truck in the sandpit then leaves to find some friends. Sally finishes her breakfast and goes out to play in the sandpit. She buries a spade in the sandpit. Again two memory questions, 'What did Tom put in the sandpit?' and 'What did Sally put in the sandpit?', and two test questions, 'What does Tom think is in the sandpit?' and 'What does Sally think is in the sandpit?', were asked.

The findings from this research revealed that children have as much difficulty with tasks where two protagonists hold alternative beliefs, even though neither of these beliefs is completely false, as they do when protagonists hold false beliefs. Furthermore, it seems that the difficulty is not entirely a result of not being able to free themselves from the current reality. If this were the case, then all incorrect responses would have indicated that both protagonists thought both toys, the car and the spade were in the sandpit. This was not the case, as most of the errors consisted of children asserting that each protagonist would think that the other toy was in the sandpit. That is, they would assert that Tom, who had hidden the car, *thought* that the spade was in the sandpit, and Sally, who had hidden the spade, *thought* that the car was in the sandpit.

The evidence from the false and alternative belief studies indicates that some time between the ages of 3 and 5 years, children are developing a more sophisticated understanding of the mind and of knowledge and beliefs as representations. The disputes amongst researchers about the actual age at which such specific developments as an understanding of false beliefs occur will probably lead to a considerable amount of further research. This might achieve very little if it focusses purely on trying to pinpoint the age at which the child has a representational theory of mind which, without question, involves the understanding that knowledge is representational and that as a result may not be an accurate reflection of reality. In the terms used by Chandler *et al.* (1989) there will continue to be *boosters* 'who advocate the first or early-onset view' (p. 1263), and *scoffers*, 'who hold out instead for more unimpeachable lines of evidence of the sort generally provided by 4- and 5-year-olds' (p. 1264).

Perhaps the greatest problem that besets this area of research, and indeed many other areas of developmental psychology, results from the tendency to assume that there will be one pure test of a particular ability, a litmus test, which will provide the definitive answer about when a particular ability develops. Associated with this is the tendency to focus on *when* an ability first appears, rather than explaining *why* it may appear in some contexts and not in others. It is unlikely that any ability develops sufficiently rapidly that it will be demonstrated by children in a range of contexts at a similar time. It is also unlikely to be possible to find pure tests of abilities that are totally valid measures of development. They will be contaminated because success on them will require other understandings as well and also because of context effects and social expectations in the test situation.

Fortunately, the research that has been conducted has provided a substantial body of knowledge which has formed the basis of theoretical descriptions of children's developing understanding of mental representations. In one of the most comprehensive of these descriptions, Wellman (1990), drawing on the findings of much empirical research, argues that children move from a non-representational understanding of desires at around 2 years of age to an early representational understanding of beliefs and hence the ability to engage in belief–desire reasoning at around 3 years of age. That is, children move from the ability to explain behaviours based on knowledge of an individual's desires, to a *limited* understanding of beliefs which allows them to explain behaviours based on both beliefs and desires.

The understanding is limited because, according to Wellman, 3-year-old children have a copy theory of representations. That is, they have an understanding that knowledge and beliefs are representational insofar as they understand their knowledge is not reality. Instead they regard it as a direct copy of reality contained inside one's head. Wellman claims that children of this age cannot cope with false beliefs because such beliefs cannot be based on a copy of current reality. However, as Wellman points out, a copy theory of representations is sufficient for children to succeed on the tasks which require judgements about knowledge and ignorance based on informational access.

During the period from 3 to 6 years of age, Wellman argues that children develop an interpretive understanding of representation which supersedes the copy theory of representations. 'Children's achievement of an interpretive understanding of representation is part and parcel of a larger achievement: an understanding of the mind itself as active and constructive' (Wellman, 1990, p. 268). The achievement is a critically important one as it reflects a much more sophisticated understanding of representations which allows for the appreciation that individuals may hold different interpretations of the same objects or events, because they have had to actively reconstruct these, rather than simply hold a copy of them. It also underlies the appreciation that beliefs may be false because they are based on representations that have been constructed without full knowledge of reality or because in constructing the beliefs, false inferences have been drawn from reality.

The theoretical description offered by Wellman, and alternative ones by, for example, Flavell (1988) and Perner (1991) (see also Olson & Campbell, Chapter 2), provide accounts of the possible changes that underlie children's developing understanding of the representation of knowledge. All descriptions provide informative ways of explaining both the naturalistic and experimental data that have been accumulating on children's developing theory of mind and give direction to future research. Nevertheless, none of the theories has addressed fully what leads to the changes in understandings about representations. Even with the wealth of data available, theoretical explanations of the causes of the changes remain a matter for considerable speculation.

In the previous section, I argued that it may well be as a result of unsuccessful attempts to establish joint attention that children start to develop an awareness of the links between the processes involved in acquiring knowledge and knowledge itself, which will form the basis for treating knowledge as a separate, mental entity. Wellman makes a parallel argument in suggesting an explanation for the shift from a copy theory to an interpretive one. When discussing situations that will appear anomalous to a copy theorist, because a person's actions are based on a false belief, he states that, 'Such situations may be the first breeding ground for an under-standing of false belief specifically and for the eventual overthrow of a direct copy theory of representation more generally' (Wellman, 1990, p. 263).

It is certainly likely that throughout development anomalous or unexpected outcomes will lead to conflict within the individual (between what was expected and what eventuated) that triggers further develop-ment. This, of course, relies on there being a basis for the appreciation that there is conflict. With respect to knowledge, it is possible that as children draw distinctions between knowing and other mental events such as dreaming and imagining, they do so on the basis that knowledge is a reflection of reality. As much knowledge is not only a representation of reality but an *accurate* representation of reality, it may be that children ini-tially overgeneralise their assumptions about the representations under-lying knowledge and beliefs. They assume that knowledge is always based on accurate representations of reality in contrast to dreams and imaginary events. This overgeneralisation could well occur in a parallel manner to the overgeneralisations that occur in other systems of representation during the phases of development documented by Karmiloff-Smith (1979, 1986). However, once this order has been brought to the system, children have the basis to realise that there are occasions when their own actions, and those of others, cannot be accounted for by assuming that knowledge always mirrors reality. When presented with these conflicts, further development takes place.

Dunn (1991) argues that there is another form of conflict, namely social conflict, that can lead to development in children. In considering children's developing understanding of other people, based on naturalistic data from families with young children in England and the United States, Dunn points out that 3-year-old children demonstrate their most mature behaviours during disputes over rights and interests. In her research, it was often the case in disputes that the children would make reference to their intentions or the intentions of others. They would, for example, make it clear that something had or had not been done *on purpose* in an attempt to manipulate the outcome of a dispute. Dunn speculates that these social conflicts may well lead to further development for one of two reasons. It may be that the dispute leads to emotional arousal that heightens children's 'vigilance and attentive powers' which in turn leads to further learning. Alternatively, it may be that during disputes, particularly disputes over rights, adults are more likely to reason with children and provide fuller explanations which may allow the child to develop more sophisticated understandings. As Dunn states, further work is required to investigate these explanations.

Our knowledge of children's understanding of the representational nature of knowledge and related mental entities has increased substantially in the past decade. Nevertheless it is evident that more attention must be paid in future work to developing an understanding of the mechanisms that lead to developmental changes, and the interplay of innate and social factors in development. I will return to this point briefly in the final section.

CONCLUDING COMMENTS

This chapter has documented children's developing understanding of knowledge, from the period when they engage in activities that lead to knowledge acquisition, to the point when they have sufficiently sophisticated understandings of knowledge that they can reflect on the knowledge status of self and others and understand the representational nature of knowledge to the extent that it will not always coincide with reality. There is, of course, much more that needs to be discovered by children, and by psychologists who wish to understand the developmental processes involved in children's developing understanding of knowledge and knowledge acquisition.

Beyond developing an understanding of knowledge and the ability to reflect on it, children in many cultures will also come to appreciate the value placed on knowledge and the interest taken by many in their culture in assessing knowledge and making judgements based on these assessments. In the social context of school, they will develop an understanding that when a teacher asks a question, the teacher frequently does not want to know the answer, but wants to know if a particular child knows the answer (see, for example, Pratt, 1985). As such question and answer routines are very common in the public arena of the classroom, children also become acutely aware that individuals, including themselves, will at times give wrong, even 'stupid', answers to questions. (Some children will of course have the additional opportunity to learn that other adults — developmental psychologists—visit schools and preschools, and ask lots of questions about such things as where Maxi thinks the chocolate is, while taking a great deal of interest in their answers.)

Moreover, it will not only be teachers and psychologists who make judgements about children's knowledge. Children will also begin to form their own judgements about their peers and, in their own social worlds in the school playground and beyond, they will often make such informed comments as, 'Sam's thick', 'deadhead' or 'teacher's pet' (the latter one labelling the child who receives constant praise from the teacher for correctly answering lots of questions).

There is evidence that the understanding of the fact that knowledge is being assessed by others develops from around 5 years of age onwards (Pratt, 1988; Galpert & Dockrell, 1991). In the study by Pratt (1988), which was undertaken to investigate children's conception of the conservation task, children in the age range $5\frac{1}{2}$–7 years were asked several questions about a conservation task they had been given by another adult earlier in the day. When asked why the experimenter had asked them questions, several children made reference to the assessment of knowledge, including comments such as, 'to see if I was right, to see if I was smart', 'to see if I knew' and, at a more general level, 'She probably wanted to ask everyone these questions to see who could answer the most of them—to see how others learn things'. There was also evidence from one 5-year-old non-conserver indicating that children of this age do form opinions about the intellectual ability of others. This child conceded that, following the transformation, 'Billy might (say it was the same) because sometimes he does not watch properly—Billy often gets things wrong'. Thus children are developing an understanding that knowledge is something that is being assessed. They are also forming opinions about the intellectual abilities of others (see Wellman, 1990; Yussen & Kane, 1985), though it may be some time before they develop a full understanding of the value placed on intellectual ability by certain cultures and particular sections within a culture.

Many challenges lie ahead for developmental psychologists and others interested in developmental processes. There is still a great deal that needs to be documented including, as suggested above, children's understanding of the reliability of sources and of the importance of assessing the veracity of knowledge. There are even more fundamental issues concerning explanations of the causes of development and the mechanisms involved in developmental change. As Gopnik (1990) comments, 'It is unfortunately all too typical of developmental psychology that we are much better at saying what develops, when, than we are of giving causal explanations for these developments' (p. 102). It is evident that one of the major challenges that lies ahead is to develop testable explanations of developmental processes which take account of children's developing understanding of the representation of knowledge and of knowledge as representations. Such explanations should also aim to take into account the interweaving of the development and use of many different systems of representation and the importance of social interaction for development.

ACKNOWLEDGMENTS

The author wishes to acknowledge the support provided by the Australian Research Council (Grant number A78932007).

REFERENCES

Astington, J.W. and Gopnik, A. (1991). Theoretical explanations of children's understanding of the mind. *British Journal of Developmental Psychology*, **9**, 7–31.

Astington, J.W., Harris, P.L. and Olson, D.R. (eds) (1988). *Developing Theories of Mind*. New York: Cambridge University Press.

Baldwin, D.A. (1991). Infants' contribution to the achievement of joint reference, *Child Development*, **62**, 875–890.

Baldwin, D.A. (in press). Infants' ability to consult the speaker for clues to word reference, *Journal of Child Language*.

Bretherton, I. (1991). Intentional communication and the development of an understanding of mind. In D. Frye and C. Moore (eds), *Children's Theories of Mind: Mental States and Social Understanding* (pp. 49–75). Hillsdale, New Jersey: Lawrence Erlbaum.

Butterworth, G.E. and Cochran, E. (1980). Towards a mechanism of joint visual attention in human infancy, *International Journal of Behavioral Development*, **3**, 253–272.

Butterworth, G.E. and Grover, L. (1988). The origins of referential communication in human infancy. In L. Weiskrantz (ed.), *Thought Without Language* (pp. 5–25). Oxford: Oxford University Press.

Butterworth, G.E. and Jarrett, N. (1991). What minds have in common is space: spatial mechanisms serving joint visual attention in infancy, *British Journal of Developmental Psychology*, **9**, 55–72.

Chandler, M., Fritz, A.S. and Hala, S. (1989). Small scale deceit: deception as a marker of two-, three-, and four-year olds' early theories of mind, *Child Development*, **60**, 1263–1277.

Chong, S.L. (1990). Children's understanding of alternative beliefs, false beliefs, and the appearance–reality distinction in their acquisition of theory of mind. Unpublished Honours thesis, The University of Western Australia, Perth, WA.

Dunn, J. (1991). Young children's understanding of other people: evidence from observations within the family. In D. Frye and C. Moore (eds), *Children's Theories of Mind: Mental States and Social Understanding* (pp. 97–114). Hillsdale, New Jersey: Lawrence Erlbaum.

Flavell, J.H. (1988). The development of children's knowledge about the mind: from cognitive connections to mental operations. In J.W. Astington, P.L. Harris and D.R. Olson (eds), *Developing Theories of Mind* (pp. 244–267). New York: Cambridge University Press.

Frye, D. and Moore, C. (eds) (1991). *Children's Theories of Mind: Mental States and Social Understanding*. Hillsdale, New Jersey: Lawrence Erlbaum.

Galpert, L. and Dockrell, J. (1991). Is understanding the experimenter's intentions the clue to conversation ability? Paper presented at the British Psychological Society, Developmental Section Annual Conference, Cambridge.

Garton, A.F. (1992). *Social Interaction and the Development of Language and Cognition*. Hove: Lawrence Erlbaum.

Garton, A.F. and Pratt, C. (1989). *Learning to be Literate: The Development of Spoken and Written Language*. Oxford: Basil Blackwell.

Gopnik, A. (1990). Developing the idea of intentionality: children's theories of mind, *Canadian Journal of Philosophy*, **20**, 89–114.

Gopnik, A. and Astington, J.W. (1988). Children's understanding of representational change and its relation to the understanding of false belief and the appearance–reality distinction, *Child Development*, **59**, 26–37.

Gopnik, A. and Graf, P. (1988). Knowing how you know: young children's ability to identify and remember the sources of their beliefs, *Child Development*, **59**, 1366–1371.

Hala, S., Chandler, M. and Fritz, A.S. (1991). Fledgling theories of mind: deception as a marker of three-year-olds' understanding of false belief, *Child Development*, **62**, 83–97.

Hogrefe, J., Wimmer, H. and Perner, J. (1986). Ignorance versus false belief: a developmental lag in attribution of epistemic states, *Child Development*, **57**, 567–582.

Karmiloff-Smith, A. (1979). Micro- and macro-developmental changes in language acquisition and other representational systems, *Cognitive Science*, **3**, 91–118.

Karmiloff-Smith, A. (1986). From meta-processes to conscious access: evidence from children's metalinguistic and repair data, *Cognition*, **23**, 95–147.

Lewis, C. and Osborne, A. (1990). Three-year-olds' problems with false belief: conceptual deficit or linguistic artifact? *Child Development*, **61**, 1514–1519.

Moses, L.J. and Chandler, M.J. (1992). Traveler's guide to children's theories of mind, *Psychological Inquiry*, **3**, 286–301.

Moses, L.J. and Flavell, J.H. (1990). Inferring false beliefs from actions and reactions, *Child Development*, **61**, 929–945.

O'Neill, D.K. and Gopnik, A. (1991). Young children's ability to identify the sources of their beliefs, *Developmental Psychology*, **27**, 390–397.

Perner, J. (1991). *Understanding the Representational Mind*. Cambridge, Massachusetts: MIT Press/Bradford Books.

Perner, J., Leekam, S.R. and Wimmer, H. (1987). Three-year-olds' difficulty with false belief: the case for a conceptual deficit, *British Journal of Developmental Psychology*, **5**, 125–137.

Pillow, B.H. (1989). Early understanding of perception as a source of knowledge, *Journal of Experimental Child Psychology*, **47**, 116–129.

Pratt, C. (1985). The transition to school: a shift from development to learning, *Australian Journal of Early Childhood*, **10**, 11–16.

Pratt, C. (1988). The child's conception of the conservation task, *British Journal of Developmental Psychology*, **6**, 157–167.

Pratt, C. and Bryant, P.E. (1990). Young children understand that looking leads to knowing (so long as they are looking into a single barrel), *Child Development*, **61**, 973–982.

Pratt, C. and Maiolo, T. (1991). Children's understanding of alternative beliefs. Paper presented at the Experimental Psychology Conference, Adelaide, South Australia.

Pratt, C. and Maiolo, T. (in prep.). Children's understanding of knowledge and alternative beliefs.

Premack, D. (1991). The infant's theory of self-propelled objects. In D. Frye and C. Moore (eds), *Children's Theories of Mind: Mental States and Social Understanding* (pp. 39–48). Hillsdale, New Jersey: Lawrence Erlbaum.

Premack, D. and Woodruff, G. (1978). Does the chimpanzee have a theory of mind? *The Behavioral and Brain Sciences*, **1**, 515–526.

Scaife, M. and Bruner, J. (1975). The capacity for joint visual attention in the infant, *Nature*, **253**, 265–266.

Sodian, B., Taylor, C., Harris, P.L. and Perner, J. (1991). Early deception and the child's theory of mind: false trails and genuine markers, *Child Development*, **62**, 468–483.

Sullivan, K. and Winner, E. (1991). When 3-year-olds understand ignorance, false belief and representational change, *British Journal of Developmental Psychology*, **9**, 159–171.

Tizard, B. and Hughes, M. (1984). *Young Children Learning: Talking and Thinking at Home and School*. London: Fontana.

Trevarthen, C. (1980). The foundations of intersubjectivity: development of inter-personal and cooperative understanding in infants. In D. Olson (ed.), *The Social Foundations of Language and Thought: Essays in Honor of Jerome S. Bruner*. (pp. 316–342). New York: W.W. Norton & Co.

Trevarthen, C. (1983). Interpersonal abilities of infants as generators for transmission of language and culture. In A. Oliverio and M. Zapella (eds), *The
Behaviour of Human Infants* (pp. 145–176). London: Plenum Press.

Trevarthen, C. and Hubley, P. (1978). Secondary intersubjectivity: confidence,
confiding and acts of meaning in the first year. In A. Lock (ed.), *Action, Gesture
and Symbol: The Emergence of Language* (pp. 183–229). London: Academic Press.

Wellman, H.M. (1990). *The Child's Theory of Mind*. Cambridge, Massachusetts: MIT
Press/Bradford Books.

Wellman, H.M. and Bartsch, K. (1988). Young children's reasoning about beliefs,
Cognition, **30**, 239–277.

Wells, C.G. (1985). *Language, Learning and Education*. Slough: NFER-Nelson.

Whiten, A. (1991). *Natural Theories of Mind: Evolution, Development and Simulation of
Everyday Mindreading*. Oxford: Basil Blackwell.

Wimmer, H. and Perner, J. (1983). Beliefs about beliefs: representation and
constraining function of wrong beliefs in young children's understanding of
comprehension, *Cognition*, **13**, 103–128.

Wimmer, H., Hogrefe, J. and Perner, J. (1988). Children's understanding of
information origins as a source of knowledge, *Child Development*, **59**, 386–396.

Yussen, S.R. and Kane, P.T. (1985). Children's conception of intelligence. In S.R.
Yussen (ed.), *The Growth of Reflection in Children*. New York: Academic Press.

4 The Representation of Spoken Language in Children

ROGER WALES
University of Melbourne

One aim of this chapter is to give a sense of some of the central issues in looking at the development of children's early language. Particular attention will be given to its normal and earliest mode, that is through the medium of speech. This means that other possible modes such as sign language or (later) writing will be ignored—not because of lack of interest but because of the centrality of speech, and the constraints of space. Also some effort will be made to introduce some of the more salient aspects of speech and language development in order to try and illustrate and emphasise the fact that various aspects of speech and language develop together as a system.

Thus we will consider in turn the development of the sound system of children's language, then the development of early words and then early sentences. Although there are variations to this pattern, this is the most likely developmental sequence a child will follow in acquiring a language. While these steps will be taken as a natural progression, there will be times when some of the relevant interconnections will be highlighted. Finally we will consider briefly some of the problems of accounting for the child's ability to communicate meaningfully. This will require us to consider the ways in which we might account for the children's growing ability to extend their communicative abilities with spoken language beyond the 'straightforward' interpretations of 'literal' meanings.

In attempting this selective survey the coverage will be by no means complete. In deciding where to point the reader for further discussion and data, there will be an attempt to refer to some of the main and accessible sources and not simply to refer to the latest trendy offerings. When someone has pioneered a point of view or an empirical study which in the view of the author has not been significantly bettered, then that study is referenced in preference to later and more 'up-to-date' sources.

One other point may help the reader understand the strategy of this chapter. No effort will be made to try and say what the state of the art is regarding what is known about the 'facts' of speech and language development. This is not because this is not a worthwhile thing to do, nor because the area is lacking in the data to make such an effort appropriate.

Systems of Representation in Children: Development and Use. Edited by C. Pratt and A.F. Garton
© 1993 John Wiley & Sons Ltd

An enormous collection of facts is now available to anyone wishing to try their hand at such an enterprise. Furthermore, these facts now span a wide range of languages, so the effort is not going to be solely one of marshalling such facts for English.

Though the study of child language is inevitably dominated by the study of English, it is simply not true that it is exclusively so (it never was anyway—German and French being at least as important as English from the inception of such studies). The monumental volumes edited by Slobin (1985) demonstrate some of the richness of detail of the data available. What is becoming increasingly clear—and exciting—is the difficult but rewarding road we need to travel to make further sense of the mechanisms which underlie these data. Whether we need to commit ourselves to as radical an option as Studdert-Kennedy (1990) and his attempt to cast language acquisition within an evolutionary and recapitulatory framework is perhaps less important than the fact that such theoretical discussion can now be engaged in without losing sight of the realities of the data to be accounted for.

The important point here is that even to attempt such an enterprise requires addressing the facts from certain points of view. The latter are concerned with such issues as the aspects of the facts which do or do not make them relatively important: what aspects contribute to our understanding of the means by which the processes of development proceed. If it were otherwise, the enterprise would be like trying to understand what a butterfly is and how it comes to be that way by making a butterfly collection. Instead of a catalogue of 'facts' then, an attempt will be made to illustrate some of the ways in which researchers in this area are pursuing their goals of trying to gain insights into the processes of speech and language development. To try and do this most researchers concentrate their attention on a particular aspect, since to do otherwise could well result in studies that are too diffuse even if exalted in ambition. However, the more revealing accounts seem to be concerned also with placing the particular facts they are concentrating on in a more general context. Thus an effort will be made to follow suit as we proceed through some of the more salient aspects of early speech and language. Thus, even as we consider individual sounds, we need to remember that these are often to be interpreted within the context of words and sentences, similarly words often need a broader context of language use for their interpretation.

SPEECH SOUNDS

If we were to propose a research study of children's spoken language we would probably start by looking at what sounds children are able to produce and which sounds they are able to perceive and understand. To look at the sounds themselves would require us to be concerned with whether, and if so when and how, children could distinguish speech and non-speech sounds. Presumably a vocal cry is not a normal speech sound—when does a young child 'know' that this is the case? A click with the tongue can sometimes sound a little like a door closing, though in some languages it is part of the repertoire of speech sounds—when are these sounds heard as different, that is as speech or non-speech? These are questions about how the child puts the sounds into systematic relation to each other. None of us says words like 'bat' by simply saying the first consonant followed by the vowel as discrete segments. There is an inter-dependence in the processes of moving smoothly through the sounds which together make up words and phrases. This interdependence requires us to know something of its structure. But to say anything very meaningful about these processes, we are forced into deciding what units are the most appropriate ones. Do we concentrate on the syllable, the word, the minimal 'meaningful' contrast? Even the latter can be set at more than one level of description; for example, 'ba' and 'pa' differ minimally by virtue of a critical difference as to when the vocal chords start vibrating relative to releasing the pent-up air at the lips ('voice-onset time' or VOT). Is the contrast then the difference between the phonemes 'b' and 'p', or the feature that distinguishes them ('voicing')? It is not simply a question of what the facts are, but what is the most revealing or economical mode of description. Of course, 'revealing' and 'economical' do not necessarily coincide. And what of the little issue about what the child/person is actually using to represent such descriptions.

Given these problems so quickly arrived at, it is small wonder that there are many problems which seem fundamental to our understanding of children, and which continue to prove intractable to any deeper under-standing than relatively simple description. This is especially unsurprising given the apparent fact that the young child is not only acquiring a set of productive sounds, and a set of relations between them, but also coming to use these to communicate messages involving at least words and sentences set within a physical and social world. The child's linguistic achievement is wonderful to behold and ponder in the context of our curiosity and perplexity as to how it is achieved.

The crux of our aim must be to accomplish our descriptive task in terms which are as consistent as possible with a 'child's perspective'. It is a truism that this is the necessary perspective, yet both of the dominant traditions of recent studies of the child's emerging abilities to process speech are crucially imbued with an adult perspective (cf. Menyuk, Menn & Silber, 1986). Thus both main recent traditions—the analysis of sound systems of individual children (an early but excellent example is Smith, 1973) and the study of the perception of speech sounds by infants (good examples can be found in Yeni-Komshian, Kavanagh & Ferguson, 1981)—

are committed to the view of the 'segment' of contemporary (adult) phonological theories.

Both of these traditions have achieved a good deal, and an understanding of young children has been greatly enhanced by them so this is not to be taken as a dismissive criticism. Thus we now know that infants are sensitive to many auditory contrasts which are similar to, if not identical with, those which are at the heart of adult spoken languages. Thus we need be less perplexed as to how babies come to hear these contrasts in the first place. Similarly, assuming that they have gained receptive control over what the contrasts signify in the adult language system they are acquiring, then some illuminating observations can be made about the apparently erroneous productions of children's earliest utterances. Hence it now seems plausible to note that many a child's 'error' relative to the adult model is not a product of random processes but the consequence of a system of the child's own system which progressively approximates that of the adult. Following this insight would lead us to expect what we find, that many cases which individually might look as if the child cannot actually say a particular sound 'properly' is wrong, and that in the appropriate speech context—for the child—the sound is there for all to hear. For example, a child who says 'lellow' for 'yellow' may also say 'yes'. The question, however, is whether taking a more explicitly child-oriented view will help move our understanding even further.

Few authors have raised the issue of the child's phonological units in a direct way (though Moskovitz, 1973, did so in a somewhat speculative manner, and Ferguson & Farwell, 1975, initiated a programme of such descriptive studies at Stanford).

To evaluate this possibility I would argue that it is necessary to harness acoustic–phonetic techniques to the enterprise of studying children's speech. As we shall soon see, we need the mechanisms of independent/ instrumental techniques in order to qualify and transcend what our adult ears and brains are 'hearing', with all their overlearned assumptions about what they are listening to when they listen to a child speak. As indicated above much work has been done since 1970 in establishing that for many synthetic speech continua infants discriminate sounds in a manner consistent with categorical syllable boundaries (both Aslin, Pisoni & Jusczyk, 1983, and Burnham, Earnshaw & Quinn, 1987, provide good reviews). On this basis Eimas (1975) concludes, 'These early categories serve as the basis for future phonetic categories', and Gleitman & Wanner (1982) assert, 'No learning apparatus is required for an initial segmentation of the acoustic wave into discrete phones. The segmentation has been provided by the nervous system' (p. 16). These kinds of views are presumably based on the (incorrect) assumption that categorical perception is peculiar to speech (Harnad, 1987) and the (incorrect) assumption that it is peculiar to the human species (Kuhl & Miller, 1975; Kuhl & Fadden, 1982). They also critically presuppose 'adult' categories.

Nevertheless it seems clear that infants are predisposed to make many of the auditory discriminations relevant to their subsequent language acquisition, and that even in the first year of life there is perceptual learning relevant to the specific language in question (Werker & Tees, 1984). What is now needed therefore is more work on the interaction of perceptual and productive abilities, through which work it may be possible to delineate more clearly the segments the children are using in constructing their understanding of speech and language. It is almost a truism that comprehension leads production. It may not be true in all cases, but for the multitude of cases where it is, the question of how, and in what ways, is much less clear.

There are now a number of cases in the literature where children are shown to maintain acoustic distinctions in their speech which correspond to linguistic contrasts but which are not perceptible to adult listeners: for example in 'normal' children—Macken & Barton (1980), Kornfeld (1971) and Kornfeld & Goehl (1974), and in 'misarticulating' children—Daniloff, Wilcox & Stephens (1980) and Maxwell & Weismer (1982). With some of our students we have also found evidence of such effects in young children: for example, 'w' 'r' distinctions being carried by third formant differences only; reliable VOT differences between 't' of 'tuck' for 'truck' as compared to the 't' of 'tuck' for 'tuck'. The relevance of this observation (first demonstrated by Kornfeld) is that in adult English the VOT of a consonant like 't' is lengthened if it is part of a consonant cluster like 'tr'. What the children are doing here is showing this pattern of lengthening even when the 't' is apparently a single consonant. An adult cannot reliably hear this difference in the child's speech, and yet the contrast is apparently being made. Surely this carries important implications for our understanding of what children 'know' about the language they are speaking.

One particularly intriguing result (O'Connor, 1979) was the finding that the formant structure of the 'gwass' for 'glass' was (for some children) reliably different from that of 'gwass' for 'grass'. What was intriguing was the fact that the presence or absence of this effect seemed to be related to the developmental stage of the child. The younger children in O'Connor's sample producing 'gwass' for either 'glass' or 'grass' did not show a consistent effect of formant structure as a function of the intended target word. However, the older children producing the same 'substitution error' did show such an acoustic effect. It seems from much of the literature already referred to that speech 'errors' in children are often similar, but vary considerably in their order of occurrence in the speech of different children. Hence the difference in phonological development may be related to the phenomena suggested by this result. Clearly more children would need to be studied, and a more comprehensive picture formulated of where the particular 'error' pattern occurred relative to the child's overall phonology, before any reliable conclusion could be drawn. Nevertheless it is clear that such phenomena exist, and need to be studied more systematically. Also they cannot be systematically studied without the use of instrumental techniques, since even the trained adult ear may frequently be misled—and once misled, the adult brain may misconstrue what the child is doing.

Before moving on to speech in word form, it is important to note that another dimension of children's speech sounds not covered by reference to their segmental aspects is that involved with intonation or the melodic form of an utterance. This is an area of children's speech which is often referred to but until relatively recently less thoroughly studied than say its segmental aspects. It has been known for some time that young babies respond receptively to variations in the pitch contour of speech (Kaplan & Kaplan, 1971; Morse 1972). This fact on its own is not uninteresting. It shows that the child is receptive to one of the linguistically critical aspects of the speech environment in advance of its use by the child in a language-related context. The presence of this auditory sensitivity does raise the question of when and how it is put to use in the language acquisition context.

One set of compelling observations has been made by Fernald and colleagues (e.g. Fernald & Kuhl, 1987; Fernald & Simon, 1984; Fernald, 1989) which supports the view that the prelinguistic child is sensitive to, and responds to, the modulation in pitch which mothers typically use in speaking to their infants. This is significant since, at least in middle-class western culture, mothers are particularly prone to exaggerate pitch modulation, especially at syntactically significant junctures such as word and clause boundaries. Fernald's observations are consistent with the view that children actually do respond to these potential cues to the segmentation of the adult's utterance. Such findings are consistent with observations made by Hirsh-Pasek *et al*. (1987) that young children also are responsive to durational cues at clause boundaries. Of course pitch and duration are two of the critical acoustic cues to the interpretation of intonation and stress, otherwise inclusively referred to as prosody. The fact that young pre-linguistic children are using these acoustic cues to help in the interpretation of the segmentation of the input speech string is also consistent with the view that this interpretation will help not only the understanding of what a possible word is but also what units may make up a sentence. These two issues will now be considered in turn.

CONSTRUCTING WORDS

Plainly one of the aspects of development that may be impinging on some of these issues is the effect of what are conventionally (and probably misleadingly) referred to as 'higher order linguistic constraints'. These would include such factors as lexical, syntactic and semantic development. If this were true it would hardly be surprising given that the child is not merely acquiring an inventory of sounds but a means of achieving and interpreting communicative ends (Campbell & Wales, 1970).

Much has been said about the child's lexical development. A number of studies have indicated a fair degree of commonality in children's earliest words, and both functional and perceptual/cognitive accounts have been offered for these. The fact that each account may plausibly co-exist with the others, given the make-up of the child and the acquisition problem, makes it hardly surprising that some evidence supports each position and none seems to place a stranglehold on the existence of the alternatives. Much of the impulse for each account seems to stem from a plausible assumption that the child is using limited means (most obviously a small vocabulary) to achieve a larger communicative intent. Unsurprisingly, but consistent with the view, the child may be interpreted as recruiting already available perceptual categories (e.g. Clark, 1973, 1983), operating on functional interpretations of the immediate environment in which communication is anchored (Nelson, 1973; Grieve & Hoogenraad, 1979), or organising its linguistic word on the basis of the saliency and centrality of best instances of categories (Rosch, 1973; Mervis & Rosch, 1981). Each of these may well be correct some of the time, though clearly not in all instances. Thus Bowerman (1978a) reports evidence suggesting greater support for Clark than Nelson in a few children's early word use. However, it seems very improbable that either Clark or Bowerman would deny a fundamental role in acquisition to functional consequences of interpretation of the contexts of acquisition (cf. Griffiths, 1986).

In the area of Rosch's theorising about the acquisition of natural categories primarily in terms of their best instances (prototype), there are two other revealing aspects of similar ambiguity. It was at first assumed that Rosch's position was at variance with any account of similar phenomena in terms of contrasts or 'features'. Since Smith, Shoben & Rips (1974), that notion has been called into question, although how best to represent natural categories and their prototypes remains problematic. It was also assumed by most that Rosch's approach to category membership was necessarily opposed to the traditional conception that a bird is a bird is a bird. Thus in her approach it seemed possible to talk of relative birdness—a robin was a better instance of 'bird' than was a chicken, and that better than an emu. Perhaps, however, the relativity lies more in the ease with which a member can be accessed as being in a given category (it is easier and hence quicker to recover the fact that a robin is a bird, than that an emu is a bird). If so, this casts the interesting work stemming from Rosch and her followers (e.g. Lakoff, 1987) in another light. It may still be the case that the appropriate representation calls for ('the fact') of all-or-none category membership. An emu either is or is not a bird. Given this view, it is not the representation but the processes involved in acquiring and/or accessing it which are reflected by children's acquisition of words and concepts, with the latter apparently driven by such factors as salience and similarity to the prototype.

While children are constructing meanings for words, they are also constructing forms. As already observed, these forms are made up of sound sequences, and there is evidence that quite early in life some of the main variations beyond the level of the basic word are already known. For example, children as young as 2 years will give you the appropriate plural form for nonsense words (e.g.wug (z) *vs* dax (ez)—Berko, 1958). A year or so later they seem to acquire the rule for regular past tense forms and overgeneralise this to irregular forms already available to them. So they will develop forms like 'goed' and 'foughted' after having earlier said 'went' and 'fought'. There is some question as to whether the earlier 'correct' irregular forms are understood by the child as being the past tenses of the present tense forms. It may be that they are initially construed as two different verbs with the same interpretation in two different temporal contexts. Nevertheless it has been standard to assume that when children do overgeneralise, they do so because (a) they recognise the verbal correspondence, and (b) they apply a rule, since they certainly have not acquired this (very characteristic) behaviour as a result of imitating the input—the spoken language they have heard.

In recent years there has been some attempt to question the need to postulate a 'symbolic representation' (i.e. a rule governed system) to account for this behaviour. Some interesting attempts have been made (Rumelhart & McClelland, 1986) to show that an associationist ('connectionist') model can reproduce the behaviour of children, without any need to postulate the need for access to morphological (word structure) information. Although an interesting challenge to the more traditional view, as Pinker & Prince (1988) point out, there are a number of critical shortcomings to the account given by McClelland & Rumelhart. These shortcomings are both with regard to the substance of what their model does and how that relates to what children are known to do. There is no doubt that connectionist models may well be able to simulate the acquisition processes at this point, but it is much less clear whether they can do so without at least tacit access to morphological (and hence independent symbolic) information.

Studies of the child's early ability to handle inflections have been much influenced by the fact that the earlier forms often seem to be driven by what Slobin (1980) has termed *transparency*—the relative ease with which the inflectional form accords with natural semantic interpretation (but see Bavin, 1991, for examples of the difficulty of applying the principle). Derwing & Baker (1979) showed that, of several derivational patterns studied in a task like Berko's, only the noun compound was used productively by a substantial number of children. This result is supported by Clark & Hecht (1982) where their youngest subjects created novel compounds out of familiar elements, for example 'build-man' for 'builder'. Clark & Hecht advance three theoretical principles for their results: (a) that of semantic transparency (following Slobin), (b) productivity or the effect of frequency or 'rule strength', and (c) conventionality, which refers to the process (whatever it may turn out to be) whereby the child moves from its own innovations (e.g. 'build-man', 'don't broom my mess') to the conventional forms of its adult speech community. The studies point to productive processes in the use of constituent elements of their morphological structure.

A complementary set of observations has been made by Bowerman (1978b) adducing the structural relationships that may underlie the meaning, errors' that her daughters were making up to the age of 5 years or so. One of the dominant characteristics of these 'errors' was using words intersubstitutively which were semantically related but where both words also had been apparently used correctly for some time. Bowerman interprets these as errors in word selection indicating meaningful connections being established, where the meanings of each word had previously been semantically isolated. Bowerman's observations are not only interesting but of course suggest another domain where (if her interpretation were to be taken at face value) a connectionist account might be usefully tested. On the other hand, Griffiths (1986) has pointed out that these data may be more the product of the developing processes of speech production than signs of lexical structure. Taken together with the arguments over the most appropriate way to represent prototypicality—intrinsic or the product of access issues—it is clear that an important focus of the next decade of research in language acquisition should be the attempt to distinguish more sharply the products of representation and process. This in itself will require a close examination of the ways in which both 'representation' and 'process' are themselves understood.

PUTTING WORDS TOGETHER

Of course children do not speak in single words, not for long anyway, and even when they do, some scholars have tended to follow De Laguna (1927) in suggesting that the child's earliest single word utterances are marked with sufficient contextual interpretative constraint that they should be better interpreted as propositional in their main character. Certainly it is typical that the young child, once speaking, will acquire vocabulary with great but uneven rapidity. One avenue of study has been to try and establish what is the basis for the unevenness in growth. In the earliest period of recent, Chomsky-inspired, grammatical description of children's language, Braine (1963) and Brown (1973) sought to use the differential rate of growth of different 'categories' as a basis for establishing the underpinnings of the child's first syntax. This possible insight was soon lost to the zeitgeist emphasising the semantic antecedents of children's 'grammars' even though the evidence against the former and in favour of the latter is equally weak. More recently, Garman (1979) has indicated a possible connection between the rate of vocabulary growth and the development of a syntax to use the vocabulary available. With respect to all these sorts of issues there are some critical questions. To what extent does it make sense to speak of a child acquiring a grammar? If a child does so, how does it do so? What is the relevance of the (apparently self-evident) fact that children acquire a language (a grammar?) to communicate with?

Let us take these in turn. A grammar is an abstract representation of relations between words. Given that our speech is rule-like in following constraints that are useful/essential for selecting and hence communicating messages, it seems not unreasonable to presume that the knowledge we acquire to achieve these ends may be said to be like acquiring a grammar. This is not to dispute the important caveat of Miller (1990) that much of our 'grammatical scholarship' is informed more by literary than natural speech constraints. Miller hence argues that many of the difficulties said to be inherent to the acquisition of grammar may be at the least overstated if looked at from the perspectives of the paradigm case of natural language, namely speech. From Miller's perspective, many problems taken to be critical for syntactic development may not be problems at all, or at the very best very delayed, for example that of long distance dependencies (i.e the fact that such principles as agreement of number need to be maintained regardless of a potentially indeterminate number of intervening elements).

One area where this argument may have particular usefulness is that involving the issue of 'learnability'. The latter is the effort to provide formal grounds for accounting for both what is learned and how it is learned. In 1967, Gold reported some fundamental results regarding this. They included the proof that without 'negative evidence' (strings/sentences explicitly marked to indicate their exclusion from a given grammatical language) no grammar more complex than a context-free phrase structure grammar could be acquired. Since the latter was generally deemed, following Chomsky (1957, 1965), to be insufficiently complex to describe a true natural language, this was a potentially devastating result. Various efforts have been made to tackle the problem that syntax of a complexity necessary for describing a natural language seemed unlearnable. The response of the majority working on children's language is simply to ignore the problem. (Perhaps the problem *will* eventually go away, but evidently not because of their scholarly efforts!)

One seminal approach was that of Hamburger & Wexler (1973) and Wexler & Culicover (1980). They produced a model capable of acquiring a transformational grammar by both enriching the information in the input signal, and making available to the model some constraining principles about what and how inputs could be processed. These additions amounted to explicit claims about what innate mechanisms might need to look like to accomplish the end of acquiring such a grammar. The achievement was that, with these principles made explicit, a proof could be given demonstrating the intended learning.

Since then, there have been a number of corollaries to such work on learnability. One has been to show (as indicated in the section on speech sounds) how prosody might be used as a grouping mechanism, and hence to simplify further the process of acquisition (Morgan, 1986). Another has been to turn away from this way of conceptualising the grammatical-learning problem itself. One approach here is (in very summary form) to assume that the grammatical information is encoded as part of the lexicon and to develop the kinds of strategies that might enable the child with this information to construct appropriate arguments through their sentences (Pinker, 1989). Another is to try and capitalise on intriguing aspects of the revision of Chomsky's Linguistic Theory (e.g. Chomsky, 1988). Here the essential point seems to be that there are a number of principles ('parameters') which together define any given natural language. Thus any particular language is a product of the way in which each parameter is realised in it. The child's task is to use this innately given information to determine whether for each parameter it is represented within its language; failing information to the contrary, it is taken as being the default value. How this approach might be related to the realities of children's behaviour is argued by such work as Roeper & Williams (1987) and Radford (1990). It will be clear that here, as elsewhere, we do not have consensus. What is also increasingly clear, however, is that only by tackling some of these hard questions are we likely to advance our under-standing of children's language much beyond an extended catalogue of what they do.

An associated enterprise likely to advance this is the re-evaluation of the formal constraints which need to be acquired to satisfy the status of a description of 'natural language'. One exemplary such effort is that by Bresnan (1982), another that of Gazdar (1982). Not only do we need to know more about the properties of what is acquired, we need to know more about the how. Peters (1983) has persuasively suggested that there are different strategies that children combine to different extents in the acquisition process. Some are more analytic and, starting from individual words, combine in various ways as syntactic abilities allow. Others are more 'synthetic', starting from formulaic utterances of whole phrases or sentences and only subsequently disentangling the internal relations of the constituent elements. This latter strategy is perhaps yet another instance of the use of limited resources to achieve larger ends (a strategy that we have observed before). Yet another instance could be use of such terms as 'that' or 'this', 'there' or 'here', to orient the listener to the intended subject of discourse without necessarily knowing how to achieve accurate referential expressions anchored appropriately in the spatial and temporal contexts of the utterance (Wales, 1986).

To understand more about the use of these devices should further constrain the structure of the learnability problem, and also serve to inform how the child's linguistic knowledge is put to productive use in interpreting and understanding messages. Studies such as Karmiloff-Smith (1979) and Hickman (1980) have shown that there is often a gap between children having basic linguistic resources and their ability to extend the use of those resources to new and more complex linguistic contexts. This is hardly surprising in itself. However, the existence of the gap and the ways it is transcended indicates that the process of acquisition is not from message contexts to linguistic structure but more the other way about, though in turn probably constrained by cognitive capacities to combine the appropriate structural information, and by social constraints, on the recognition of the need to extend the linguistic resources. Beyond this is the relevance to the child of the social setting and expectations which further determine both the structure, content and style of the child's utterances (Romaine, 1985).

GOING BEYOND THE LITERAL

One last reflection should address the place of metaphor in children's spoken language. Figurative expressions are of course called to mind when considering the many early (and often cute) utterances that children make—utterances which seem to have their own sense, yet clearly do not follow the conventions of adult literal usage. It seems to be misleading and a misnomer to call these 'metaphors' unless we have information suggesting that the child intended a contrast to the literal, or at least can demonstrate elsewhere that that contrast is available. For someone learning French it is a bit bizarre to claim that chicken is a metaphor for fish because the word 'pousson' has been used instead of 'poisson'! Yet this is the form of the claim to which some students of child language seem committed.

As with other aspects of child language, there are a growing number of studies exploring the processes of the development of metaphoric language use (e.g. Winner, 1988; Vosniadou & Ortony, 1983; Wales & Coffey, 1986). A good review and discussion is provided by Vosniadou (1987). These studies attempt to make sense of the constraints imposed by such factors as the level of semantic and syntactic understanding which the child brings to the task of understanding metaphors, and the relation between this understanding and the child's other cognitive abilities at the time. In doing so these studies aim to bring the behaviourally central topic of children's metaphor into the mainstream of child language research, rather than leaving it either to the disregard and disparagement of the grammatical literalists or the fanciful interpretations of the figuratively inclined.

A key issue in this area which continues to exercise the majority of current studies is the extent to which the child's capacity to handle meta-phorical language is a function of the child's intrinsic language com-petence, or is more a function of broader cognitive abilities. As Vosniadou points out, an earlier trend had been to assume that there was a 'stage-like' developmental sequence to the child's metaphorical language use —some even positing a 'metaphorical' stage, others claiming a direct association with the development of some aspect of cognitive development (e.g. the development of cross-classificatory abilities). However, it is fairly clear that children can handle some kinds of metaphor much earlier than others, and that there is no clear evidence of this ability being a direct consequence of any particular cognitive ability. This is not, however, to assert that there is not, as common sense would expect, some relation between the cognitive demands of the metaphor and the child's likelihood of understanding it.

What is now the main focus of study in this area is not the evaluation of global claims of dependence/interdependence of the cognitive and the metaphorical/semantic. Rather it is to disentangle the relative contributions of inference rules applied across general linguistic processes, and the influence of specific knowledge domains. Only by disentangling these are we likely to be able to say much more about the processes by which chil-dren come to understand and use metaphorical language productively. In short, it is still not certain whether we are primarily concerned with making sense of metaphorical language or metaphorical thinking in chil-dren. In order to tackle the latter issue it seems certain that more attention in the developmental studies will need to to be paid to recent efforts to consider metaphor within an interdisciplinary setting, thus taking into account not only psychological and linguistic issues but also those arising from philosophy and artificial intelligence. The constraints imposed by the latter in particular may be especially useful in the attempt to provide a com-putationally effective model of what a metaphor may need to look like. Two distinct and interesting attempts in this direction are provided by MacCormac (1985) and Way (1991). As with the issues discussed under learnability and before that with respect to the analysis of the child's speech sounds, it is interesting to note the increasing weight being given to the role that formal models are playing in our attempts to make sense of the processes by which children acquire their language. This is unsurprising given the fact that such models enable us to evaluate more precisely exactly what the nature of our claims are, and the extent to which the claims relate to the facts they purport to explain.

REFERENCES

Aslin, R.N., Pisoni, D.B. and Jusczyk, P.W. (1983). Auditory development and speech perception in infancy. In M. Haith and J. Campos (eds), *Carmichael's Manual of Child Psychology, Vol. 2*. New York: Wiley.

Bavin, E. (1991). The acquisition of Warlipiri. In D. Slobin (ed.), *The Cross-Linguistic Study of Language Acquisition, Vol. 3*, Hillsdale, New Jersey: Lawrence Erlbaum.

Berko, J. (1958). The child's learning of English morphology, *Word*, **14**, 150–177.

Bowerman, M. (1978a). The acquisition of word meaning: an investigation into some current conflicts. In N. Waterson and C. Snow (eds), *The Development of Communication*. Manchester: Wiley.

Bowerman, M. (1978b). Systematising semantic knowledge in changes over time in the child's organisation of word meaning, *Child Development*, **49**, 977–987.

Braine, M. (1963). The ontogeny of English phrase structure in the first phase, *Language*, **39**, 1–14.

Bresnan, J. (ed.) (1982). *The mental representation of grammatical relations*. Cambridge, Massachusetts: MIT Press.

Brown, R. (1973). *A First Language: The Early Stages*. London: Allen and Unwin.

Burnham, D.K., Earnshaw, L. and Quinn, M.C. (1987). The development of categorical identification of speech. In B.E. McKenzie and R.H. Day (eds), *Perceptual Development of Early Infancy: Problems and Issues*. Hillsdale, New Jersey: Lawrence Erlbaum.

Campbell, R. and Wales, R. (1970). The study of language acquisition. In J. Lyons (ed.), *New Horizons in Linguistics*. Harmondsworth: Penguin Books.

Chomsky, N. (1957). *Syntactic Structures*. The Hague: Mouton.

Chomsky, N. (1965). *Aspects of the Theory of Syntax*. Cambridge, Massachusetts: MIT Press.

Chomsky, N. (1988). *Language and Problems of Knowledge: The Managua Lectures*. Cambridge, Massachusetts: MIT Press.

Clark, E.V. (1973). What's in a word? In T.E. Moore (ed.), *Cognitive Development and the Acquisition of Language*. New York: Academic Press.

Clark, E.V. (1983). Meanings and concepts. In P. Mussen (ed.), *Carmichael's Manual of Child Psychology, Vol. 3*, 4th edn. New York: Wiley.

Clark, E.V. and Hecht, B. (1982). Learning to coin agent and instrument nouns, *Cognition*, **12**, 1–24.

Daniloff, R., Wilcox, K. and Stephens, M.I. (1980). An acoustic-articulatory description of children's defective /s/ productions, *Journal of Communication Disorders*, **19**, 346–363.

De Laguna, G. (1927). *Speech: Its Function and Development*. New Haven: Yale University Press.

Derwing, B. and Baker, W. (1979). Recent research on the acquisition of English morphology. In P. Fletcher & M. Garman (eds), *Language Acquisition, 1st edn*. Cambridge: Cambridge University Press.

Eimas, P. (1975). Auditory and phonetic coding of the cues for speech: discrimination of the /r-l/ distinction by young infants, *Perception & Psychophysics*, **18**, 341–347.

Ferguson, C.A. and Farwell, C.B. (1975). Words and sounds in early language acquisition, *Language*, **51**, 419–439.

Fernald, A. (1989). Intonation and communicative intent in mothers' speech to infants: is the melody the message? *Child Development*, **60**, 1497–1510.

Fernald, A. and Kuhl, P. (1987). Acoustic determinants of infant preference for motherese speech, *Infant Behavior and Development*, **10**, 279–293.

Fernald, A. and Simon, T. (1984). Expanded intonation contours in mothers' speech to newborns, *Developmental Psychology*, **20**, 104–113.

Garman, M. (1979). Early grammatical development. In P. Fletcher and M. Garman (eds), *Language Acquisition, 1st edn*. Cambridge: Cambridge University Press.

Gazdar, G. (1982). Phrase structure grammar. In P. Jacobson and G. Pullins (eds), *The Nature of Syntactic Representation*. Dordrecht: Reidel.

Gleitman, L. and Wanner, E. (1982). Language acquisition. In E. Wanner and L. Gleitman (eds), *Language Acquisition: The State of the Art*. Cambridge: Cambridge University Press.

Gold, F. (1967). Language identification in the limit, *Information and Control*, **10**, 447–474.

Grieve, R. and Hoogenraad, R. (1979). First words. In P. Fletcher and M. Garman (eds), *Language Acquisition, 1st edn*. Cambridge: Cambridge University Press.

Griffiths, P. (1986). Early vocabulary. In P. Fletcher and M. Garman (eds), *Language Acquisition, 2nd edn*. Cambridge: Cambridge University Press.

Hamburger, H. and Wexler, K. (1973). A mathematical theory of learning transformation grammar, *Journal of Mathematical Psychology*, **12**, 137–177.

Harnad, S. (ed.) (1987). *Categorial Perception*. Cambridge: Cambridge University Press.

Hickman, M. (1980). Creating referents in discourse. *Chicago Linguistic Society Papers: Parasession on Anaphora*. Chicago: Chicago University Press.

Hirsh-Pasek, K., Kemler-Nelson, D.G., Jusczyk, P.W., Wright Cassidy, K., Druss, B. and Kennedy, L. (1987). Clauses are perceptual units for young children, *Cognition*, **26**, 269–286.

Kaplan, E. and Kaplan, G. (1971). The prelinguistic child. In J. Eliot (ed.), *Human Development and Cognitive Processes*. New York: Holt Reinhart.

Karmiloff-Smith, A. (1979). *A Functional Approach to Child Language: A Study of Determiners and Reference*. Cambridge: Cambridge University Press.

Kornfeld, J. (1971). What initial clusters tell us about a child's speech sounds, *MIT RLE Quarterly Progress Report*, **101**, 218–221.

Kornfeld, J. and Goehl, H. (1974). A new twist to an old observation: kids know more than they say. *Chicago Linguistic Society Papers: Parasession on Natural Phonology*, pp. 210–219. Chicago: Chicago University Press.

Kuhl, P. and Fadden, D.M. (1982). Enhanced discriminability at phonetic boundary for the voicing feature in macaques, *Perception & Psychophysics*, **32**, 542–550.

Kuhl, P. and Miller, J.D. (1975). Speech perception by the chinchilla: voiced–voiceless distinctions in alveolar plosive consonants, *Science*, **190**, 69–72.

Lakoff, G. (1987). *Women, Fire and Dangerous Things*. Chicago: Chicago University Press.

MacCormac, E. (1985). *A Cognitive Theory of Metaphor*. Cambridge, Massachusetts: MIT Press.

Macken, M. and Barton, D. (1980). The acquisition of the voicing contrast in English: a study of voiced-onset time in word-initial stop consonants, *Journal of Child Language*, **7**, 41–74.

Maxwell, E. and Weismer, G. (1982). The contribution of phonological acoustic and perceptual techniques to the characterisation of a misarticulating child's voice contrast for stops, *Journal of Applied Psycholinguistics*, **3**, 29–43.

Menyuk, P., Menn, L. and Silber, R. (1986). Early strategies for the perception and production of words and sounds. In P. Fletcher and M. Garman (eds), *Language Acquisition, 2nd edn.* Cambridge: Cambridge University Press.

Mervis, C. and Rosch, E. (1981). Categorisation of natural objects, *Annual Review of Psychology*, **32**, 89–115.

Miller, J. (1990). Unpublished manuscript, University of Edinburgh.

Morgan, J. (1986). *From Simple Input to Complex Grammar.* Cambridge, Massachusetts: MIT Press.

Morse, P. (1972). The discrimination of speech and non-speech sounds in early infancy, *Journal of Experimental Child Psychology*, **14**, 477–492.

Moskovitz, A.I. (1973). The acquisition of phonology and syntax. In K. Hintikka, J. Moravsik and P. Suppes (eds), *Approaches to Natural Language.* Dordrecht: Reidel.

Nelson, K. (1973). Structure and strategy in learning to talk, *Monographs of the Society for Research in Child Development*, **38**(1–2), Serial No. 149.

O'Connor, G. (1979). Unpublished MSc thesis, University of Melbourne.

Peters, A. (1983). *The Units of Language Acquisition.* Cambridge: Cambridge University Press.

Pinker, S. (1989). *Learnability and Cognition.* Cambridge, Massachusetts: MIT Press.

Pinker, S. and Prince, A. (1988). On language and connectionism: analysis of a parallel distributed processing model of language acquisition, *Cognition*, **28**, 73–193.

Radford, A. (1990). *Syntactic Theory and the Acquisition of Syntax.* Oxford: Basil Blackwell.

Roeper, T. and Williams, E. (eds) (1987). *Parameter Setting.* Dordrecht: Reidel.

Romaine, S. (1985). *The Language of Children and Adolescents.* Oxford: Basil Blackwell.

Rosch, E. (1973). The internal structure of perceptual and semantic categories. In T.E. Moore (ed.), *Cognitive Development and Language Acquisition.* New York: Academic Press.

Rumelhart, D. and McClelland, J. (1986). On learning the past tenses of English verbs. In J. McClelland and D. Rumelhart (eds), *Parallel Distributed Processing, Vol. 2, Psychological and Biological Models.* Cambridge, Massachusetts: MIT Press.

Slobin, D. (1980). The repeated pathway between transparency and opacity in language. In U. Bellugi and M. Studdert-Kennedy (eds), *Signed and Spoken Language: Biological Constraints on Linguistic Form.* Weinheim: Verlag Chemie.

Slobin, D. (1985). *The Cross-Linguistic Study of Language Acquisition.* Hillsdale, New Jersey: Lawrence Erlbaum.

Smith, E., Shoben, E. and Rips, L. (1974). Structure and process in semantic memory: a featured model for semantic decisions, *Psychological Review*, **81**, 214–241.

Smith, N. (1973). *The Acquisition of Phonology: A Case Study.* Cambridge: Cambridge University Press.

Studdert-Kennedy, M. (1990). Language development from an evolutionary perspective. *Haskins Laboratories Status Report on Speech Research*, No. 101/102, New Haven, Connecticut: Haskins Laboratories and (in press) in N. Krasneger, D. Rumbaugh, R. Schiefelbusch and M. Studdert-Kennedy (eds), *Language Acquisition: Biological and Behavioural Determinants.* Hillsdale, New Jersey: Lawrence Erlbaum.

Vosniadou, S. (1987). Children and metaphors, *Child Development*, **58**, 870–885.

Vosniadou, S. and Ortony, A. (1983). The emergence of the literal-metaphorical anomalous distinction in young children, *Child Development*, **54**, 154–161.

Wales, R. (1986). Deixis. In P. Fletcher and M. Garman (eds), *Language Acquisition, 2nd edn.* Cambridge: Cambridge University Press.

Wales, R. and Coffey, G. (1986). On children's comprehension of metaphor. In C. Pratt, A.F. Garton, W.E. Tunmer and A.R. Nesdale (eds), *Research Issues in Child Development*. Sydney, Australia: Allen and Unwin.

Way, E. (1991). *Knowledge Representation and Metaphor*. Dordrecht: Kluwer.

Werker, J. and Tees, R. (1984). Cross-language speech perception: evidence for perceptual reorganisation during the first year of life, *Infant Behavior and Development*, **7**, 49–63.

Wexler, K. and Culicover, P. (1980). *Formal Principles of Language Acquisition*. Cambridge, Massachusetts: MIT Press.

Winner, E. (1988). *The Point of Words*. Cambridge, Massachusetts: Harvard University Press.

Yeni-Komshian, G., Kavanagh, J. and Ferguson, C. (eds) (1981). *Child Phonology* (2 vols). New York: Academic Press.

5 Spatial Representation in Infancy and Early Childhood

J. GAVIN BREMNER

University of Lancaster

The aim of this chapter is to examine key parts of the literature on the development of spatial representations in infancy and early childhood with a view to making suggestions about the processes leading to development of spatial representations and the form these representations take. With respect to infancy, the dominant account until recently was Piaget's, with its emphasis on the gradual construction of representations through action in the world. However, a mass of evidence has now accumulated indicating that his account is at least wrong in detail, and the task is to build alternative models of the development of spatial representations during this period. The literature on spatial representation in early childhood also has its roots in Piagetian work, and again the literature of the past 30 years has been largely critical of his claims, but has done relatively little to build alternative models of development of childhood spatial representations. Additionally, this literature has remained essentially separate from the work on infancy. Thus, in addition to making suggestions about the processes that may lead to development of representations in these two age periods, comparisons will be made between the emerging models with a view to establishing common developmental themes.

RELATIONS BETWEEN PERCEPTION AND REPRESENTATION IN EARLY INFANCY: WHAT DEVELOPS?

Piaget's account

The development of spatial representation has a central role in Piaget's (1954) theory of sensori-motor development. In his account, during the first 2 years of life the infant gradually constructs an external reality through action in the world. While this construction is initially based on actions rather than on mental activity, it culminates in mental representations of reality that support understanding of the physical world independent of action in it. There is no sense in which young infants know the world around them as an objective arrangement of objects in a space separate from self. Perceptual inputs are initially treated as bodily sensations

Systems of Representation in Children: Development and Use. Edited by C. Pratt and A.F. Garton
© 1993 John Wiley & Sons Ltd

linked to particular acts, and there is no awareness that they originate from objects in an external world. This knowledge only emerges fully around the end of the second year with the development of representations of objects and spatial relations.

For the young infant, then, space is not something that exists 'out there' *a priori*: it is a construction that is gradually imposed on the infant's percep- tions through action in the world. In the early months, through watching their actions on objects, infants begin to construct an external space, but one that is limited in two ways. First, its three-dimensionality extends only as far as the infant can reach. Second, the relations constructed in this space are *egocentric*, that is objects' positions are related to the infant but not to each other.

This second limitation leads to one of the best known Piagetian phenomena—search failure at around 6 months. Because infants are unable to relate one object to another, when an object is hidden by an occluder they are only able to relate the occluder to self and consequently the hidden object's position cannot be represented. As infants progress through subsequent stages, objective relationships of this sort are gradually constructed, leading to object search when static relations are involved and then, some months later, to the ability to make inferences about an object's movements in space even when these are not seen. But one vestige of egocentrism lingers on right to the penultimate stage of the sensori-motor period. Even once objective spatial relations are constructed between objects, infants still do not treat themselves as objects that are bound by the same spatial principles. Self remains a privileged spatial centre until the final sensori-motor stage, when infants' representational capacities allow them to step outside the constraints of egocentric perception to view themselves as objects in external space.

Recent evidence against Piaget

Recent research has presented a considerable challenge to some of Piaget's main claims. In particular, studies of visual perception have indicated perceptual capacities that appear to go well beyond those that Piaget would have attributed to young infants. Many of the most recent advances have arisen from ingenious adaptations of the *visual habituation technique*. Probably the most productive of these has been the *habituation–novelty* technique, in which the infant is habituated to a single stimulus and is then presented with that stimulus paired with a novel one. Prior habituation should lead infants to look less at the habituated stimulus and conse- quently more at the novel stimulus *provided* they can discriminate between them. This technique has proved to be a sensitive method of detecting dis- criminations in young infants, and its relevance to questions about young infants' spatial awareness is that we can apply it to three-dimensional stimuli to investigate, for example, whether infants discriminate on the basis of the retinal form of stimuli or in terms of their true shape.

Discrimination on the basis of true shape involves *shape* constancy, something that Piaget claimed was beyond infants until they were around 9 months old. However, recent research suggests otherwise. Caron, Caron & Carlson (1979) habituated 3-month-old infants to one shape (a rectangle or trapezoid) presented at different tilts to the line of sight. After this, they presented either the same shape in a tilt not used during habituation or a novel shape. They found clear dishabituation only to the novel shape, despite the fact that both dishabituation stimuli projected novel retinal images, and concluded that 3-month-olds have shape constancy. Testing newborns, Slater & Morison (1985) used a *habituation–novelty* version of the technique used by Caron *et al.* (1979). After habituation trials in which one shape was presented at various angles, newborns showed a strong preference for a novel shape over the original stimulus presented at an angle not previously encountered. So again, there is evidence for shape constancy, this time right at birth. This has implications for newborn space perception, since shape constancy involves perception of the third dimension: it is only through picking up the orientation of the stimulus in the third dimension that its true shape can be derived from the retinal form. Additionally, the ability to perceive constant forms despite changes in viewing angle is a very basic aspect of spatial awareness.

Another major principle of space perception that according to Piaget only emerged around the age of 9 months is *size constancy*. In order to exhibit size constancy, it is necessary to perceive the distance of the object and compute its true size from its distance and the retinal image size. Quite some time ago Bower (1964) presented evidence that infants under 2 months were capable of both depth perception and size constancy. Until recently, however, other workers failed to obtain evidence of size constancy in infants under 6 months (McKenzie, Tootell & Day, 1980). But it now appears that this arose because the habituation techniques that they used were not sufficiently sensitive, since, adopting the *familiarization* technique used in the case of shape constancy, Slater, Mattock & Brown (1990) obtained evidence for size constancy at birth.

The image of early infancy emerging from this work is very different from the one presented by Piaget. It would appear that even at birth infants pick up three-dimensional information sufficiently well to perceive an objective reality. Shape and size constancy do not have to be constructed as early forms of spatial representation but are present at birth. This evidence is supplemented by work with slightly older infants which indicates even more impressive awareness of the rules of spatial relations. For instance, 5-month-olds (Baillargeon, Spelke & Wasserman, 1985) and even some 3-month-olds (Baillargeon, 1987) show surprise if a screen rotates from horizontal to vertical to occlude an object placed behind it and then continues to rotate, appearing to move right through the space that the object occupies. By contrast, they were not surprised if the screen rotated to occlude the object, but stopped before violating the object's space. Spelke (1985) suggests that infants perceive the persistence of an object when it is out of sight and realize how this constrains the movement of another object, a conclusion that is further supported by the finding that 6- to 8-month-olds show surprise when a moving object apparently moves through another object placed in its path (Baillargeon, 1986).

There are two main schools of thought with regard to the basis of these early abilities. Baillargeon & Spelke conclude that primitive representational abilities exist that permit infants to perceive the persistence of objects and to detect violations of normal spatial rules. In contrast, Gibson (1979) argues against the need to invoke representation at all: the structure of the world is specified in the optical flow reaching the subject, and this dynamic information is sufficiently rich to specify objects even when they are temporarily out of sight. The strength of this view is its identification of perception as a dynamic process with continuity over time. The issue is no longer how a series of flat retinal snapshots are integrated and used as the basis for a constructed three-dimensional world: three-dimensionality is just there in the perceptual flow. Information about three-dimensionality is specified in perception and infants do not need to construct representations of reality from impoverished perceptual data.

Persuasive as this may be, however, a good deal seems to be left out. Nothing is said, for instance, about the form of the perceptual structures required for extraction of this information. No matter how rich the perceptual flow, the quality of the information extracted can only be as good as the system doing the extracting, and we must assume a sophisticated perceptual system to support the processes that Gibson proposes. But whatever the modifications required in Gibson's theory, it has to be said that the accumulating data pointing to the richness of newborn perception fit more easily with his account than with conventional views of perceptual and cognitive development.

If we focus solely on the evidence for early perceptual competence it is easy to reach the conclusion that there is little to be developed in infancy. However, a quick look at the realities of infancy indicates that this is far from being the case. No matter how perceptually competent newborns appear, we are left with the fact that infants do not show these competencies in spontaneous behaviour for quite some time. Even if young infants are sophisticated perceivers, they have a limited ability to act on the world. And development of action is not just a matter of motor development: the infant has to construct proper relations between perception and action. Consequently, I believe we can recast Piaget's constructionist account to emphasise a different sort of spatial representation that develops through action. Although the physical world may be objectively perceived from birth, infants still have to construct the relationships between that objective world and their developing action systems. Thought of this way, infants are in the business of constructing *functional* representations of the world, functional because rather than specifying the physical properties of objects and space they specify relations between these physical properties and the infant's action systems. This is really very close to Gibson's concept of affordances, and it may well be that some functional properties of the world are simply discovered through action. For instance, while learning to walk the infant will discover that some surfaces support walking while others do not (Gibson *et al.*, 1987). However, I shall argue that there are also forms of knowledge that are not simply picked up, and that infants and young children construct organisations of space that are not so much inherent in space itself as relevant to their current plans for action.

SPATIAL REPRESENTATION IN INFANCY

Reference systems for coding positions in space

One focus of infancy research concerns the forms of reference systems that infants develop to code positions in space and how these systems change developmentally. In other words, the interest is in what sorts of representations infants develop that allow them to organise space. Generally speaking, two different sorts of system are identified. Infants might code an object's position relative to self, that is at a given angle and distance relative to the body axes, or they might code the object's position relative to other objects or relative to some external framework that is either provided by the spatial structure or is imposed on space mentally. This distinction has often been labelled *egocentric* versus *allocentric* spatial coding (e.g. Bremner & Bryant, 1977; Harris, 1973).

There is a danger, however, that applying such a dichotomy oversimplifies or misrepresents the problem. Firstly, given Piaget's emphasis on egocentrism as a limitation of infant cognition, the term *egocentric coding* suggests a limitation in spatial organisation. However, the primary goal of most spatial activities is to maintain the relationship between self and particular environmental features or goals. For this reason, I prefer to use the term *self-referent coding*, and the developmental issue becomes not when infants abandon self-referent coding in preference for allocentric coding, but how allocentric coding can be used to help them to update self-referent codings during movement. The advantage of self-referent coding is that it relates directly to infants' actions on the world; they need to know the self-referent position of an object in order to act on it. The disadvantage is that, used on its own, this system requires constant updating during the infant's movements. However, if some allocentric coding is employed (e.g.

the goal is 'near to the window'), the infant can then move around and attend elsewhere, but can instantly update the self-referent position of the goal by reference to its allocentric position coding.

Secondly, some means of coding position have both self-referent and allocentric components. For instance, if one object is coded as 'to the left' of a landmark, there is both an allocentric component, since the object is being related to an external feature, and a self-referent element, since 'to the left' depends on the subject's position in space, and would no longer be correct if, for instance, the subject viewed the array from the opposite side of the room.

For these reasons, we need to be wary of oversimplifying our analysis of position coding, even when dealing with its early manifestation in infancy. As we shall see, the infant's ability to perform spatial updating during self-movement depends on the type of movement, the environment in which it occurs, and whether or not the movement was controlled by the infant. I shall argue that all these factors can be accounted for in terms of the spatial orientation problems that arise as the infant progressively gains control over visual and, later, locomotor exploration of the environment.

A good deal of the initial work on infant spatial coding was related directly to one of the Piagetian search phenomena. His observation was that once infants began to search for hidden objects, they would only search in one place, failing to take account of a change of hiding locus. This task has been analysed in terms of the position coding involved (Bremner, 1978a; Bremner & Bryant, 1977; Butterworth, 1975; Harris, 1973), and one hypothesis is that the error is due to failure to update the object's self-referent location during the move (Butterworth, Jarrett & Hicks, 1982). There are, however, other accounts and conflicting findings (for a review, see Bremner, 1985), and I shall concentrate instead on studies that have looked directly at spatial reference during infant movement.

An early study (Bremner, 1978b) involved the search task illustrated in Figure 5.1. Infants were faced with an array of two hiding locations and watched an object being hidden in one. Before being allowed to search, however, they were moved round to the opposite side of the array. The issue was whether they updated their self-referent coding of the object's position, in which case accurate search would result, or whether they failed to update, in which case they would search at the opposite place in the array. The task was presented in two cueing conditions: in one case the table sides were different colours and in the other case the covers for the locations were different colours. There were also two comparison conditions in which the table rather than the infant was rotated after the object was hidden. The results indicated that two factors determined the accuracy of search. The more direct cover cues led to better performance, and infants performed better after their own movement than after a rotation of the table.

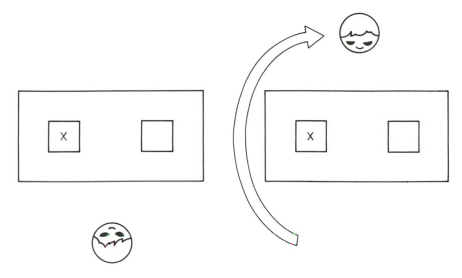

Figure 5.1 The method used by Bremner (1978b) to investigate spatial updating during movement. The dependent measure was search for an object (X) hidden before movement

The first finding seems straightforward enough: it would make good sense to find that strong spatial cues help infants to search accurately, either by providing the structure to which an external position coding can be attached, or by directly cueing the correct location. The second finding, however, was a little more puzzling, since the movement of the infant was a good deal more distracting than the table rotation. The favoured conclusion was that self-movement cued the use of a different strategy. Infants at this age are beginning to crawl, and as a direct result must encounter many situations in which updating spatial locations relative to self is necessary.

Other methods have been used to assess spatial orientation ability in infancy. For instance, Acredolo (1978) used anticipative looking rather than object search as her dependent measure. Testing took place in a rectangular room. Initially, infants were trained to anticipate the appearance of someone at one of two windows to their left and right: a centrally placed buzzer sounded, followed consistently by the event, always at the same window. After training, infants were moved to the opposite side of the room. The crucial question was whether, on hearing the buzzer, they looked in the same self-referent direction as before, and hence at the wrong window, or whether they updated the event location during movement and so made the opposite head turn to fixate the correct window. Acredolo carried out this task in a marked condition, in which the event window was marked by a colourful star pattern, and in an unmarked condition, in which both windows looked the same. She found that 6-month-olds in both conditions turned in the same direction after movement, and hence fixated the wrong window. At 11 months, performance was still poor in the unmarked condition, while only half of the infants in the marked condition turned the wrong way, indicating that spatial cues were beneficial at this age. By contrast, at 16 months performance was good in both conditions, so it would seem that by that age infants' spatial orientation is good enough not to need the support of strong direct cues. Subsequently, Acredolo & Evans (1980) found that by presenting even stronger position cues they could elicit correct updating from the majority of 9- and 11-month-olds, although the performance of 6-month-olds under these conditions was still poor.

The advantage of this anticipation method is that it can be used with infants who have not begun to search for hidden objects. However, a potential disadvantage is that the training of a fixed response may lead to a form of perseveration that could conceal spatial ability. McKenzie, Day & Ihsen (1984) circumvented this problem by modifying the training phase so that no single response was trained. They trained infants to anticipate an event at one place on a circular surround but varied the infant's orientation during training so that different head-turns were required on different trials. After this training, 6- and 8-month-olds showed the ability to fixate the correct location despite body rotations of up to 90°. Additionally, Meuwissen & McKenzie (1987) showed that 8-month-olds use spatial landmarks as a primary guide to orientation in this sort of task. Note, however, that the movement in this task was a simple bodily rotation without a displacement, and infants of this age do not seem to be able to take account of rotations greater than 90°, a result in keeping with an earlier finding that they could not deal with 180° rotations (Cornell & Heth, 1979). So there are limits to their ability even when sensitive methods are used, and current evidence suggests that the ability to take account of relatively small bodily rotations precedes the ability to take account of larger rotations or movements involving both displacement and rotation.

Action and spatial orientation

As already noted, it may be no coincidence that the ability to take account of bodily movements involving displacement as well as reorientation emerges at around 9 months. Infants begin to crawl sometime between 6 and 9 months and it seems plausible that the exercise of this new ability presents new demands that lead infants to adopt new ways of organising space. Before beginning to crawl they are, of course, carried around by their parents, but the resulting experience may not be as effective as that arising from self-controlled movements, where visual experiences relate directly to their activities.

The notion that active experience is important is not new. As well as being an important part of Piaget's theorising, it crops up in other work. For instance, Held & Hein (1963) found that active perceptual experience was important for normal perceptual development in animals. The notion here is that visual experience has to occur in parallel with vestibular and kinaesthetic information about normal active movement to be properly interpreted. In addition, we can look for a role for active movement that differs from both of these accounts. In the case of passive movements, infants are not faced with the problem of execution. Active movement, on the other hand, throws up a range of spatial problems that the infant has to solve—detour problems being one example—and solution of these problems is likely to require new spatial representations.

With respect to human infants, the issue of active movement and development was first investigated in connection with performance on the 'visual cliff'. The original finding was that infants over the age of 6 months showed wariness of large vertical drops, refusing to crawl on glass over a large drop but doing so when the glass covered a solid surface (Gibson & Walk, 1960). However, more recent work indicates that infants only become wary of the visual cliff after they have been crawling for some time (Campos et al., 1978). Additionally, Svejda & Schmid (1979) found that with age held constant, those infants who could already crawl showed evidence of wariness on the visual cliff (indicated by an increase in heart rate), whereas those who were still immobile did not. However, as Campos et al. (1982) point out, infants who crawl early may do so because they are generally more advanced, cognitively as well as motorically. Indeed, the direction of causality could even be in the opposite direction, with crawling onset motivated by cognitive advance rather than permitted by motor developments. This means that simply holding test age constant is no guarantee of controlling all relevant factors other than mobility. But strong evidence for a causal link between locomotor experience and spatial awareness comes from the finding (Campos et al., 1981) that infants supplied with baby-walkers at 5 months were more likely to be wary of the visual cliff than a matched group not given this early mobility advantage.

The interpretation of these relations that springs from the Held & Hein work is that the onset of crawling permits active exploration of the environment that has a crucial role in 'tuning up' infants' space perception. A viable alternative, however, is that active exploration does not so much 'tune up' perception as lead to discovery of the implications of certain perceptual experiences for newly developed action: vertical drops become particularly dangerous when infants begin to crawl. It is worth noting that this discovery may be at least partly socially mediated, since Sorce et al. (1985)

found that the mother's emotional expression could determine whether or not infants crossed the deep side of an intermediate-height visual cliff.

Given the results with visual cliff avoidance, it would be reasonable to expect a similar relation between locomotion and spatial ability to apply to the spatial orientation tasks discussed in the previous section. After all, these tasks involve just the sorts of spatial transformations that occur when the infant crawls. Surprisingly, however, direct research on crawling and spatial orientation is a recent development and is still sparse. What research there is has pursued two slightly different lines.

Two studies have investigated whether accuracy of spatial orientation is affected by whether the infant moves actively or passively within the task itself (Acredolo, Adams & Goodwyn, 1984; Benson & Uzgiris, 1985). In both cases, the two-position object search task was adapted by placing screens on three sides of the array. From the side opposite to the unscreened section, infants watched the object hidden, so that to search for it, they had to crawl around to the unscreened side in order to get through the screen. Both Acredolo *et al.* (1984) and Benson & Uzgiris found that infants who made the movement themselves were more accurate at relocating the object than a comparison group who were moved passively. This is a striking finding, since the active group perform better despite the fact that their attention must be partly directed to executing the detour.

Other workers have tried to show a relationship between crawling experience and spatial orientation. So far, the work here is rather contradictory. McComas & Field (1984) found no relationship between amount of crawling experience and spatial orientation in a task of the sort used by Acredolo (1978). However, possible reasons for their negative results are that they did not hold test age or crawling onset age constant and they compared infants with different degrees of crawling experience rather than comparing crawlers to non-crawlers. In contrast, Campos & Bertenthal (1988) claim positive relationships between crawling experience and spatial orientation on Acredolo's task. In addition, two studies have shown a positive relation between crawling experience and performance on object permanence related search tasks (Horobin & Acredolo, 1986; Kermoian & Campos, 1988). However, what performance on these tasks indicates about spatial coding is not entirely clear, and more work is needed before definite conclusions can be drawn.

Probably we should not limit our attention to the onset of locomotion, since it may well be the case that infants find out a good deal about the relationship between self and environment through simpler sorts of active movement. In this respect, the achievement of sitting up unaided may be very important. Young infants lack the postural control to support themselves, and the external support supplied by baby chairs or the floor generally impedes the infant's head and body movements further. In contrast, once infants achieve the sitting posture, they become capable of exercising reasonably fine control over rotational movements of head, and later the trunk—movements of just the sort produced in the spatial rotation studies carried out by McKenzie and her colleagues.

There is a striking chronological agreement here which seems unlikely to be a coincidence. On average, infants sit unaided at 6 months, and begin to execute rotational movements of the trunk about a month later (Illingworth, 1973). This matches up with the finding that 6-month-olds are capable of taking account of relatively limited rotational movements (McKenzie *et al.*, 1984), while 8-month-olds extended this ability to larger rotations (Keating, McKenzie & Day, 1986).

This analysis has interesting implications for the development of spatial reference systems. Once infants can sit unaided, control over head movements precedes control over movements of the trunk. This leads to the possibility that we may need to distinguish between position relative to the body, position relative to the head, and position in the external world, since while infants are only capable of head movements, the relation between body and world remains fixed (as far as actively achieved changes are concerned). Thus the body-centred system is confounded with any stable external system. On the other hand, position relative to the head is dissociated from position in an external system whenever a head movement is executed. If active movements of this sort have an important effect on spatial development, the prediction is that from quite an early age infants should be able to dissociate position defined by a head-based system from position in the external world, but that they should take longer to dissociate a body-centred system from external systems.

A model of spatial development in infancy

In the section, 'Recent evidence against Piaget' (pp. 68–71), findings were reviewed pointing to high-level spatial perception from birth onwards, and it was suggested that a major aspect of spatial development concerned the establishment of relations between objective perception and developing action. The section that followed reviewed evidence on development of position coding and drew links between this and development of action. There are several ways in which development might be mediated by action. Firstly, according to Gibson (1979) perception is an active extraction process that occurs as the organism moves through the environment. An implication of this is that as infants gain greater control over bodily movement they should become capable of extracting more information from the world. But according to Gibson this does not involve construction of representations: the information is just there to be picked up as the infant becomes more active. In addition, as locomotion is achieved, new affordances should emerge that relate to this new activity. For instance, infants will come to detect surfaces which support locomotion and those that do not. It may well be that the visual cliff avoidance data fit in here. Although it is possible that locomotion leads to enhanced depth perception, we need to remember that the dependent measure in these studies is *wariness* of vertical drops. It seems more likely that active locomotion leads infants, either directly or through social mediation, to realise the danger of vertical drops in connection with acts of locomotion.

While it is likely that this is an important part of the story, other considerations suggest that we also need to view the infant as a spatial problem-solver. Development of control over movement may well reveal new spatial structures in the world, but the new-found motor ability yields new possibilities for acting within these structures, which in themselves throw up new problems that infants must solve if they are to use these new actions effectively. For instance, the onset of crawling makes it necessary to develop allocentric codings of space that allow for updating of the self-referent system during movement. Also, detour problems crop up when certain spatial structures offer barriers to direct approach to a goal. Interestingly, these detour problems may well become particularly common for those infants who move around using furniture as a support, since this mode of locomotion rarely allows direct approach to a goal.

The suggestion is that infants develop new representations of space through solving these problems. However, these representations, rather than being complete internal replicas of space, are imposed organisations that are particularly useful for the infant's mode of action in the world at the time. For the 6-month-old who can sit upright, some form of self-referent organisation may be adequate, while for the mobile 9-month-old the addition of an allocentric system may be necessary. Put in this way, it may seem that the sequence of cognitive development is determined by the sequence of motor development. However, these representations, once developed, are used to guide action. So actions are partially determined by the form of current internal representation as well as by the infant's motor maturity. Thus there is a constant interplay between level of representation, form of action, and the new problems consequent on that form of action, so that current representation indirectly determines the form of representation to follow.

SPATIAL REPRESENTATION AFTER INFANCY

The roots of work on spatial representation in childhood can again be found in Piaget's work, the best known being his work with Inhelder on children's perspective-taking ability (Piaget & Inhelder, 1956). The main task required children to identify the view of a doll observing three model mountains from a position that differed from their own, either by constructing the view using cut-outs of the mountains, or by selecting the picture that they believed represented the doll's view. Using these methods,

Piaget & Inhelder traced the development of perspective taking, from complete failure at 4 years to full success at 10 years, and two major factors emerged. Firstly, at around 6 years of age (younger children were unable to understand the task at all), they did not just fail to identify the other observer's view; they showed a strong tendency to construct their own view and to select a picture that either represented their view or contained all the information that they could see from there. To Piaget and Inhelder this indicated the fundamental egocentrism of pre-operational thought. Such a child is unable to apply logical transformations to his or her own view in order to construct other views, and in consequence has no conception that other views exist: '... he appears to be rooted in his own viewpoint ... so that he cannot imagine any perspective but his own' (Piaget & Inhelder, 1956, p. 242). Secondly, once children have begun to recognise that other views exist, they still have difficulty in constructing them if the array contains object relations in both near–far and left–right planes. The argument, supported by other work (Piaget, Inhelder & Szeminska, 1960), was that although they are capable of imposing a unidimensional organisation on space, they are unable to apply a coordinate reference system relating objects in orthogonal dimensions.

There is now a considerable literature indicating that children are capable of performing such tasks better or sooner than Piaget & Inhelder indicated, showing, for instance, that use of familiar materials or simplified response methods yields much better performance (Borke, 1975), or that children of 3–5 years expect a view to change when they move (Shantz & Watson, 1970). The main studies that I want to focus on here, however, are ones that analyse the representational abilities required to perform perspective taking and related spatial tasks. Piaget & Inhelder identified two component abilities in perspective taking—the ability to recognise that different views exist and the ability to construct these other views on the basis of the child's own view. According to their data, the latter ability follows some time after the former, a predictable enough result since there is clearly a lot more to constructing another view than simply realising that it exists.

Piaget & Inhelder treated spatial cognition within the same framework as the rest of Piagetian theory; spatial tasks of this sort had to be performed by logical manipulation of spatial relations. For instance, an opposed view would be constructed by reversing relations in both near–far and left–right dimensions, very much a logical, rule-based solution. However, there are other ways in which another view might be arrived at. Suppose children mentally represent their own movement around the array into the new position. A full representation of this event would include the progressive updating of their view until it corresponded with the perspective to be taken, and the representational process would be more in the form of a mental analogue of perception than a logical manipulation of relations.

Alternatively, children might mentally rotate the array through the appropriate angle and so effect an equivalent transformation. A study by Huttenlocher & Presson (1973) bears on this issue. They showed children an array which was then screened, at which point children were asked to say how the array would appear from a new location. One group were asked to do this from their observation position, the usual perspective-taking task, whereas the other group actually adopted the new position and made their judgement from there. The latter group performed much better, and Huttenlocher & Presson concluded that, in tasks involving movement of the subject, performance was mediated by a mental rotation process, and that updating was made simpler by the child's movement being actual rather than imaginary.

Huttenlocher & Presson appear to favour the notion that children mentally rotate the array as part of the process of arriving at the new perspective. In contrast, Harris & Bassett (1976) suggest that children imagine a rotation of self around the array to a new position from which they reconstruct the array. However, while either of these alternatives are plausible possibilities, neither Huttenlocher & Presson nor Harris & Bassett provide direct evidence for the operation of a rotation strategy. For this reason, Bremner, Knowles & Andreasen (1992) performed a study designed to produce direct evidence on the form of solution used by young children. A search task was employed in which the child watched an object being hidden at one of four locations and then walked around to the opposite side of the array before searching. The sides of the array were screened to prevent children from solving the task by simply fixating the correct location while moving around.

Two different arrangements of locations were used, as shown in Figure 5.2, the reason for this choice being as follows. If children attempt to solve

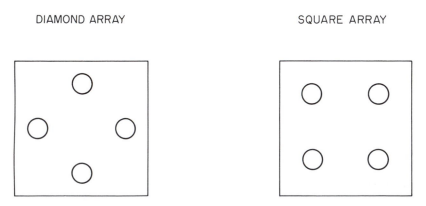

DIAMOND ARRAY   SQUARE ARRAY

Figure 5.2 The hiding arrays used by Bremner, Knowles & Andreason (1992) to investigate young children's spatial updating strategies

the task by defining the search location through a coordinate reference system, the two arrays should present different levels of difficulty. In the diamond array, each position can be defined in relation to the others through use of one dimension alone (near, far, left or right). In contrast, in the square array, each position can only be uniquely defined relative to the rest through use of two dimensions, that is, a position is not simply 'near', but is 'near-left' or 'near-right'. The Piagetian prediction would be that young children would fail to apply a two-dimensional definition of this sort, and so we would expect the square array to be harder to deal with than the diamond array. In contrast, if children use a mental rotation strategy, the two arrays should present equal difficulty since there is no obvious reason why one should be harder to 'rotate' than the other. In addition, errors should take the form of failure to compensate fully for the movement around the array, and would relate to the direction in which the child moves around the array.

Children between 18 months and 4 years old were tested on one or other of these arrays. The main findings were that the error rate was similar for both arrays, and that by 3 years of age children were performing with few errors. Also, there was no indication in the error pattern that children were updating one dimension but not another. There was, however, evidence in the error pattern for use of a 'mental rotation' strategy. The predominant error involved searching at the position that was one place further round in the direction in which the child had travelled. This suggests that children were adopting a rotational compensation for their movement which was often successful, but which was not always complete and so yielded errors of the sort obtained.

This does not mean, of course, that young children are unable to use coordinate reference systems. Instead it may indicate that for this sort of spatial orientation task in relatively small-scale space another perfectly effective method is available that puts less of a cognitive load on the child. And in fact there is evidence from a number of studies indicating that from the age of 4 years onwards children are capable of coordinating spatial dimensions.

The first suggestion that this was the case came from a study by Hughes & Donaldson (1979). The primary aim of this study was to test Piaget & Inhelder's claims about perspective taking, and an example of the arrangement is shown in Figure 5.3. Two walls intersected at right angles at their mid-points, two policemen were placed so that their lines of sight were orthogonal, and the child's task was to place a model boy so that he would be out of sight from both policemen. Children as young as $3\frac{1}{2}$ years made few errors on this task, and performance remained above chance if an additional wall and third policeman was added. This led Hughes & Donaldson to conclude that young children could identify the perspective of another

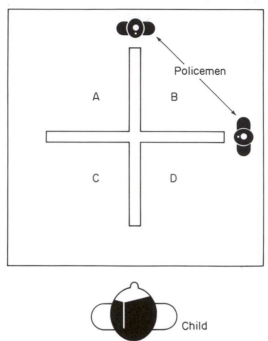

Figure 5.3 The task used by Hughes & Donaldson (1979) to investigate coordination of perspectives by young children. This task was first described in Donaldson (1978), *Children's Minds*, and is reproduced by permission of the publisher, Fontana, an imprint of HarperCollins Publishers Ltd

and that they could coordinate orthogonal dimensions, in this case the lines of sight of the policemen.

The second claim is questionable, since we do not know the basis on which children were making their judgement. Hughes & Donaldson's assumption was that they identified the perspectives of the policemen and coordinated them. However, it is equally possible that they used a sort of 'ostrich principle' of the form, 'If I can't see them, they can't see me'. Indeed, there is evidence for use of this principle even when it does not lead to effective concealment (Bridges & Rowles, 1985). Thus they may have placed the boy where he could see neither policeman, something that requires perspective taking but not coordination of dimensions. But there is even reason to question the first claim. Another likely strategy in hide-and-seek is to get as far from the 'seeker' as possible and, within the constraints of the task, placement of the boy as far as possible from both policemen also involves placing him out of sight of both.

Work by Somerville & Bryant (1985) provides an unambiguous test of coordination of dimensions. Several tasks were used, but the one used with 4-year-olds was designed to be as meaningful as possible in terms of

children's everyday experience, and involved two people facing in orthogonal directions. The child was asked to identify the point at which their
paths would cross if they started walking in straight lines. Children had
four points to choose from, arranged in a square array so that three points
lay on the path of one or other person but only one lay on the path of both.
Four-year-olds also showed some ability to identify the correct point,
although significant success was only achieved by a minority.

The general issue of task familiarity appears in a number of parts of this
literature. It has, for instance, been claimed that poor performance on the
three mountains task was partly due to the unfamiliar stimuli used (Borke,
1975), and an important part of Donaldson's (1978) argument is that tasks
should make *human sense* if they are to yield accurate estimates of children's abilities. However, this emphasis produces its own problems. It is
not obvious which task settings will make more sense to a child, nor is it
transparent what *sort* of sense a child will make of these tasks. To predict
the latter in particular, we would have to know, in advance, how children
think, and it is precisely because we do not know this that cognitive
developmental research is carried out. There is a strong possibility that
children may solve more 'everyday' tasks through some heuristic that
serves them well in everyday life (like the 'ostrich principle' above) but that
does not embody the logical structure that the investigator seeks to study.
Thus, it is really necessary to expose the whole issue of *human sense* (or
rather, *child sense*) to empirical analysis if we are to get to grips with its
contribution. The factor is clearly important enough to demand systematic
investigation.

One starting point for such an analysis would be to compare different
task settings, holding the task constant. Bremner *et al.* (1992) adopted this
approach in a series of studies using a three-dimensional adaptation of
Somerville & Bryant's task. On a series of trials, children had to locate an
object that they had not seen hidden. There was a choice of four locations,
and cues were provided to help the child identify the correct location.
These cues were arranged as shown in Figure 5.4 so that their correct use
involved coordination of dimensions.

A number of factors had an important effect on performance. Embedding
the task in a meaningful context enhanced performance. If the cues were
in the form of people and children were told that the correct location was
at the point where their paths would cross, performance was better than
if the cues were simply discs. Performance was even better, however, if
children were told that both people were looking at the right location, so
line of sight appears to be a particularly effective way of introducing
implicit orthogonals. However, before concluding that there was something really special about the line-of-sight cue, we judged it necessary to
provide a comparison condition in which more abstract but explicitly directional cues were used. The reasoning was that use of cues such as arrows

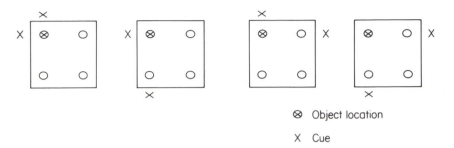

⊗   Object location

X   Cue

Figure 5.4   Forms of the task used by Bremner *et al*. (1992) to investigate coordination of dimensions by 4-year-old children

would not create the same everyday meaningful context as the line-of-sight condition would, but would present cues that were quite explicitly directional. Thus it would be possible to see whether the directionality implicit in the meaning of line-of-sight was more or less effective than explicit directionality in the form of the cues themselves. It turned out that although arrow cues were more effective than the disc cues used earlier, they were not as effective as line-of-sight cues.

From these results it appears that casting this task in the meaningful line-of-sight setting is the most effective way of enhancing the performance of 4 year olds. It seems very likely that the better cues are effective because they help the child to extrapolate from cue to target, and further work is needed to establish the degree to which children's difficulties relate to extrapolation or to simultaneous use of two dimensions.

We also investigated whether the three-dimensionality of the task was important (Bremner, Kendall & Andreasen, 1992). On the one hand, a three-dimensional task might be seen by young children as relating more to everyday experience, so one would guess it would be relatively high in 'human sense'. On the other hand, a two-dimensional representation simplifies the array and could well make the extrapolation task simpler through the imposition of a plan view. The second alternative received more support. Six-year-old children performed better in a two dimensional task than in a three-dimensional one. Additionally, the two-dimensional task appeared to serve as good preparation for performance in three dimensions, since children performed better in the latter if it followed testing in the former.

These results have a potential bearing on the nature of early spatial representations. The argument put forward by Donaldson is that quite sophisticated abilities are to be found early, embedded in everyday experience. According to this view, the best performance will only emerge in tasks that make everyday sense to children. However, as noted already, it is not at all clear what will make sense to children, and our research indicates that it is not enough to rely on our intuitions in deciding what will make a human sense setting. On the one hand, introducing a meaningful task setting in the form of line-of-sight cues was particularly effective. On the other hand, making the task two-dimensional, and hence apparently less 'everyday', can improve performance.

Our suspicion is that two particular factors need closer analysis. *Firstly*, spatial tasks need to be analysed in terms of their information-processing requirements. The tasks considered here require extrapolation of imaginary lines and also identification of the point at which they intersect. It may well be that children are capable of either component of the task singly but have difficulty in performing both together. Thus, use of line-of-sight cues may be effective through reducing the difficulty of the extrapolation component, leaving the child with more capacity to deal with the coordination problem itself. For similar reasons, other more abstract manipulations such as use of arrow cues or two-dimensional presentation may improve performance. According to this analysis, different tasks are likely to yield different patterns of data. For instance, in the case of map reading we would expect a three-dimensional equivalent (provision of a model instead of a map) to be simpler, since it eliminates the need for transformation between three and two dimensions.

We can extend this analysis to the perspective-taking literature to link up with points that have been made in the past. Different perspective-taking tasks have placed different cognitive demands on children, ranging from simply judging whether or not something can be seen by another observer to actually constructing the detail of another's view. These issues have been discussed by Flavell (1974) in terms of three levels of perspective taking. Children are first aware of the objects others can see but not of their specific view of them (Level 1). Then they gain the ability to identify others' views of objects that they can see themselves (Level 2). However, this ability is limited to manipulation of the spatial array itself, and it is only in Level 3 that children gain the ability to identify the other's view in terms of the visual projection of the scene at that standpoint. This sort of analysis needs to be carried even further to investigate the information-processing requirements presented by different forms of spatial tasks, including perspective-taking ones.

Secondly, in predicting the task settings most likely to yield good performance, we need to consider the context in which particular abilities first come to be needed by the child. Spatial orientation problems are encountered early on in the child's everyday environment, so we might expect to reveal the child's orientation skills best in tasks embedded in a setting that makes everyday sense, for instance in three-dimensional tasks that relate closely to everyday experiences. On the other hand, although O'Keefe & Nadel (1978) claim that there is a neural substrate for Euclidean spatial organisation, there is little evidence that dimensional coordination is a skill required for everyday spatial orientation. It seems more likely that a polar coordinate system is primary in spatial orientation since it maps directly onto action, and dimensional coordination may first be required when the child is faced with particular geometric problems in the school setting. Thus, we should not expect a 'more real' three-dimensional setting of a coordination task to have a positive effect, and indeed, once the child encounters graphs and maps, the effect may be the opposite, with tasks presented on paper being solved more easily than tasks set in three-dimensional contexts simply because the more abstract setting is the familiar one.

CONCLUSION

In ending, I should make explicit the strong link that I see between the account I have developed about spatial ability in childhood and the earlier model of infant spatial development. The common theme is that particular representations come into play to deal with the specific needs or problems that children encounter at different points in their development. To some extent these new problems are determined by the child's own development, as in the way the onset of locomotion presents the child with new goals and resulting spatial problems. However, particularly later in development, the need for new skills will be imposed from outside when parents or teachers decide the time is right. In this respect, coordination of dimensions may have little place in everyday spatial orientation, but certainly becomes important when the child is faced with paper and pencil tasks such as graph or mapping problems. It may well be that once these representations come into play they modify general representations of space. For instance, children may start to organise their spatial representations through a coordinate reference system once this system has developed through classroom experiences, and use of maps may lead cognitive 'maps' to become 'map like' simply because this is an economic way of coding spatial information. Thus, as increased control and mobility was seen as leading the infant to develop new representations of space, so new problems faced by the child entering school lead to new representations that eventually may act beyond the school sphere to influence the general form of spatial representations.

REFERENCES

Acredolo, L.P. (1978). Development of spatial orientation in infancy, *Developmental Psychology*, **14**, 224–234.
Acredolo, L.P. and Evans, D. (1980). Developmental changes in the effects of landmarks on infant spatial behaviour, *Developmental Psychology*, **16**, 312–318.

Acredolo, L.P., Adams, A. and Goodwyn, S.W. (1984). The role of self-produced movement and visual tracking in infant spatial orientation, *Journal of Experimental Child Psychology*, **38**, 312–327.

Baillargeon, R. (1986). Representing the existence and the location of hidden objects: object permanence in 6- and 8-month-old infants, *Cognition*, **23**, 21–41.

Baillargeon, R. (1987). Object permanence in 3.5- and 4.5-month-old infants, *Developmental Psychology*, **23**, 655–664.

Baillargeon, R., Spelke, E.S. and Wasserman, S. (1985). Object permanence in five-month-old infants, *Cognition*, **20**, 191–208.

Benson, J.B. and Uzgiris, I.C. (1985). Effect of self-initiated locomotion on infant search activity, *Developmental Psychology*, **21**, 923–931.

Borke, H. (1975). Piaget's mountains revisited: changes in egocentric landscape. *Developmental Psychology*, **11**, 240–243.

Bower, T.G.R. (1964). Discrimination of depth in premotor infants, *Psychonomic Science*, **1**, 368.

Bremner, J.G. (1978a). Spatial errors made by infants: inadequate spatial cues or evidence for egocentrism? *British Journal of Psychology*, **69**, 77–84.

Bremner, J.G. (1978b). Egocentric versus allocentric coding in nine-month-old infants: factors influencing the choice of code, *Developmental Psychology*, **14**, 346–355.

Bremner, J.G. (1985). Object tracking and searching in infancy: a review of data and a theoretical evaluation, *Developmental Review*, **5**, 371–396.

Bremner, J.G. and Bryant, P.E. (1977). Place versus response as the basis of spatial errors made by young infants, *Journal of Experimental Child Psychology*, **23**, 162–171.

Bremner, J.G., Kendall, G. and Andreasen, G. (1992). The effects of array complexity and task dimensionality on coordination of spatial dimensions by 4- to 6-year-old children (in preparation).

Bremner, J.G., Knowles, L. and Andreasen, G. (1992). Young children's spatial orientation during movement: evidence for a form of spatial rotation, *Journal of Experimental Psychology*, submitted for publication.

Bremner, J.G., Andreason, G., Kendall, G. and Adams, L. (1992). Conditions for success in coordination of spatial dimensions by four-year-old children. *Journal of Experimental Child Psychology*, submitted for publication.

Bridges, A. and Rowles, J. (1985). Young children's projective abilities: what can a monster see? *Educational Psychology*, **5**, 251–266.

Butterworth, G. (1975). Object identity in infancy: the interaction of spatial location codes in determining search errors, *Child Development*, **46**, 866–870.

Butterworth, G., Jarrett, N. and Hicks, L. (1982). Spatio-temporal identity in infancy: perceptual competence or conceptual deficit. *Developmental Psychology*, **18**, 435–449.

Campos, J.J. and Bertenthal, B.I. (1988). Locomotion and psychological development. In F. Morrison, K. Lord and D. Keating (eds), *Applied Developmental Psychology*. New York: Academic Press.

Campos, J., Hiatt, S., Ramsay, D., Henderson, C. and Svejda, M. (1978). The emergence of fear on the visual cliff. In M. Lewis and L. Rosenbloom (eds), *The Development of Affect*. New York: Plenum Press.

Campos, J., Svejda, M., Bertenthal, B., Benson, N. and Schmid, D. (1981). Self-produced locomotion and wariness of heights: new evidence from training studies. Paper presented at the meeting of the Society for Research in Child Development, Boston, Massachusetts.

Campos, J.J., Svejda, M.J., Campos, R.G. and Bertenthal, B. (1982). The emergence of self-produced locomotion: its importance for psychological development in infancy. In D. Bricker (ed.), *Intervention with At-Risk and Handicapped Infants*. Baltimore: University Park Press.

Caron, A.J., Caron, R.F. and Carlson, V.R. (1979). Infant perception of the invariant shape of objects varying in slant, *Child Development*, **50**, 716–721.

Cornell, E.H. and Heth, C.D. (1979). Response versus place learning by human infants, *Journal of Experimental Psychology (Human Learning & Memory)*, **5**, 188–196.

Donaldson, M. (1978). *Children's Minds*. Glasgow: Fontana.

Flavell, J.H. (1974). The development of interferences about others. In T. Mischel (ed.), *Understanding Other Persons*. Oxford: Basil Blackwell.

Gibson, E.J. and Walk, R.D. (1960). The 'visual cliff', *Scientific American*, **202**, 64–71.

Gibson, E.J., Riccio, G., Schmuckler, M., Stoffregen, T., Rosenberg, D. and Taorimina, J. (1987). Detection of the traversability of surfaces by crawling and walking infants, *Journal of Experimental Psychology (Human Perception & Performance)*, **13**, 533–544.

Gibson, J.J. (1979). *The Ecological Approach to Visual Perception*. Boston: Houghton Mifflin.

Harris, P.L. (1973). Perserverative errors in search by young infants, *Child Development*, **44**, 28–33.

Harris, P.L. and Bassett, E. (1976). Reconstruction of the mental image. *Journal of Experimental Child Psychology*, **21**, 514–523.

Held, R. and Hein, A. (1963). Movement produced stimulation in the development of visually guided behaviour, *Journal of Comparative and Physiological Psychology*, **56**, 872–876.

Horobin, K. and Acredolo, L. (1986). The role of attentiveness, mobility history and separation of hiding sites on stage IV behaviour. *Journal of Experimental Child Psychology*, **41**, 114–127.

Hughes, M. and Donaldson, M. (1979). The use of hiding games for studying coordination of viewpoints, *Educational Review*, **31**, 133–140.

Huttenlocher, J. and Presson, C.C. (1973). Mental rotation and the perspective problem, *Cognitive Psychology*, **4**, 277–299.

Illingworth, R.S. (1973). *Basic Developmental Screening: 0–2 Years*. Oxford: Blackwell Scientific.

Keating, M.B., McKenzie, B.E. and Day, R.H. (1986). Spatial localization in infancy: position constancy in a square and circular room with and without a landmark, *Child Development*, **57**, 115–124.

Kermoian, R. and Campos, J.J. (1988). Locomotor experience: a facilitator of spatial cognitive development. *Child Development*, **59**, 908–917.

McComas, J. and Field, J. (1984). Does early crawling experience affect infants' emerging spatial abilities? *New Zealand Journal of Psychology*, **13**, 63–68.

McKenzie, B.E., Day, R.H. and Ihsen, E. (1984). Localization of events in space: young infants are not always egocentric, *British Journal of Developmental Psychology*, **2**, 1–9.

McKenzie, B.E., Tootell, H.E. and Day, R.H. (1980). Development of visual size constancy during the first year of human infancy, *Developmental Psychology*, **16**, 163–174.

Meuwissen, I. and McKenzie, B.E. (1987). Localization of an event by young infants: the effect of visual and body movement information, *British Journal of Developmental Psychology*, **2**, 1–9.

O'Keefe, J. and Nadel, L. (1978). *The Hippocampus as a Cognitive Map*. Oxford: Clarendon Press.

Piaget, J. (1954). *The Construction of Reality in the Child* (trans. M. Cook). New York: Basic Books (originally published in French, 1936).

Piaget, J. and Inhelder, B. (1956). *The Child's Conception of Space*. London: Routledge and Kegan Paul.

Piaget, J., Inhelder, B. and Szeminska, A. (1960). *The Child's Conception of Geometry*. New York: Norton.

Shantz, C.U. and Watson, J.S. (1970). Assessment of spatial egocentrism through expectancy violation, *Psychonomic Science*, **18**, 93–94.

Slater, A.M. and Morison, V. (1985). Shape constancy and slant perception at birth, *Perception*, **14**, 337–344.

Slater, A.M., Mattock, A. and Brown, E. (1990). Size constancy at birth: newborn infants' responses to retinal and real size, *Journal of Experimental Child Psychology*, **49**, 314–322.

Somerville, S.C. and Bryant, P.E. (1985). Young children's use of spatial coordinates, *Child Development*, **56**, 604–613.

Sorce, J., Emde, R.N., Campos, J.J. and Klinnert, M. (1985). Maternal emotional signaling: its effect on the visual cliff behaviour of one-year-olds, *Developmental Psychology*, **21**, 195–200.

Spelke, E.S. (1985). Perception of unity, persistence, and identity. In J. Mehler and R. Fox (eds), *Neonate Cognition: Beyond the Blooming Buzzing Confusion*. Hillsdale: Lawrence Erlbaum.

Svejda, M. and Schmid, D. (1979). The role of self-produced locomotion in the onset of fear of heights on the visual cliff. Paper presented at the Meeting of the Society for Research in Child Development, San Francisco.

6 Symbolic Development in Young Children: Understanding Models and Pictures

JUDY S. DELOACHE and NANCY M. BURNS
University of Illinois

Avid fans of *Yes, Prime Minister* (Lynn & Jay, 1986) may remember the following interaction between Prime Minister James Hacker and his assistant Dorothy. In this skirmish in the never-ending power struggle between the PM and Sir Humphrey, Dorothy is complaining that Humphrey has changed her office assignment in a way she finds unacceptable.

'[I've been moved to] the bloody attic,' she snapped. 'Look!' And she started to move things around on my desk. 'This desk is a plan of Number Ten. This file is the Cabinet Room, where we are now. Through the doors here'—she placed a book at one end of the file—'is your private office. This ruler is the corridor from the front door—here. This corridor'—and she grabbed a paper knife and put it down alongside the file and the book—'runs from the Cabinet Room and connects up to the locked green-baize door, on the other side of which is the Cabinet Office, which is this blotter, where Sir Humphrey works. This coffee cup is the staircase up to your study. And this saucer is the gents' loo—here. And this is—was—my office,' She put an ashtray down beside the file that represented the Cabinet Room. 'Now, my desk faced out into the lobby and I always kept my door open. What could I see?'

I stared at it all. 'You could see,' I said slowly, 'everyone who came in from the front door, or the Cabinet Office, or in and out of the Cabinet Room, or the Private Office, or up and down the stairs.'

She remained silent while I pondered this. Then, pressing home her advantage, she picked up the saucer and put it down again. 'And I was opposite the gents' loo. I have to be opposite the loo.'

I asked her if she'd seen a doctor about this, but apparently I was missing the point. 'The gents' loo,' she reminded me. 'Almost everyone in the cabinet is a man. I could hear everything they said to each other, privately, when they popped out of Cabinet meetings for a pee. I was able to keep the last Prime Minister fully informed about all their little foibles.'

'Was that any of his business?' I asked.

'When they were plotting against him, yes!'

She's brilliant! No wonder Humphrey turned her office into a waiting room and banished her to the attic.

Systems of Representation in Children: Development and Use. Edited by C. Pratt and A.F. Garton
© 1993 John Wiley & Sons Ltd

Later, the Prime Minister tries to communicate his alternative plan to his private secretary, Bernard:

> 'And then there's the lobby, here!'. I indicated my desk.
> Bernard looked blank. 'Where?'
> 'There,' I said. 'Look. Between the ashtray, the cup and the saucer.'
> He looked at the desk, then back to me, wide-eyed with confusion.
> 'Between the coffee cup and the saucer?'
> He is so *dense* sometimes. 'The saucer is the gents' loo, Bernard,' I told him.
> 'Wake up!'
> I sometimes wonder if Bernard's mind is agile enough for this job.

Every reader of this chapter, regardless of whether you have ever seen or read *Yes, Prime Minister*, can readily follow and interpret this passage. You understand Dorothy's use of common desk-top objects to stand for full-size rooms and other architectural features. You easily comprehend her intent and may even be able to construct an image of the spatial layout she is describing.

Not one of our readers, we would wager, had the slightest reluctance or difficulty letting the ashtray stand for Dorothy's old office or having the saucer represent the men's room. None of you thought, 'But that's a saucer; it can't be a loo.' In other words, it was a simple and straightforward matter to think of a set of objects as representing or standing for—that is, as symbolizing—something other than themselves. Furthermore, the use of the objects enabled you to think about their referents and to come to new insights about those referents. Dorothy's symbolic use of the desk-top items helped the notoriously dim Jim Hacker to appreciate the strategic importance of the placement of her office.

This example illustrates some of the wonderful flexibility adult humans display in symbolization. We use a variety of symbols so easily and automatically that it is difficult for us to realize that they are not necessarily obvious to others. (Witness Hacker's irritation with Bernard's literal response to his use of the desk-top paraphernalia as symbols rather than objects.) Indeed, it is our capacity for creating and using symbols that is the hallmark of human cognition.

Humans have invented a large variety of symbol systems to record and communicate their experience. In the first few years of life, young children are expected to master or begin to master some of these symbol systems. In western industrialized societies, virtually all children need to learn to read and write, to count and do maths. They discover how to interpret pictures and television, and many learn to read music and maps. Failure to acquire the symbolic tools of the culture excludes an individual from full participation in and benefit from that culture. In modern western societies, illiteracy is a serious social and intellectual handicap; in other cultures, failure to understand important religious rituals could be similarly problematic.

For several years we have been studying very young children's understanding of two types of symbols—pictures and models. Pictures are pervasive in our culture and in the experience of infants and young children. Nevertheless, surprisingly little is known about young children's understanding of the symbolic or representational role of pictures. Unlike pictures, scale models are relatively rare in the everyday life of young children. Nevertheless, research on 2- and 3-year-old children's understanding of models has revealed several interesting and important facets of early symbolic development, some of them previously unsuspected.

In this chapter, we will discuss symbolic functioning in very young children, considering their understanding first of scale models and then of pictures. As will become clear, in their initial encounters with some kinds of symbolic representations, young children display the same sort of confusion evidenced by the PM's secretary. Young children often have trouble in achieving *representational insight*, that is understanding that a particular entity stands for something other than itself. As we shall see, they have particular difficulty with real objects that are used as symbols; Bernard's difficulty in understanding Hacker's use of the saucer to stand for the men's room is mirrored in 30-month-old children's difficulty in understanding that a miniature room—a scale model of a full-sized room— stands for that room. In addition, very young children seem to experience special problems in appreciating that a symbol such as a picture or a model stands for some specific reality rather than for a general class or concept.

SCALE MODELS

A scale model is a symbol: it represents a particular, larger entity, typically a larger space. Atop the computer on my desk is a small cardboard model of the Radcliffe Camera at Oxford University. My tiny model stands for that large, lovely building. It contains many of the distinctive features of the Radcliffe, and the spatial relations among those features are accurately represented. Thus, the model is round, it has a domed roof with a cupola at the top, there are no windows on the ground level but many windows appear higher up, and so forth.

At the same time that my model symbolizes and calls to mind a particular building thousands of miles away, it is a real object. I can pick it up, turn it around to inspect the different parts of it, dust it, use it to hold down a paper, and so forth.

This object thus has a dual reality: (1) it is a symbol for the actual Radcliffe Camera, and (2) it is itself a real object with its own physical properties.

I can respond to the symbolic content of the object, to the object itself, or to both. Young children do not show such flexibility when they encounter scale models. As will become clear, they find it very difficult to appreciate the dual nature of models, to think about both the objects themselves and what they represent at the same time.

We have extensively studied young children's understanding of scale models (DeLoache, 1987, 1989a, 1989b, 1990, 1991; DeLoache, Kolstad & Anderson, 1991). Scale models are not familiar items in the everyday environment of young children. Although most children in our culture have access to numerous representational toys, these items do not bear the kind of highly specific relation to what they stand for that a scale model does. Unlike my miniature Radcliffe Camera, a child's doll's-house does not stand for any particular house; rather it represents houses in general. Nevertheless, in spite of their lack of familiarity with true models, young children's response to scale models reveals many important aspects of early symbolic development.

Our research with scale models uses a simple object-retrieval game in which 30- and 36-month-old children search for an attractive toy that is hidden somewhere in a natural location in a room (e.g. behind the couch, under a chair or pillow). The child watches as an experimenter hides a tiny plastic dog (introduced to the child as 'Little Snoopy') somewhere in a scale model of the room. The child is told that 'Big Snoopy' (a stuffed toy dog) will be hidden in the 'same place' in the big room. For example, a child might observe the miniature dog being placed behind the small couch in the model and then search for the larger dog that is concealed behind the full-sized couch in the room. To succeed in this task, the child must: (1) recognize the correspondence between the model and the room, (2) map the elements of one space onto those of the other, and (3) use his or her knowledge of where the miniature toy was hidden to figure out where the larger toy must be.

The children are always explicitly told about the correspondence between the two spaces. At the beginning of the session, they are instructed that, except for size, the two toys are alike and that the room and model are alike. On every trial, they are told and then reminded that the larger toy is in the place in the room corresponding to where the miniature toy is hidden in the model. ('I'm hiding Little Snoopy here. I'm going to hide Big Snoopy in the same place in his room.')

Each trial in this task consists of three parts: the hiding event in the model, retrieval of the larger toy in the room (retrieval 1), and retrieval of the miniature toy in the model (retrieval 2). The second retrieval is necessary to make sure that any poor performance on retrieval 1 is not simply due to forgetting the location of the original toy or to lack of motivation to search for the toys.

The focus of this task is thus to determine to what extent very young children notice and exploit the symbolic relation between the model and the room. Specifically, can they use their memory for the hiding event in the model as a guide to search for the large toy in the room? We know that very young children are fully competent at retrieving objects when instructed to do so; children as young as 14 months respond to commands to fetch familiar objects that are out of sight (Huttenlocher, 1974). In a pilot study using the same rooms and objects as in the current research, we established that 24-month-olds could follow verbal instructions to retrieve a hidden toy. The experimenter simply said, 'Big Bird is hiding in the basket. Can you go find him?' The children went directly to the toy 82% of the time. Therefore, if our subjects fail to retrieve the larger toy after seeing the smaller one being hidden in the model, it is unlikely to be because they cannot remember what we told them or cannot follow instructions to retrieve objects. Rather, such failure would suggest that they do not understand the relation between the model and what it represents.

In the original study using this task, a large difference was found in the performance of young children only a few months apart in age (DeLoache, 1987). As Figure 6.1 shows, 36-month-old children who had observed a miniature toy being hidden in the model knew where to find the corresponding larger toy in the room (retrieval 1). Their rate of errorless retrievals was 77%. In contrast, extremely few 30-month-olds had any idea where to find the hidden toy, and their retrieval 1 performance was only 15%.

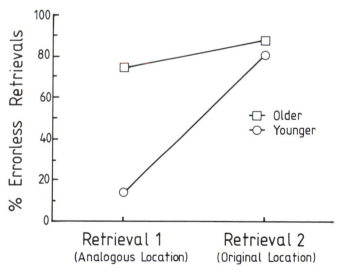

Figure 6.1 Percentage of errorless retrievals achieved by two age groups

The large discrepancy in the success of these two age groups was not due to differences in memory or motivation. When asked to retrieve the toy they had originally observed being hidden (retrieval 2), both groups were highly successful (88% and 83% for the older and younger children, respectively). The dramatic age difference and the absolute levels of performance have been replicated several times in our laboratory (DeLoache, 1989a, 1989b, 1990, 1991; DeLoache et al., 1991) as well as in other laboratories using different stimuli (Dow & Pick, 1992; S.J. Resnick, 1991, personal communication).

In our studies, the 30-month-old children have seemed to understand everything about the task except the critical fact that the room and model are related and, hence, that what happened in one space told them something about the other. They understood that there was a toy hidden in the room and that they were supposed to search for it. What they failed to realize was that they had any way of knowing where it was. They were happy to search for it, but they treated the task as a guessing game. What the 36-month-olds achieved, and the 30-month-olds failed to achieve, is *representational insight*—awareness of the symbolic relation between the model and what it stands for.

In using the term, 'representational insight', we do not mean any kind of conscious or verbalizable awareness. Almost none of the young subjects in our studies—even those children who are highly successful—can articulate the model–room relation. Thus, our use of the term insight is similar to that of Kohler when describing the problem-solving of his apes. He used insight to refer to the apes' sudden solution of a problem, their abrupt realization that one thing was (or could be) related to another. These apes were obviously even less able to describe the nature of their awareness of the relation than our subjects are, but insight nevertheless seems the appropriate descriptor in both cases.

Why is it so difficult for 30-month-olds to detect the correspondence between a scale model and a larger space? The dual nature of models—the fact that a model is both a symbol and a real object—seems to be an important factor. To succeed in the model task, the child must respond to the model in two different ways at the same time—as the object that it is *and* as a symbol for something it is not.

The 30-month-old children in this research clearly represented the model as a concrete object; they were highly successful at retrieving the toy they had observed being hidden in the model. Focusing on the model as an attractive object, they did not appreciate its symbolic role; they failed to detect the correspondence between the model and the room. As a consequence, they had no basis for understanding that what they saw happen in the model had implications for the unseen event in the room. A major challenge for the young child is thus the necessity for *dual representation*—representing something both in terms of the object itself and in terms of what it stands for. Responding to the model as an object seems to block appreciating its symbolic function. This reasoning led to a counter-intuitive prediction: 30-month-old children should be more successful if given information about the location of a hidden object by pictures, rather than by a model, because pictures should not require a dual representation to the same extent that a model does.

A picture is, of course, a real, tangible object and hence has a certain 'double reality' (Sigel, 1978). However, its primary function is as a representation of something else. When we look at a picture, we normally think only of its referent, of what is depicted in it, and not of the picture as an object itself. To use a picture, we do not have to keep in mind both object and referent. Thus, from the point of view of dual representation, 30-month-old children should be better able to find a toy concealed in a room if its location is communicated via pictures than by a three-dimensional model.

On other grounds, however, the prediction is counterintuitive. We normally think of objects as being more interesting, more salient, more informative than pictures. We expect young children to do better with real objects than with pictorial stimuli, and there are numerous experiments showing such effects in a variety of tasks (e.g. Daehler, Lonardo & Bukatko, 1979; DeLoache, 1986; Hartley, 1976; Sigel, 1953; Sigel, Anderson & Shapiro, 1966; Sigel & Cocking, 1977; Sigel & Olmsted, 1970; Sorce, 1980; Steinberg, 1974).

Three different studies have supported the picture-superiority prediction of the dual representation hypothesis (DeLoache, 1987, 1991). In two of these studies, 30-month-old children participated in two tasks, with task order counterbalanced across subjects. On one day, they experienced the standard model task described above in which they watched the experimenter hide a miniature toy in the model and then searched for its larger counterpart in the room. On the other day, they were given a picture task in which the experimenter pointed to a picture to indicate to the child where the toy was hidden. In one study, there were four colour photographs, each depicting one of the hiding places in the room. In the second study, either a wide-angle colour photograph of the room or a lightly coloured line drawing was used. Both pictures depicted all the hiding places in the room. The experimenter simply pointed to the appropriate picture or part of a picture, telling the child, 'This is where Snoopy is hiding in the room. He's hiding back [under] here.'

The results provided strong support for the dual representation hypothesis. Figure 6.2 shows the data from the study using the four photographs (DeLoache, 1987). The 30-month-olds successfully exploited the information in the pictures to retrieve the hidden toy. Having seen the experimenter point appropriately to the picture, they knew where to search in the room. The same children performed very poorly (significantly

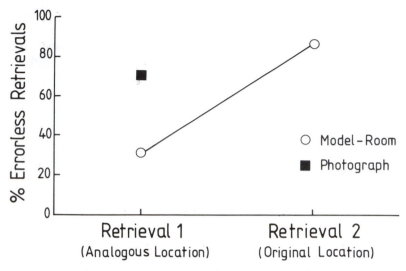

Figure 6.2 Percentage of errorless retrievals by 30-month-olds for pictures versus model

worse than with the pictures) in the model task. The results from the studies with the wide-angle photo and line drawing were the same; indeed, performance with those pictures was even slightly better. These picture studies thus support the idea that 30-month-old children have difficulty with the model task because it is hard for them to represent a concrete object (the model) and what it stands for (the room) at the same time.

One potential problem with these data, however, is that not only did the medium (picture vs model) by which the relevant location was communicated to the child differ, but the method by which the information was conveyed also differed. In the model task a miniature toy was hidden behind an item of furniture, whereas in the picture task the experimenter simply pointed to that item. It would not be surprising if it were more difficult to form a mental representation of a hiding event involving the relation between two objects than to represent a simple point to a single object. Thus, the picture-superiority effect just described could have been due to this difference in the method of communication rather than, as hypothesized, to the difference in medium. If so, the results would not support the dual representation hypothesis.

Accordingly, an experiment was designed to separate the effects of medium and method (DeLoache, 1991). There were four conditions, two of which were replications of previous tasks. In Hide–Model, the child watched as the experimenter hid a miniature toy in the model (the standard model task), and in Point–Picture, the experimenter pointed to the relevant location in one of the same four photographs used in the original picture study. The crucial condition was Point–Model, in which the experimenter simply pointed to the correct place in the model. If 30-month-olds' poor performance in the standard model task is due to the necessity of representing a hiding event, then performance should be good in this condition. In the fourth condition, Hide–Picture, the experimenter hid the miniature toy behind one of the four pictures.

The results of this study (retrieval 1 data only) are shown in Figure 6.3. Performance in the two replication conditions, Hide–Model and Point–Picture, was just as expected—very poor in the former and very good in the latter, replicating previous results.

Performance in the crucial condition, Point–Model, was as predicted by the dual representation hypothesis. It was *exactly* the same as in the Hide–Model condition. In other words, our young subjects did not know where the toy was hidden in the room, regardless of whether they had watched the experimenter hide the miniature toy in the model or simply point to the correct place in the model. This result supports our reasoning. If 30-month-olds' poor performance in the model task is due to the need for a dual representation, then it should not matter how the specific hiding place is communicated; because they fail to detect the model–room correspondence in the first place, performance should be poor either way. In other words, if a young child responds to the model only as an object and

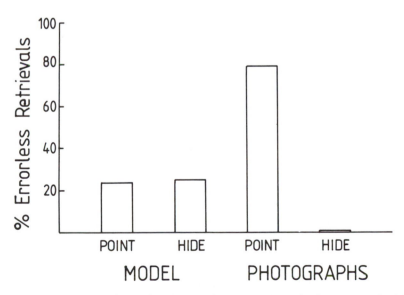

Figure 6.3 Percentage of errorless retrievals (retrieval 1 only) by 30-month-olds as a function of medium (scale model vs pictures) and method (hiding vs pointing)

not also as a symbol, then that child will connect neither pointing nor hiding in the model with anything in the room.

Further support for the dual representation hypothesis came from the fourth condition, Hide–Picture, in which the child watched as the experimenter hid the miniature dog behind one of the four pictures. Our 30-month-olds found this condition incomprehensible; not a single child made a single successful retrieval.

Why should this condition have been so devastating? First, it required a dual representation, although in a different way from the model. Here, we were asking our young subjects to treat something (a picture) both as a symbol (a picture of something) and as an object (a hiding place). They apparently succeeded in responding to the pictures as objects; the children had very high retrieval 2 scores, indicating that they represented the pictures as locations of the hidden toy. However, responding to the pictures as objects seems to have blocked interpreting them as symbols of something else—the depicted places in the room. After watching Little Snoopy being hidden behind the picture of the couch, the children knew where to find that toy (behind the couch picture); however, they did not know that Big Snoopy was behind the real couch.

The second factor making this condition extraordinarily difficult was that it violated the normal symbolic function of pictures. Pictures are not normally treated as objects. Our subjects knew that pictures are to be interpreted in terms of what they depict, not as objects in themselves. Thus, the Hide–Picture condition involved an anomalous use of symbols. Their retrieval score of 0 suggests that the children did indeed find the situation anomalous.

The Hide–Picture condition thus lends further support to the dual representation hypothesis, and it demonstrates the inflexibility of early symbolic functioning. These 30-month-old children knew quite a lot about pictures; indeed, they knew the most crucial thing of all—that pictures are representations of something other than themselves. However, having learned to respond to pictures only in terms of their representational content, our subjects were stymied by the demand to treat them as both object and symbol.

These studies thus provide support for the dual representation hypothesis by showing better performance by young children with pictures than models. Even more direct evidence comes from two recent studies that explicitly investigated it. According to the dual representation hypothesis, the more salient a symbol is as an object, the more difficult it should be for very young children to become aware of its symbolic potential. Conversely, the less salient a symbol is as an object, the easier it should be to achieve a dual representation of it.

In one study (DeLoache, 1990), we attempted to *decrease* the salience of a scale model as an object. To do so, we placed the model behind a window. The child never touched the model or its contents, nor did the experimenter. To indicate the location of the toy in the room, she simply pointed to the appropriate location in the model. (Recall that pointing in the model produces exactly the same results as hiding a toy does.)

The prediction was that this rather bizarre modification would *improve* the performance of 30-month-old children—the age group who typically fail the model task. Distancing the model behind the glass should make its nature as a real object less salient. Hence, it should be easier to achieve a dual representation of the model, thus enabling these children to appreciate the model–room correspondence.

The results, shown in Figure 6.4, were as predicted. Performance was significantly better for those children who were denied access to the model than it was for the comparison group in the standard model task. Half (7 of 12) of the 30-month-olds in the window condition were successful (vs only 1 of 8 in the comparison group). Thus, physically separating the children from the model helped them to achieve psychological distance from it (Sigel, 1970).

In the second direct test of the dual representation hypothesis, we took the opposite tack: we attempted to *increase* the salience of the model as object, predicting a subsequent decrement in children's performance. The

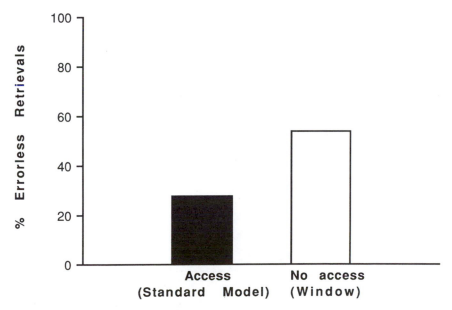

Figure 6.4 Percentage of errorless retrievals (retrieval 1 only) by 30-month-olds with access to the model (standard condition) and without access (window condition)

subjects for this study were 36-month-olds, the age group that typically succeeds in the standard model task.

The experimental manipulation was extremely simple: one group of children was given a small amount of extra experience with the model. When the children arrived at the laboratory, the model was situated in the middle of the room, and they were encouraged to play with it for approximately 5–10 minutes. The model was then replaced in its usual place in the small room next door, and the standard model task ensued.

The prediction here was that their extra experience with the model as an object would make it more difficult for these 36-month-old children to appreciate its symbolic role in the model task. The prediction was supported. As Figure 6.5 shows, performance of the children given the extra experience with the model was significantly poorer in the model task than performance of a group of the same age tested in the standard task in which they had much less experience with the model. Interaction with the model as an object apparently made it more difficult for these children to interpret it as a symbol.

The dual representation hypothesis has thus received strong support from a series of counterintuitive results: (1) young children performed better with two-dimensional stimuli than with three-dimensional stimuli; (2) putting a barrier between young children and the experimental

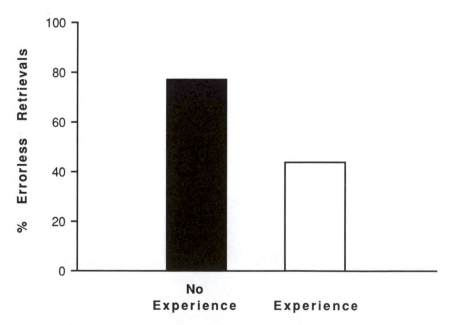

Figure 6.5 Percentage of errorless retrievals (retrieval 1 only) by 36-month-olds with standard or extra experience with the model

materials improved their performance; and (3) familiarizing young children with the experimental materials decreased their performance. The outcomes of these studies were predicted from the dual representation hypothesis; everyday reasoning or any other approach we can think of would predict the opposite in all cases.

To what extent is the pattern that we have observed for 30- and 36-month-olds in our model studies specific to this age group and this task? We believe representational insight is actually a common problem, and we have evidence that achieving it can be extremely difficult for children with media other than models. It comes from research that we have recently conducted on even younger children's understanding of pictures (Burns, 1990). Because pictures are much more familiar stimuli for young children than are scale models, the finding of similar patterns argues for the importance and generality of the concept of representational insight.

PICTURES

Pictures are pervasive in modern, western culture, and they are encountered by its youngest members. Middle-class children are commonly introduced to pictures via picture-books during or near the end of their first year of life, and picture-book interactions are a very common form of parent–child interaction (DeLoache & DeMendoza, 1987; Ninio & Bruner, 1978). Because infants and toddlers name pictured objects appropriately in their earliest encounters with pictures, it is often assumed, by parents and researchers alike, that they understand pictures in more or less the same way as older individuals do. In particular, the assumption is made that children interpret pictures as representations, that they understand that pictures can stand for something that exists apart from the picture. We will present data that argue that this assumption is not warranted.

Several years ago, Sigel (1978) noted that pictures constitute a 'deceptively simple problem' and stressed the need to separate picture perception and picture comprehension. We agree and argue for the need for even more distinctions. We have chosen a single term, 'pictorial competence', to include the many different aspects of recognizing, interpreting, using and understanding pictures (DeLoache & Burns, 1991). It is intended to encompass the simplest perception of pictured information and the most sophisticated understanding of the conventions and techniques of the pictorial media. In choosing a single term, we do not want to disregard or blur any of the distinctions among these disparate aspects; indeed, we seek to emphasize that in considering the development of pictorial competence, it is crucial to give full attention to these distinctions.

When do children understand pictures? The answer depends on what type of picture you are referring to and what kind of understanding you mean. It also depends on the cultural group in which you are interested.

For now, we will limit consideration to very simple pictures (realistic photographs or drawings of single objects or simple scenes) and to children growing up in literate, western societies in which pictures and other symbols are abundant. The research reviewed in the following section clearly illustrates the need to distinguish between simple recognition of pictorial content and understanding pictures as representations.

Young children's understanding of pictures as representations

A primary use of pictures, especially photographs, is to convey information. Learning new information from pictures is a common experience in our everyday lives. The historic photographs of the earth from space provide a perceptual and conceptual experience most people could never have directly. Posters alert the citizenry to the FBI's list of most-wanted criminals. Photographs at the finish line serve as incontrovertible evidence of which horse won by a nose. An aerial photograph of Paris shows the eager tourist where the Eiffel Tower is located with respect to the Seine and the Louvre.

In a series of studies (Burns, 1990; DeLoache & Burns, 1991), we asked when children first come to appreciate the relation between photographs and the reality they depict. Specifically, we examined young children's use of photographs as a source of information.

In this research, we used the same simple object-retrieval game described above, but pictures were used to show our young subjects where in the room the toy was hidden. Two pictures were used in the first study: the wide-angle colour photograph of the room, showing all of the items of furniture that would serve as hiding places, and the line drawing of the same scene (the same pictures used in DeLoache, 1991).

There were two age groups in this study: 24-month-olds and 30-month-olds. Each session began with a fairly extensive orientation phase in which the experimenter explicitly described the correspondence between the pictured pieces of furniture and their real counterparts: 'This is a picture of Snoopy's room. There's his couch in the picture, and here is that couch. They're the same.' The picture was held up to each piece of furniture as the correspondence was pointed out. On each of the four hiding/retrieval trials, the experimenter and child were in a small room adjoining the larger experimental room. The experimenter showed the child the picture of the large room. She pointed to the location where the toy was hidden and asked the child to retrieve it: 'This is where Snoopy is hiding in his room; can you find him?'

Figure 6.6 shows the results for the two age groups on the first two and the last two trials. The 30-month-olds were quite successful (72% overall); the 24-month-olds were remarkably unsuccessful (13%). One of the eight 24-month-olds found the toy on every trial; the other seven together *never*

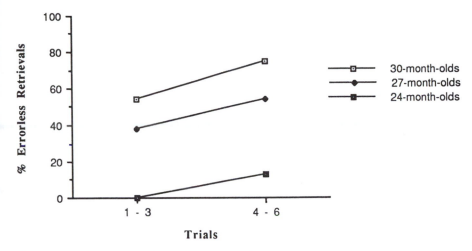

Figure 6.6 Percentage of errorless retrievals by two age groups in two trial blocks

had a single errorless retrieval. Performance did not differ for the two pictures.

The results thus show that the 30-month-olds used the information in the pictures to find the toy. When they looked at the picture, they formed a belief about the current location of the toy based on the depicted information.

On the other hand, the 24-month-olds (with one notable exception) gave no evidence of making the connection between the room and the picture of the room. Their extremely poor performance was somewhat surprising on several grounds. For one thing, children of this age have typically had a great deal of experience with picture-books and other pictures, and they are adept at identifying pictured objects. For another, the children in our study could identify (by naming and/or pointing to) the items in our pictures. Finally, the extremely poor performance of the 24-month-olds is surprising in view of the extremely good performance of the older children who were only a few months older.

Before drawing any conclusions about a basic lack of knowledge on the part of our 24-month-old subjects, we thought it advisable to explore the possibility that our task did not tap their true level of competence. There are certainly many examples of developmental research with young children in which their skills have been seriously underestimated. Often, relatively minor changes in experimental procedures produce considerably enhanced performance. Thus, in a subsequent study, we tried to simplify our task in an effort to elicit whatever pictorial competence 24-month-olds might possess.

The same object-retrieval task was used, but the nature of the pictures was changed. There were two aspects of the pictures in the first study that we thought might have been problematic for our younger subjects. (1) Each picture showed the entire room, including several different items of furniture (hiding places). Perhaps 24-month-old children would find it easier to understand the correspondence between a single item and a picture of that item. (2) The picture only showed the front view of the hiding place and did not depict the hidden toy. Thus, to formulate a search, the child had to generate an image of the toy in the place pointed out by the experimenter. The younger children might have found it difficult to construct such an image. If so, their failure to retrieve the hidden toy might have been more indicative of limits on their imaginative capabilities than on their understanding of pictures.

Accordingly, in the next study, the pictures showed the toy in its hiding place. On each of six test trials, the child was shown a photograph that depicted a Big Bird doll hidden in, under or behind one of the pieces of furniture in the room. For example, one photograph showed Big Bird hidden behind the large chair, and another depicted Big Bird in the basket. These pictures thus showed a view of the object (furniture) that the child could see only after approaching very close to it or walking around to the side or back of it. The procedure was the same as in the preceding study.

Three age groups were tested in this study—the same two ages as in the preceding experiment (24- and 30-month-olds), and an intermediate age group of 27-month-olds. As Figure 6.7 shows, the results for the comparable age groups replicated those of the previous study. The 30-month-olds were very successful at using the pictures to guide their search for the hidden toy: they were 75% correct on the last half of the trials. The 24-

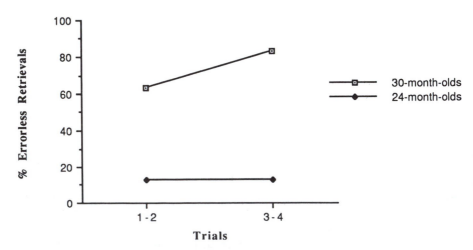

Figure 6.7 Percentage of errorless retrievals by three age groups in two trial blocks

month-olds performed just as poorly here: none of them had a single correct retrieval on the first block of trials, and all of the apparent increase over trials was due to one subject who got all of the last three trials right. The intermediate age group was in between the other two, but more similar to the performance of the older group.

The extremely poor performance by the 24-month-olds was not due to simple deficits. It did not reflect a total absence of ability to respond correctly to pictures. These children were capable of labelling the objects in the picture, and many spontaneously named Big Bird. Their poor showing was also not due to a failure to grasp the overall nature of the task. Upon being asked to find Big Bird, they immediately went into the room, and they usually searched for the toy. Finally, their low success rate did not reflect simple random searching. On the contrary, they were fairly systematic, but wrong. On half of their trials (54%), they searched at a location that had been a hiding place on a previous trial, with most of these errors being searches of the most recent hiding place. Thus, where they had last seen the real toy (on the previous trial) took precedence over the photograph they had just seen. After looking at the picture of Big Bird in the basket, they did not consider the basket a likely hiding location. It was not until they had actually seen the toy in the basket that they searched there—on the following trial when the toy was hidden somewhere else!

One way to characterize the behavior of the 24-month-olds is that, in deciding where to search for the toy, they gave precedence to their previous direct experience with that object, disregarding the pictorial information. When the experimenter pointed at the picture and said, 'Here's where I've hidden Big Bird', these children apparently thought only of the referent—Big Bird—and ignored the location information in the picture and the experimenter's statements regarding it. The only representation that systematically guided their searching was their memory for where they had seen the actual toy before.

The results of both of these studies thus suggest that our 24-month-old subjects did not interpret the pictures as relevant information about the current location of the toy. Could we do something to help them appreciate the relevance of the pictures? In the third study in this series, we took great pains to familiarize explicitly a new group of 24-month-old children with every element of the experimental situation: (1) the experimenter showed the child all of the hiding locations that would be used and labelled each one; (2) with the child watching, the experimenter placed the toy in each of those locations; (3) the test photographs, each of which depicted the toy hidden in one of the locations, were also shown to the child in relation to the actual scenes they depicted; (4) the experimenter explicitly pointed out the relation between the picture of the hidden toy and the toy in that location. Thus, before the test trials began, the child had seen all of the experimental materials, had seen the toy in each of the hiding places, and had had the correspondence between each picture and its referent explicitly described.

The effect of this extensive orientation is easy to summarize: there was none. The 24-month-olds who received these special instructions performed no differently from the children of the same age who received the standard orientation in the previous study (16% vs 6%).

The results of the first three experiments were extremely consistent for our 24-month-old subjects: only a very few children in this age group gave any evidence of understanding the relevance of the picture–referent relation, in spite of our efforts to simplify the task and make the relation explicit and more salient. In a final study in this series, we adopted a different approach. Rather than modifying aspects of the task and the stimuli, we attempted to highlight the photograph–referent relation directly. To do so, we used a Polaroid camera, demonstrating and explaining its use during the orientation. We did not, of course, expect our young subjects to know or learn anything about the inner workings of cameras. However, we did think it possible that they might be sensitized to the picture–referent relation by watching an adult point the camera at a particular scene and then seeing a picture of that scene emerge from the camera.

On each of the six test trials, the experimenter explained to the child that she was going to hide the doll in the room and take a picture of it. The experimenter then entered the room, hid the toy, and snapped the camera and flash. She returned to the control room with the appropriate (pre-taken) photograph and showed it to the child, saying, 'This is where Big Bird is hiding right now. Can you go and find him?'

The performance of the 24-month-olds tested in the Polaroid condition was slightly (27%) but not significantly better than that of the same age group in the standard picture condition (6%). Two of the children in the Polaroid condition seemed to understand the picture–referent relation, compared with a single subject in the standard condition who caught on midway through his six trials.

Why have the vast majority of our 24-month-old subjects found our picture task impenetrable? Why have they failed to extract the simple information from the pictures and apply it in the room next door? As noted before, it is not because they are incapable of perceiving or interpreting the picture itself. All of our subjects know that the pictures depict Big Bird, and they can label the other objects (e.g. couch, basket, pillow) in the pictures as well. Nevertheless, they appear to assume that the pictures have nothing to do with the finding game they are playing.

We have concluded that the results of our picture studies reveal the importance of the type of *representing relation* between symbol and referent. In our tasks, the models and pictures all have what we have called *representational specificity*: this term denotes a symbolic relation in which the symbol stands for a specific, existing reality (DeLoache & Burns, 1991). To our knowledge, the developmental importance of this aspect of symbolization has not previously been recognized (although Olson, 1989, has discussed the general concept).

It is necessary to distinguish between *generic* and *specific representation*. Many (perhaps most) symbols stand for a general concept of class of objects or other entities. The word 'dog', for example, stands for any of the millions of exemplars of that species. 'Australian shepherd' refers to dogs of a specific breed, but there are still vast numbers of dogs to which this label appropriately applies. Both of these terms are generic symbols. 'Biggles', on the other hand, is a specific symbol, referring, as it happens, to a particular Australian Shepherd curled up at my feet as I write. Biggles, like any proper name, thus refers to one particular entity. It is a specific representation.

The pictures in our research have representational specificity. The picture of the Big Bird toy behind the chair shows that particular object in that particular location. Our subjects, however, treat this (and the other pictures) like generic representations; as noted before, they can label the toy and the other objects in the pictures, yet in spite of explicit instructions to do so, they do not use the pictures as a guide to the actual state of affairs in the room next door. These 24-month-olds show remarkable tenacity in their generic interpretation of the pictures.

This developmental difference in children's understanding of generic and specific representation, with generic symbols being correctly interpreted earlier than specific ones, is also true in our model studies. Even when they fail the model task (i.e. when they do not understand the correspondence between the model and the room), 30-month-old children respond to the model as a miniature room. They see the tiny couch as a toy couch and Little Snoopy as a toy dog. In both cases, what the children fail to appreciate is the relevance of the symbol to the specific reality it represents. They fail to do so in spite of the close temporal and spatial contiguity of the symbols and their referents and in spite of the extensive instructions and demonstrations we provide about the correspondences.

There are two obvious possibilities to explain why there is a developmental difference in the appreciation of generic vs specific representation. One is that children may have an early bias to treat all symbols as generic representations. A child's initial assumption upon encountering any new symbol could be that it stands for a class of entities, not for a particular one. The well-documented over-extensions of early words could reflect such a bias, for example the infant who uses 'Daddy' to refer to all men, just as she uses 'doggie' to label all four-legged mammals.

Another possibility is that some of their initial symbolic experiences predispose young children to a generic bias. One aspect of children's early experience with pictures that might lead them to interpret pictures generically is the kind of pictures to which they are exposed. Virtually all of the pictures in infants' and young children's books are generic representations, regardless of whether they are drawings, paintings or photographs. A picture of a ball in a baby alphabet book stands for balls in general, not for any specific ball. Hence, when shown a picture of Big Bird behind the chair in our laboratory, 24-month-olds fail to interpret it as representing that specific state of affairs.

CONCLUSION

We have made three main points in this chapter:

(1) Understanding the relation between a symbol and what it stands for can be a formidable challenge for very young children. Even a symbol that is highly iconic and patently obvious to an adult or older child can be virtually incomprehensible to a younger one. Achieving *representational insight* is thus a considerable feat. The age at which such insight is achieved depends on the symbolic medium involved, as well as a variety of characteristics of the particular task.

(2) One of the hurdles in young children's symbolic path is *dual representation*—the ability to think about a symbol and its referent at the same time, in particular the ability to represent both the symbolic object itself and what it stands for. Scale models are problematic for 30-month-olds because they have a strong response to a model as an attractive object, which makes it difficult for them to simultaneously recognize its symbolic content.

(3) A second hurdle is *representational specificity*. Young children seem to be predisposed initially to treat symbols as generic representations. Only later do they interpret a symbol such as a picture as standing for an actual state of affairs and providing new information about reality.

The most obvious practical implication of our research has to do with designing appropriate materials for very young children. Virtually all adults in our culture place great value on literacy and competency in other symbol systems. A common intuition of adults is that we can facilitate our children's interest and understanding if we provide them with appealing, evocative materials. Hence, nearly every home in America in which a toddler or preschool-aged child lives has plastic magnetic letters competing for space on the refrigerator with children's art work. We purchase these letters and display them on the assumption that they will help our children become familiar with letters and hence give them a leg up on reading.

It should be clear from the research with models, and specifically the dual representation hypothesis, that this ubiquitous intuition is probably dead wrong. Far from facilitating any appreciation or understanding of letters, these letters-cum-objects should actually impede it. The toddler is likely to respond to them and play with them simply as objects. The more the child enjoys forming patterns on the refrigerator door with the magnetic shapes, the more difficult it should be to realize that these objects are meant to stand for something. Only if a child has already achieved representational insight with respect to letters should such objects have any salutary potential.

This everyday example and the laboratory studies summarized here illustrate forcefully that our adult intuitions are often off base when it comes to early symbolic development. We are so steeped in symbols and so experienced and adept at using and interpreting them that it is difficult for us to imagine being unaware of such relations. But young children obviously do not yet share in much of our symbolic experience. Relations that are transparent to us are opaque to them. Research like that discussed in this chapter makes it even more obvious what a marvellous accomplishment it is to become a proficient interpreter and user of symbols.

ACKNOWLEDGMENTS

This research and the preparation of this chapter were partially supported by HD-25271 from the National Institute for Child Health and Human Development and by HATCH grant 60-309 from the University of Illinois Agriculture Experiment Station. We are deeply indebted to Kathy Anderson for her extremely capable assistance at all stages of this research.

REFERENCES

Burns, N.M. (1990). Emergence of the understanding of pictures as symbols in very young children. Unpublished master's thesis, University of Illinois, Urbana-Champaign, Illinois.
Daehler, M.W., Lonardo, R. and Bukatko, D. (1979). Matching and equivalence judgement in very young children, *Child Development*, **50**, 170–179.
DeLoache, J.S. (1986). Memory in very young children: exploitation of cues to the location of a hidden object, *Cognitive Development*, **1**, 123–137.
DeLoache, J.S. (1987). Rapid change in the symbolic functioning of very young children, *Science*, **238**, 1556–1557.
DeLoache, J.S. (1989a). The development of representation in young children. In H.W. Reese (ed.), *Advances in Child Development and Behavior, Vol. 22* (pp. 1–39). New York: Academic Press.
DeLoache, J.S. (1989b). Young children's understanding of the correspondence between a scale model and a larger space, *Cognitive Development*, **4**, 121–139.
DeLoache, J.S. (1990). Young children's understanding of scale models. In R. Fivush and J. Hudson (eds), *Knowing and Remembering in Young Children* (pp. 94–126). New York: Cambridge University Press.
DeLoache, J.S. (1991). Symbolic functioning in very young children: understanding of pictures and models, *Child Development*, **62**, 736–752.
DeLoache, J.S. and Burns, N.M. (1991). Early understanding of the representational function of pictures. Unpublished manuscript.

DeLoache, J.S. and DeMendoza, O.A.P. (1987). Joint picturebook reading of mothers and one-year-old children, *British Journal of Developmental Psychology*, **5**, 111–123.

DeLoache, J.S., Kolstad, V. and Anderson, K. (1991). Physical similarity and young children's understanding of scale models, *Child Development*, **62**, 111–126.

Dow, G.A. and Pick, H. (in press). Young children's use of models and pictures as spatial representations, *Cognitive Development*.

Hartley, D.G. (1976). The effects of perceptual salience on reflective-impulsive performance differences, *Developmental Psychology*, **12**, 218–225.

Huttenlocher, J. (1974). The origins of language comprehension. In R.L. Solso (ed.), *Theories in Cognitive Psychology: The Loyola Symposium*. Hillsdale, New Jersey: Lawrence Erlbaum.

Lynn, J. and Jay, A. (1986). *Yes, Prime Minister: The Diaries of the Right Hon. James Hacker, Vol. I* (pp. 115–116). London: BBC Publications.

Ninio, A. and Bruner, J. (1978). The achievement and antecedents of labelling, *Journal of Child Language*, **5**, 1–15.

Olson, D.R. (1989). Making up your mind, *Canadian Psychology*, **30**, 617–627.

Sigel, I.E. (1953). Developmental trends in the abstraction ability of children, *Child Development*, **24**, 131–144.

Sigel, I.E. (1970). The distancing hypothesis: a causal hypothesis for the acquisition of representational thought. In M.R. Jones (ed.), *Miami Symposium on the Prediction of Behavior, 1968: Effect of Early Experiences* (pp. 99–118). Coral Gables, Florida: University of Miami Press.

Sigel, I.E. (1978). The development of pictorial comprehension. In B.S. Randhawa and W.E. Coffmann (eds), *Visual Learning, Thinking, and Communication* (pp. 93–111). New York: Academic Press.

Sigel, I.E. and Cocking, R.R. (1977). *Cognitive Development from Childhood to Adolescence: A Constructivist Perspective*. New York: Holt, Rinehart & Winston.

Sigel, I.E. and Olmsted, P. (1970). Modification of cognitive skills among lower-class black children. In J. Hellmuth (ed.), *The Disadvantaged Child, Vol. 3*, (pp. 300–338). New York: Brunner-Mazel.

Sigel, I.E., Anderson, L.M. and Shapiro, H. (1966). Categorization behavior of lower and middle class Negro preschool children: differences in dealing with representations of familiar objects, *Journal of Negro Education*, **35**, 218–229.

Sorce, J. (1980). The role of operative knowledge in picture comprehension, *Journal of Genetic Psychology*, **136**, 173–183.

Steinberg, B.M. (1974). Information processing in the third year: coding, memory, transfer, *Child Development*, **45**, 503–507.

7 Drawing: Public Instruments of Representation

NORMAN H. FREEMAN
Department of Psychology, University of Bristol

The most direct start to understanding children's drawing is to look at one. Figure 7.1 is immediately recognisable as a scene with human figures and a snowman. A snowman is a stylised representation of a human figure, stylised because of the constraints of the sculptural medium. Would it be correct to term the picture of the snowman 'a representation of a representation'? Even worse, do you, as observer of the picture, form a mental representation of that representation of a representation? Clearly, matters are liable to get out of hand in any theoretical formulation of levels of representations. It is prudent to constrain the term 'representation' to what occurs in the mind, and accordingly a picture is an *instrument* of representation deployed by an artist and taken up by an observer. The artist intends the observer to recognise that a scene is depicted. The scene-recognition in Figure 7.1 is based on a capacity which both artist and observer share—the capacity to recognise members of one's own species. An account of depiction as the triggering of recognition can be found in Schier (1986), and a computational approach to the minimal shapes which trigger a specifically human-figure recognition can be found in Marr (1982). So a fundamental strand of an account of the development of drawing has to be an analysis of when children come to realise that their pictures have to trigger particular recognitions in the minds of others, and how they discover ways of organising their depictions so that recognitions will get triggered.

But that is, at best, only a quarter of the story. You may have noticed that the figures lack a nose. Yet the chances are that you were not so naively realistic as to conclude that the referents were tragically mutilated persons. Why not? If drawings are defined solely in terms of how faithfully they project onto real referents it is inescapable that the referents must be nose-less children at play. This shows that crude 'photographic realism' criteria fail to capture a fundamental fact about pictorial instruments of representation whereby observers seem to know that there is a crucial difference between merely not drawing a nose and positively depicting someone as noseless. It might be supposed that that is a very banal point, for how could one depict a noseless person except by not drawing a nose? But the

Systems of Representation in Children: Development and Use. Edited by C. Pratt and A.F. Garton
© 1993 John Wiley & Sons Ltd

Figure 7.1 Snowball fight by Sarah, aged $6\frac{1}{2}$ years

point is actually a most important one, and in the next section a picture will be discussed in which the child has apparently drawn a deformity but observers recognise the scene as *not* containing that deformity. In short, the intolerable constraint of 'photographic realism' is that it keeps one's mind focused on *what* is possibly depicted rather than *how* things are depicted. A conception of *how* depictions are organised is a cornerstone of an intuitive 'theory of depiction' in the following sense. Children come to categorise pictures as being objects which people use as instruments of representation, and as Neisser (1987) put the matter in general: 'To categorise an object, I believe, is to assert that it bears a particular relation to a particular set of ideas' (p. 4). People hold implicit theories which justify both what is to *count as a class of depictions* and what is *to qualify as good depictions* as tokens of their type. When do young children come to hold a coherent 'theory of art', a set of concepts which they believe explains why some pictures look good and others do not, to their eyes (Freeman, 1991)?

But if you talk to children about their drawing, it becomes clear that all of the above has got one only half way. Children use three types of discourse: how referents look, how referents are structured, and how a drawing 'goes'. They use the language of perception, knowledge and action when explaining how they draw as they do. They have a rough-and-ready conception of the *labour of production* of depiction. One component of that is a conception of the amount of *pre-planning* which they can do, and another is entirely implicit in the ways they respond to graphic puzzles which they themselves have generated—their on-the-spot graphic decisions. One strand of an account must be the developmental course of the typical balance between planning and 'playing it by eye' (see Allik & Laak, 1985; Duthie, 1985; Freeman, 1987; Thomas & Silk, 1989). Freeman (1980) for instance, argued that 'missing' noses and hands are indices of serial problems in drawing one thing at a time for which preschoolers have not yet developed a plan. The general temptation of 'graphic end anchoring' has been well expounded by van Sommers (1984).

Finally, what is left? So far the outline has been entirely prosaic, as competence-accounts usually are, with no mention of symbol systems, art, aesthetics or creativity. The analogy would be with an account of language which was confined to simple declaratives with no expressive language (such as 'nice' or 'hello'), no poetry and no jokes. Drawing is not boring for children—it is fun and it harnesses visual pleasure. More, it is a source of *power* for children—they can make things come true with drawing, they can control what happens on a blank page to allow visual order to emerge. By the time they are 5 years old, they have characteristic individual styles which outside observers can detect over and above the topics being depicted (Hartley *et al.*, 1982). Children have an understanding of how to appropriate for themselves the fact that there are different ways of drawing. Where does their conception of *artistry* come from? And where does it stop?

The evidence is that a love of pictures is often powerfully operative in the third year of life, which clearly flowers in the early school years. But drawing is difficult and relatively solitary (Freeman, 1990), and perform-ance persistently falls short of competence, often much to the vexation of the artist. A spirited account of how graphic errors can come home to roost is to be found in van Sommers (1984). At some time in the early years of schooling, children reach the point at which their untutored theory of pictorial representation both recognises the peculiarity of visual art and sets that to work in a generative mode to make deeper and deeper pictorial discoveries about the nature of representation. The remainder of the chapter follows through a very few of the implications of the paragraphs so far, with a little interweaving.

WORKING WITH REPRESENTATIONS

We begin by bracketing the problem of characterising a pictorial attitude. In cultures where pictures are common and communally valued (i.e. iconophilia is fostered within the culture), it is usual for children to begin picture-making long before anyone could understand what their pictures are about (the scribbling stage occurring in the second year of life). One route into pictorial competence comes from the more general representa-tional activity of the very young child. The child *pretends* to be an artist. Between the ages of 5 and 7 years, children usually come both to hold and to use a naive realist theory of art which channels their picture-production through a rather narrow bottle-neck. They have a conception of 'getting a picture right so that you can see what it's about' (see Willats, 1984). Some researchers rather deplore the restriction (Gardner & Wolf, 1987; Taylor, 1989), while others see it as a stepping-stone to a grasp of what is peculiarly rich and universal about visual aesthetic experience (recently, Parsons, 1987). Perhaps the balance can tip different ways in different children in differing environments? Irrespective of what the outcome might be, between the ages of $1\frac{1}{2}$ and 7 years, the average child makes rapid progress in coming to grasp a coherent set of fundamental principles about pictorial representation, some of which can be traced to concerns expounded by DeLoache (Chapter 6).

The emergence of pictorial competence involves both looking at pictures and at things which can be depicted, and the active making of pictures from scratch, bringing visual order onto a blank page. To borrow a formulation from Searle (1983), both perceiving and acting are the 'biologically primary forms of Intentionality'—both are directed to ensuring a 'mind to world fit' in a special, active way. He adds that, 'Beliefs and desires are not the primary forms, rather they are etiolated forms of more primordial experiences in perceiving and doing. Intention, for example, is not a fancy form of desire; it would be more accurate to think of desire as a faded form of intention ...' (p. 36). The study of picture-production and picture-inspection brings one straight to the 'primordial' level of representations. Harrison (1978) discussed how the 'rationality of making' becomes harnessed to the production of art-works.

Let us now widen the scope of enquiry to give an indication of the sources of evidence with which a competence account has to reckon. From the basic dichotomy of perceiving and doing, it follows that there are as many ways of interacting with pictures as human intentionality will allow. Here is an incomplete list from Eisner (1989): 'There are four major things that people do with art. They make it. They look at it. They understand its place in culture over time. They make judgements about its quality' (p. 127). It is necessary to add that pictures are widely generated, exchanged, discussed, displayed, reworked, copied, loved, admired, coveted, and so forth. Yet cultures do not license promiscuous interactions amongst those categories—children are allowed to rework their own pictures but not usually to draw on other people's pictures. Some classes of picture are regarded as ephemeral, others held up as enduring and authoritative, some are classified as private property, some are public, and so forth. Considered as a commodity-production-and-circulation *system*, cultures promote some pictorial attitudes and inhibit others. The emergence of the child's theory of pictorial representation will ultimately have to be explained in terms of what *facts* about depiction the system presents them with, how they conceive of the *human labour* which goes into producing and using pictures, and how an endogenously-driven developmental advance allows their minds *to take instruments of representation as an input and to yield as output representations of representations*. Anyone who passes a critical comment on a picture is engaged in some way, no matter how superficially, in that complex of mental activities. Parsons (1987)

commented: 'Young children start with much the same basic understanding of what paintings are about [as adults], and they restructure that
understanding in much the same ways as they grow older. They do this
to make better sense of the works of art they encounter' (p. 5). One may
add that they do this in order to improve the works of art they produce.
But is a pictorial-attitude account useful? And what is a basic level of
understanding of art?

THE PICTORIAL ATTITUDE AT WORK

Consider a picture made at what many identify as a peak time of children's
productivity. As Gardner & Wolf (1987) put it: '... the ages 5 to 7 seem to
us a very special time, one that deserves to be termed the flowering of
symbolisation' (p. 314). Figure 7.2 is a 6-year-old's drawing, and it is quite
important that you look at it without having access to a caption which
explains the artist's intention. The first question is what scene do you think
is depicted? There is *clearly* an adult and child, it *apparently* depicts an
outsize apple-core, and it depicts a *relation* between child and apple-core
in which something is *happening*. If that is roughly what you concluded,
you would be correct. We shall unpack those several aspects shortly. For
the moment, the important point is that that is more or less what Debbie
intended an outside viewer to conclude. The child and yourself share a
pictorial attitude which has shaped both *her* labour of production and some
part of *your* response to the product.

  How should the pictorial attitude be characterised? I suggest that the
opening sentence from page 1 of Searle (1983) is close to what is needed:
'As a preliminary formulation we might say: Intentionality is that property
of many mental states and events by which they are directed at or about
or of objects and states of affairs in the world. If, for example, I have a
belief, it must be a belief that such and such is the case ...'. The reason why
Debbie's intentionality was transmitted to you, no matter how imperfectly,
was because you both regarded the picture as her statement about some
state of affairs. But what enabled this producer–consumer couple to
contract such a relationship? It is not enough to say hopefully that the
picture *looks like* a state of affairs, though in some sense it surely does.
Resemblance will not do as a *foundation-stone* for a competence account of
the pictorial attitude. As Plato pointed out, everything resembles everything else up to a point. Indeed, one flat picture resembles another flat
picture more closely than either resembles the people whom they may be
about. Further, as Goodman (1976) showed, whilst resemblance is a tran-
sitive relation, depiction is intransitive: that is, if X resembles Y, then Y
resembles X, but one needs something else to tell one whether X and Y are
tokens of the same type (two trees for example) or if one is a representation
of the other, and if so whether it is X that represents Y or vice versa.

Figure 7.2 A scene which impressed a 6-year-old: explanation in text

Representation is asymmetrical: a real brick does not represent a picture of a brick any more than it represents the word 'brick' or the proposition, 'This is a brick'. Schier (1986) is a useful source for tracking the problem of characterising the asymmetry.

Now put together the asymmetry and the intentionality. The traditional question is what is corrigible: could the picture be wrong in any sense? Clearly if the picture is meant to refer your mind to a state of affairs, and it does not do so, one could ask the artist to redraw or repair the picture. Artists develop styles of drawing and repair which can often be detected across their tackling of different topics (e.g. in the style of Degas to which children often become sensitive in early adolescence, see Wolf & Perry, 1988). The possibility of drawing in a common way across referents arises from the following proposition: *anything that can be drawn can be drawn differently*. That follows as a necessary truth from the foundation proposition of the pictorial attitude that *anything that can be visually recognised can be depicted* (Freeman, 1990). As Schier (1986) argued, a picture does not work by mapping directly onto a referent but by inducing viewers to access their normal recognition of the referent. If both artist and viewer have similar recognitional capacities, a similar repertoire of primary representations of states of affairs, then a picture is a device for mapping between the artist's mental representation and the viewer's. Let us take two visual puzzles from Figure 7.2 to expose an intuitive flexibility in producer and viewer which Debbie has exploited, with varying degrees of success.

One puzzle concerns the apple-core. Is it really meant to be that big? As it happens, the answer is that it is—it was a giant sculpture (recall the snowman in Figure 7.1). But things could have been otherwise. Debbie was faithfully conserving scale in her statement of fact; but what she had then not grasped was that more elaborate rules would be needed for an *authoritative* statement of a *pictorial* fact. Her theory of art had not yet developed that far. To that extent, her naive realism was rather literal-minded, as Gardner & Wolf (1987) term the limitation. One way of expressing the limitation, taken from Harrison (1990), is that the relative sizes of child and apple-core accurately depict the *relation* between the two but that thereby casts into doubt the status of the apple-core as one pole of the relation (i.e. as a *relatum*). It could conceivably have been the case that the topic of the picture was of Snow White pointing in horror to the poisoned apple before collapsing. The second puzzle is of the same type. Debbie's extended arm is lengthened in the interests of showing the relation between herself and the sculpture, literally so, since she drew the sculpture first, then her torso, then connected the two. The lengthening of the arm is not a property of one arm as a relatum—Debbie had no such deformity. The odd thing is that most viewers, from preschoolers to adults, immediately intuitively grasp that fact in their first impression. In informal interviews with a range of informants, many of them commented that the picture could surely have been 'drawn better' but none regarded the pictorial lengthening as a compelling statement about the relatum. You may have noticed in the crouching boy in Figure 7.1 a false attachment between the arms; no-one takes that to be a statement of one arm related to the other as an outgrowth but as a hopeful stab at depicting partial occlusion of one relatum.

What the pictorial puzzles have in common is that they expose a resolutely non-realist strand of the pictorial attitude, an understanding that the interpretation of lines can shift between relation and relatum, and which interpretation one opts for is a matter of pictorial *plausibility* (Duthie, 1985). Such flexible interpretation is simply something one does not do with the perception of real objects except under obscure viewing conditions. Here is a simple proof of that, which exposes one visual puzzle that does not occur—no-one regards the heavy black outline of the two human figures as a relatum. It is taken for granted that the artist is not committed to an assertion that the referents have heavy black outlines. No-one carries a resemblance-criterion that far. None of the people I interviewed thought that the picture would automatically have been better if the outlines had been sketched in very faint pencil. Wolf & Perry (1988) classify decisions about line-texture as pertaining to the category 'rendition': a category which they assert to be developed around the age of 6 years as a distinct component of the child's drawing competence. Everyone understands that it is difficult to draw smooth, rounded objects on a flat page. If anything qualifies for being a peculiarity of visual art, it is the squashing of the third dimension onto a two-dimensional surface, often with the use of 'fictional lines', lines which are not to be taken literally as representations of relata.

Let us now sum up. Perceiving and making pictures are basic forms of intentional action. Both involve mental representations, and the picture is a public, external instrument of representation. The child's pictorial attitude develops along the lines of an intuitive theory involving the mental representation of the instruments. The foundation-stone of the intuitive theory is that anything which can be visually recognised can be drawn. But a drawing is not a replica of the whole, or even of bits, of the referent, but a map of relations, and it follows as a necessary truth that any map which is drawn can be drawn differently. Children discover that for themselves very early on in their attempts at picture-production. If the bare account is at all true, three things follow. One is that the earliest drawings will often arise from a form of intentional action which is itself non-pictorial—from pretend play—which becomes *narrowed* onto pictures. The second is that a large part of the development of drawing-skill will be explicable as increasingly sophisticated attempts to preplan the balance between (a) getting relations on the page to map onto relations in the referent and (b) making clear what each separate relatum looks like. Fenson (1985) traced one development in human-figure drawing to a move away from assembling relata towards outlining the whole figure to allow relata to be moulded from the relations. Finally, if pictures are rooted in normal non-pictorial visual recognition, children's drawings will often be dominated by attempts to use non-pictorial vision as a guide in shaping their drawings. According to the computational approach to vision (inspired by Marr, 1982), the visual system is well designed to yield object-centred representations (that is, representations not tied to a temporary specific viewpoint) as an output. There should be a way of detecting that that level of representation serves as input into the child's representation of representations.

THE FIRST TWO STEPS INTO THE PICTORIAL ATTITUDE

Gardner & Wolf (1987) summarise one route into the pictorial attitude in the following words: 'Consider ... when the child of $1\frac{1}{2}$ or 2 is asked to draw a truck ... a typical child will grab a marker, move it across the paper back and forth rapidly, and then say "Vroommm, Vroommm" as if the marker were itself a vehicle' (p. 310). Here the drawing itself arises out of the gestural system: a way of playing which represents one aspect of a truck is harnessed to picture-making. I suggest that we classify such a picture as a *record* of an activity, but it is little more. Its value as a record lasts as long as what inspired it can be recalled. In sum, as gestures are evanescent, so are such records of them, though the records physically linger on and often look beautiful. Figure 7.3 shows one such record in which something about a referent has 'mapped itself' onto the paper.

The second route into drawing also arises during the second year of life. In pretend play, the child generates representations by creating alternative models of the world, often with the support of physical objects which play

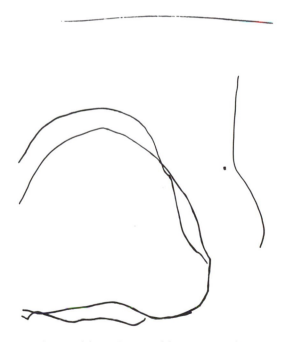

Figure 7.3 A pictorial record by a 2-year-old: a car moving

the role of props to the self-generated drama. The roles are *stipulated* by the child: a blob of clay may be stipulated to be a cake. Children discover the same route into drawing—they stipulate what the scribble represents. If an adult writes the stipulation on the drawing as a caption, that preserves its representational life. The caption is a record of the child's *intentionality* in picture-production. Without the caption, Figure 7.4 would be completely uninterpretable to an outsider observer, and indeed perhaps not discriminable from a record.

To characterise this stage of life one can put forward two general propositions which at first sight seem too commonplace to be worth noting, but which together point to the next advance. The example of the record was confined to a truck moving, but of course it is generalisable to many types of movement and many types of referent—a rabbit hopping, for example.

Figure 7.4 A stipulated representation: five attempts at a person by child aged 3 years 2 months

Wolf (1988) discusses some of these referents. The general proposition is that anything in reality which can be gesturally *simulated* can be recorded on the page by allowing mapping to occur. Recording, then, represents the intentionality of doing, and that is one of Searle's two primordial forms.

Stipulation has something in common with recording, in that a publically unrecognisable set of marks is the product. But there is also a crucial difference: in stipulation the marks are not just allowed to occur as a result of simulation but are made to happen as a marker of intentionality. The child is pretending to be an artist whereby the manner of drawing is shaped with a view to the form of the end-product. The general proposition which characterises stipulation is that anything in reality which can be stipulated as existing in imagination can be stipulated as represented in any end-product. The question then is what implicit theory of pictorial representation does the scribbler hold? Is it really the case that 'anything goes', that any end product is as good as any other for the purpose of pretending to be an artist?

The answer seems to be that in or by the third year of life, the scribbler has grasped the intentionality of perception. The proof is that if an adult defines a joint activity as that of picture-making, and produces sufficient markings on the page to trigger a visual recognition in the child, then the child will join in appropriately by shaping her stipulation to fit the representation. Figure 7.5 is an example of that occurring with a child aged 25 months. Consider the right-hand figure where George said 'nose': this

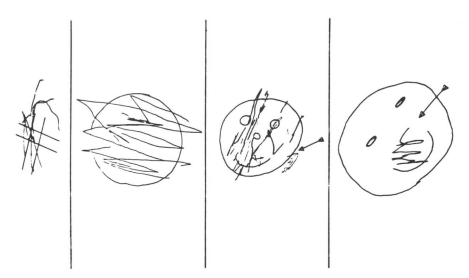

Figure 7.5 Scribbles by George, aged 25 months, over predrawn shapes. An arrow marks where his pen hit when he announced an ear and a nose as the relata (from Figures 5 and 6 in Freeman, 1977, by permission of Plenum Press)

first step was literally to point with his pen to the place where the nose should be, and then he scribbled. That is not an isolated phenomenon, and Freeman (1980) discussed the occurrence of such 'localisation skills' in several places in his book. Two points are relevant here. The first is that the graphic pointing is actually an elegant way of using the most basic form of dramatic gesture, pointing, and allowing it to record—where the pen hits, there the mark starts. The second is rather more fundamental; it is an answer to the question of why did the child say 'nose' at all in the first place? Clearly we, as adults, find it rather an unsurprising thing to do, given a depiction of a face. But that banal fact is enough to show that the scribbler is not *confined* to a pretend mode in which anything goes—a cushion can be a cat, or a screw of paper a toffee—but even the meagre pattern in Figure 7.5 triggers an intentional perceptual stance.

THE NEXT STEPS IN THE PICTORIAL ATTITUDE

Again, the most direct entry into understanding the advances which are typical of the age range 3–5 years is to look at a picture. This time we shall use an adult sketch, to indicate the room for manoeuvre in picture-making. Figure 7.6 shows three alternative ways of sketching a face. Why do they all 'work'? Clearly, the overall pattern is the important thing—the gross relations amongst forms. That constitutes the icon of a face, and as Schier (1986) points out, no separate part can be extracted and recognised in isolation as an icon of anything (e.g. one of the dots alone does not iconify an eye). That is sometimes traced to the fact that all marks are inherently *plurifunctional*: a circle can represent a hole, disc, sphere, etc. By the same token, as Harrison (1990) points out, any mark can play the role of relation or relatum. By age 5 years, most children have developed a repertoire of forms which they use plurifunctionally, much as in Figure 7.6. They can also be adept at composing abstract designs, exploring the effects of juxtaposing various forms, and that has been harnessed to serve a visual thinking educational programme in the Weizman Institute (see Agam, 1984).

Figure 7.6 Three ways of drawing eyes in a schematic face: the substitutibility of different shapes with same relata

The simplest eyes can be dots, dashes or enclosed regions. As Willats (1987) pointed out, that series corresponds in levels of complexity to the primitives in Marr's (1982) computational approach to vision. Each primitive *refers to*, is a projection of, the same referent, an eye, but each *denotes* it by a different form. There is indeed a calculus of denotations to be formalised, and one account has been offered by Willats (1987), applied to the human-figure drawings of 3–5 year olds.

Consider what would happen if one mixed the denotations, making one eye a dot and another a dash, for instance. The picture would no longer refer to a general human face but would identify a winking face. Again, a leg can be drawn as single line or as a thin oval, but to mix them would identify a peg-legged pirate very well. Children's experimentation with a calculus of denotations makes up a large part of what Gardner & Wolf (1987) were sensitive to as 'symbolic flowering'. It provides a large part of the fun of creativity, a type of 'form-play'.

I suggest that one strand of the pictorial attitude which develops after the scribbling phase is a non-realist strand of experimenting with forms. It would not be entirely a pun to call it a formal component. The child consults her repertoire of pictorial forms to find which one can stand for an entity in the presence of other forms she has drawn or is about to draw. And yet it is not easy to select the most appropriate form on occasion. A striking account is in van Sommers (1984). In one example, 5-year-olds

Figure 7.7 A typical 'tadpole form' of the human figure by a 4-year-old

were asked to draw a comb which had two thicknesses of teeth. The wider teeth sometimes came out drawn longer instead of wider, or more densely packed instead of more spread out. Van Sommers calls this 'perceptual cross-talk'.

The above examples of form-selection were at rather a detailed level. At a more global level, there is an intriguing phenomenon where the young child seems to grasp a basic pictorial method and recycle it with increasingly difficult drawing problems. Figure 7.7 shows a typical 'tadpole form', one in which most of the whole figure is depicted by a single circle. The traditional puzzle is whether the circle represents an undifferentiated head-trunk or just a head. Different lines of argument have complementary strengths and weaknesses (see Freeman, 1987). What is clear is that *the drawing is globally intended by the child to signal a representation of the whole human figure*. The circle is a framework laid down within and around which graphic relations can be marked. The picture does not contain the basic six cylinder organisation of Marr (1982), which defines the ground-plan of human-figure recognition, though it is recognisably only one step away. What gives the clue that this is some sort of fundamental graphic strategy is the re-emergence of global intentions with other segmented figures which are very difficult to draw. It is common, for example, for even 7-year-olds to draw a cube as just an approximation to a single square. Moore (1986) elegantly showed that this was indeed a global representation by setting children to draw a dice, and observing that they packed the single square with dots from all sides of the dice. The global approach seems to be most readily understandable as the child's claim upon a pictorial working-space before she has puzzled out 'how the drawing should go'. There is quite an element of stipulation in that. Finally, another neat observation by Moore was that a few older children also produced a single square but then included only the dot from the front face of the cube. The square represented only one local part of the complex referent, after which the children stopped rather than tackling the problems of graphic differentiation. It is a salutory reminder that identical products (squares) can result from radically different production processes. To step back an age-level or two, it is entirely possible that some tadpole-drawers pre-plan their basic circle as a global torso whilst others generate it as a denotation of a head only (and then maybe see wider possibilities in it).

Clearly, the difficulty of drawing a cube is because it is difficult to depict a three-dimensional referent on a plane surface. A variety of attempts to solve that problem characterises drawings from around the age of 7 years well into adolescence (and beyond). In the next section attention is drawn to two common phenomena in three-dimensional drawing which serve to return the present account to where it began in the opening paragraph— the triggering of a recognition, the problem of projective mapping, and a computational account of vision.

Figure 7.8   A clear drawing of a cup, a canonical representation, by a 6-year-old

HOW SHOULD THE MISSING DIMENSION 'GO'?

Figure 7.8 looks like a fairly clear drawing of a cup by a 6-year-old. So it is, but the cup which served as referent had been placed so that its handle was not visible, and the child had been asked to draw precisely what she could see. She was confronted with a sort of appearance/reality conflict. The solution she failed to adopt was to cope with *occlusion* in the scene by *hidden-line elimination* on the page. That cup-problem was first documented by Freeman & Janikoun (1972), and followed up by Freeman (1980) and Davis (1985). Davis reported that children would readily solve the graphic problem when the target cup was paired with one which indeed had its handle visible. The power of *simultaneous projective contrast* was independently reported by Cox (1985) and Light (1985). The child can readily be provoked into a situation-specific change within pictorial attitude by turning the task from one of visually describing a referent, triggering a recognition of the referent, to visually identifying the referent in context, conveying what the temporary purpose of the drawing is intentionally about. It may or may not be coincidence that the first functional approach to the problem of reference in child language laid stress on the way that description gradually gives way to identification (see Karmiloff-Smith, 1986).

'Visually realistic' drawings, like a cup with a handle, induce the spectator to access an object-centred representation of the referent, a 'canonical form' of a cup. That type of mental representation is held in long-term storage, and a variety of viewpoint-dependent representations can be referred to it by the spectator. What happens if the child is faced with a graphic problem which cannot readily be solved by making a viewpoint-dependent drawing as simply as the cup-problem could be? One such problem was noted by Freeman (1980) in a test in which the cup was made transparent so that the turned-away handle was visible through the body of the vessel and looked like a straight rod. The key finding was that many children who could cope with the cup-task by using hidden-line elimination now 'regressed' to drawing the glass-handle in full view attached to the side of the glass. Presumably the glass poses a real visual puzzle: the handle cannot be omitted because it is indeed visible, but to draw it as a rod within the outline of the glass would look like a distorted or uninterpretable representation. Davis (1985) reported that the simultaneous-contrast technique largely failed to work with glasses. In sum, where children may be ready to respect the impact of the third dimension on appearance by eliminating hidden lines, they are less willing to commit themselves to a change in form. That is the case even though they readily experiment with forms for non-3D drawings of the Figure 7.2 type. That ordering, from which bits are visible to what forms are visible, reminds one of a popular ordering from appearance-reality tests (see Flavell, 1989).

But now let us enquire into how children cope when they *cannot* sidestep a form-dimension problem if they are to get their drawings to 'look right'. Such a problem is encountered whenever a drawing could never fit like a costume onto a referent. The meagre shape of a cube exposes the problem well. If you try to draw it like a Necker cube, in what is termed 'oblique projection', that respects the integrality of the cube at the expense of producing fictional angles and slopes (an example is shown in Figure 7.9). Oblique projection is characterised by the third-dimension parallels being preserved as parallels and drawn obliquely, compared with the non-parallel (converging) obliques of linear perspective (see Dubery & Willats, 1983, for a classification of projective systems). If you try to design a

Figure 7.9 Attempts to draw a cube: possibly the commonest task which gives rise to the greatest number of variant forms

costume ready to be fitted onto a real cube, you will draw disjointed squares which do not remotely look like a cube. Rather unsurprisingly, the request to draw a cube produces an enormous number of variant forms as children struggle with the alternatives (as seen in Figure 7.9). One alternative is of *explaining* the structure of the referent as a Necker-cube does (from the Latin 'ex' + 'planere'—to lay out on a surface), and the other method is to *explicate* the structure (from 'ex' + 'plicere'—to unfold). Freeman (1987) discussed the alternatives, and Caron-Pargue (1985) devoted a whole text to the interplay of solutions and errors. Let me briefly suggest a typical developmental course of problem-solving here.

It is common to begin with a single square which stands for the whole cube (as noted in the previous section). One option is to use parallels and perpendiculars to subdivide it in various ways (Mitchelmore, 1985). The trouble with this strategy is that as the internal complexity of the drawing increases, it comes to look less and less recognisable as corresponding to a canonical object-centred representation of the simple form of the referent. The square outline acts as a severe constraint on the depiction of relata—the faces—and of their relations. Accordingly one sees an age-related trend to bursting the constraint, that is towards explication whereby the various assemblages of faces are attempted without much respect for the integrality of the overall outline. But having burst the constraint, how does the child come to reassemble the bits in an explanation mode? The solution is to use obliques. These signal *changes in direction* on the picture-plane. The price to be paid is that some faces of the cube are now not depicted as squares at all. The diagonals are thus arguably a *local solution* to the problem of *joining* the separated shapes rather than a sudden grasp of a new *projective system* devoted specifically to the third dimension. Such an argument has been put forward independently by Duthie (1985), Mitchelmore (1985) and van Sommers (1984); see Freeman (1986, 1987) for discussion.

The argument can readily be cast into terms introduced in the opening sections of this chapter. The oblique solution to projection here arises from the child working on the *relations* between cube-faces and on the denotational aspect of drawing—the use of a single line to indicate a *join* between two regions rather than as the *contour* of one region. One test of the account would be to show that the use of an oblique did not generalise to another three-dimensional figure. That is because the account specifies that the child is making a discovery about the local relations of the particular referent rather than a general projective discovery about the third dimension which holds good for a class of referents. Lack of generalisation was reported by Phillips, Inall & Lauder (1985). A second prediction is that the first obliques to be discovered by the child would be those where faces join, not those occurring at the edge of the drawing. There is a lack of systematic data, but certainly it is a familiar finding that the right-hand bottom oblique is discovered last (the 'flat-bottom error'). A struggle with the problems of joining regions and reserving obliques for the third dimension occupies depictors up to and through adolescence (see Duthie, 1985). For a minority of adolescents, the struggle to impose linear perspective on pictures becomes something of an addiction.

CONCLUSION

A developing theory of art is manifest in the orderliness with which children generate pictorial problems. The pictorial attitude is a peculiarly intimate blend of doing and seeing: both intentional stances provide routes into the pictorial system. Harrison (1978) neatly summed up the intimacy as follows, in describing what is involved in a child making an art-object:

> The object itself he is making ... while importantly an 'object' in the sense of being a 'thing' is at the same time 'the object of' his activity ... (p. 18).

The preschool child claims pictures as objects of activity (intentional objects) by recording and stipulation in pretend play. She develops representations of representational work. Once launched, there is no principled reason why her theory of art should ever cease developing. It is a sad fact that unless carefully nurtured, it grinds to a halt in most people. They then end up with only the language of belief and desire ('Pictures have got to look like things' and 'I know what I like')—Searle's 'etiolated' left-over from biologically primary modes of representation, warmed up and cursorily served to the next generation of potential artists.

REFERENCES

Agam, Y. (1984). Seeing is learning—or should be! *Kidma (Israel Journal of Development)*, **8**, 1–8.

Allik, J. and Laak, T. (1985). The head is smaller than the body: but how does it join on? In N.H. Freeman and M.V. Cox (eds), *Visual Order*. Cambridge: Cambridge University Press.

Caron-Pargue, J. (1985). *Le Dessin du Cube Chez l'Enfant*, Berne: Peter Lang.

Cox, M.V. (1985). One object behind another: young children's use of array-specific or view-specific representations. In N.H. Freeman and M.V. Cox (eds), *Visual Order*. Cambridge: Cambridge University Press.

Davis, A.M. (1985). The canonical bias: young children's drawings of familiar objects. In N.H. Freeman and M.V. Cox (eds), *Visual Order*. Cambridge: Cambridge University Press.

Dubery, F. and Willats, J. (1983). *Perspective and Other Drawing Systems*. London: The Herbert Press.

Duthie, R.K. (1985). The adolescent's point of view: studies of forms in conflict. In N.H. Freeman and M.V. Cox (eds), *Visual Order*. Cambridge: Cambridge University Press.

Eisner, E. (1989). Structure and magic in discipline-based art education. In D. Thistlewood (ed.), *Critical Studies in Art and Design Education*. London: Longman.

Fenson, L. (1985). The transition from construction to sketching in children's drawings. In N.H. Freeman and M.V. Cox (eds), *Visual Order*. Cambridge: Cambridge University Press.

Flavell, J.H. (1989). The development of children's knowledge about the mind: from cognitive connections to mental representations. In J.W. Astington, P.L. Harris and D.R. Olson (eds), *Developing Theories of Mind*. Cambridge: Cambridge University Press.

Freeman, N.H. (1977) How young children try to plan drawings. In G. Butterworth (ed.), *The Child's Representation of the World*. New York: Plenum Press.

Freeman, N.H. (1980). *Strategies of Representation in Young Children: Analysis of Spatial Skills and Drawing Processes*. London: Academic Press.

Freeman, N.H. (1986). How should a cube be drawn? *British Journal of Developmental Psychology*, **4**, 317–322.

Freeman, N.H. (1987). Current problems in the development of representational picture-production, *Archives de Psychologie*, **55**, 127–152.

Freeman, N.H. (1990). Innovation in child art, *European Journal for High Ability*, **1** 52–63.

Freeman, N.H. (1991). The theory of art that underpins children's naïve realism, *Visual Arts Research*, **17**, 65–75.

Freeman, N.H. and Janikoun, R. (1972). Intellectual realism in children's drawings of a familiar object with distinct features, *Child Development*, **43**, 1116–1121.

Gardner, H. and Wolf, D. (1987). The symbolic products of early childhood. In D. Gorlitz and J.F. Wohlwill (eds), *Curiosity, Imagination and Play*. Hillsdale, New Jersey: Lawrence Erlbaum.

Goodman, N. (1976). *The Languages of Art, 2nd edn*. Indianapolis: Hackett.

Harrison, A. (1978). *Making and Thinking*. Sussex: Harvester.

Harrison, A. (1990). The minimal syntax of the pictorial. Talk given at the Bristol University Centre for Cognitive Issues in the Arts, May meeting.

Hartley, J.L., Somerville, S.C., Jensen, von C.D. and Eliefja, C.C. (1982). Abstraction of individual styles from the drawing of five-year-old children, *Children Development*, **53**, 1193–1214.

Karmiloff-Smith, A. (1986). Some fundamental aspects of language development after age 5. In P. Fletcher and M. Garman (eds), *Language Acquisition*. Cambridge: Cambridge University Press.

Light, P. (1985). The development of view-specific representations considered from a socio-cognitive standpoint. In N.H. Freeman and M.V. Cox (eds), *Visual Order*. Cambridge: Cambridge University Press.

Marr, D. (1982) *Vision: A Computational Investigation into the Human Representation and Processing of Visual Information*. San Francisco: Freeman.

Mitchelmore, M.C. (1985). Geometrical foundations of children's drawing. In N.H. Freeman and M.V. Cox (eds), *Visual Order*. Cambridge; Cambridge University Press.

Moore, V. (1986). The use of a colouring task to elucidate children's drawings of a solid cube, *British Journal of Developmental Psychology*, **4**, 335–340.

Neisser, U. (1987). Introduction: the ecological and intellectual bases of categorisation. In U. Neisser (ed.), *Concepts and Conceptual Development*. Cambridge: Cambridge University Press.

Parsons, M.J. (1987). *How We Understand Art*. Cambridge: Cambridge University Press.

Phillips, W.A., Inall, M. and Lauder, E. (1985). On the discovery, storage and use of graphic descriptions. In N.H. Freeman and M.V. Cox (eds), *Visual Order*. Cambridge: Cambridge University Press.

Schier, F. (1986). *Deeper into Pictures*. Cambridge: Cambridge University Press.

Searle, J.R. (1983). *Intentionality*. Cambridge: Cambridge University Press.

Taylor, B. (1989). Art history in the classroom: a plea for caution. In D. Thistlewood (ed.), *Critical Studies in Art and Design Education*. London: Longman.

Thomas, G.V. and Silk, A.M.J. (1989). *An Introduction to the Psychology of Children's Drawings*. London: Harvester Wheatsheaf.

van Sommers, P. (1984). *Drawing and Cognition: Descriptive and Experimental Studies of Graphic Production Processes*. Cambridge: Cambridge University Press.

Willats, J. (1984). Getting the drawing to look right as well as to be right. In W.R. Crozier and A.J. Chapman (eds), *Cognitive Processes in the Perception of Art*. Amsterdam: North-Holland.

Willats, J. (1987). Marr and pictures: an information-processing account of children's drawings. *Archives de Psychologie*, **55**, 105–125.

Wolf, D. (1988). Drawing the boundary: the development of distinct systems for spatial representation in young children. In J. Stiles-Davis, M. Kritchevsky and U. Bellugi (eds), *Spatial Cognition*, Hillsdale, New Jersey: Lawrence Erlbaum.

Wolf, D. and Perry, M.D. (1988). From endpoints to repertoires: some new conclusions about drawing development, *Journal of Aesthetic Education*, **22**, 17–34.

8 The Representation of Number in Infancy and Early Childhood

KEVIN DURKIN
The University of Western Australia

> In sum, reference is socially fixed and not determined by conditions or objects
> in individual brains/minds. Looking inside the brain for the reference of our
> words is ... just looking in the wrong place   (Putnam, 1989, p. 25).

Among the many phenomena that human beings are able to represent, numbers are particularly troublesome. First, the relationship between any spatio-temporal entity and a number is ephemeral and arbitrary: for example, an object which is 'two' in an array of six objects could be 'five' if we recounted from a different starting point, or 'three' if we reordered. This would not be the case for its other properties: a Teenage Mutant Ninja Turtle would still be 'green' and a 'Teenage Mutant Ninja Turtle' wherever we began a list of colour words or category names. Second, the words for numbers are subject to unusual constraints: they recur in a fixed order, and the last mentioned provides a summary statement about the properties of a set. This is not the case for Donatello, Raphael, Leonardo and Michaelangelo, of whom we may speak in any order and for whom the final word does not provide a meaningful summary. Further, we can repeat an adjectival description in an account of the Turtles (Donatello is green and Michaelangelo is green) but we cannot properly repeat a numerical description (if Raphael is 'two', then Michaelangelo is some other number).

Clearly, as contributors to this volume attest, children have a great deal of other problems to surmount in representation: in the midst of these, how might we expect them to fare with something as unique and abstract as number? In fact, the evidence is overwhelming that young children do very well in this domain. The ostensibly simple act of counting an array of say, 8–10 objects, which most children can perform accurately by around age 5 years (Fuson, 1988), actually involves quite sophisticated organisation (Fuson, 1988, 1991; Gelman & Gallistel, 1978) which is not available to the young or the mature of lower species (cf. Klein & Starkey, 1987). As we shall see below, even during the preschool years children can represent and use numbers in important ways, and of course ultimately mathematical skills constitute one of the human species' most powerful

Systems of Representation in Children: Development and Use. Edited by C. Pratt and A.F. Garton
© 1993 John Wiley & Sons Ltd

representational achievements and tools. Although there are certainly huge individual differences in mature competence in this area, most people are able to represent numbers in useful ways from relatively early in the lifespan.

How does this come about and how does it progress? In this chapter I assume that the development of numeracy is a multidetermined social activity and I will attempt to account for some aspects of the interactions and consequences of several key factors. To assert multidetermination of a developmental phenomenon is scarcely an original proposition, but it is at least a useful safeguard. It protects against the tendency to represent an achievement as explicable within a framework which is 'purely' cognitive, or social, or linguistic. The development of numerical knowledge and abilities involves each of these factors, and more, but the predominant bias of the current literature is to focus upon the first, perhaps assuming that because mathematical skills involve cognitive processes focused upon relatively 'cold' symbols, and are in turn fundamental to many other cognitive processes, then their ontogenesis is the preserve of cognitive developmentalists.

Unfortunately, this can lead to a misrepresentation of the nature of development as cognitive developmentalists are wont to perceive learning as a confrontation between the innocent monadic enquirer and the inherent structures or facts of a domain of knowledge. Thus, interactions between the learner and others of whatever level of knowledge are often disregarded or treated as peripheral (Bruner & Bornstein, 1989). Although there is some important work on the social contexts of mathematical development (discussed later), this has been quantitatively a minority activity in the field. Similarly, the relations between thought and language are for many cognitivists transparent (the former being the prerequisite on to which the latter is mapped), and so there seems to be little reason to investigate the linguistic features of numerical learning (Piaget, 1952, p. 29, saw children's counting as 'merely verbal'). This characterisation is not intended to detract from the many positive contributions of cognitive developmental work which, after all, has forged the major headway in the study of number and mathematical development through the last decade and resulted in many exciting lines of enquiry. In fact, other disciplines and subdisciplines which might make valuable contributions to the study of humans' number knowledge have been far more remiss. For example, as Hurford (1987) points out, numeral systems have not been central to the major intellectual debates of recent times, and have not attracted much attention from linguists, despite (or perhaps because of) their unique structures and unusual semantics. Nevertheless, it has become increasingly apparent in recent years that the traditional representation of the solo child, primarily engaged in physical, object-centred discoveries, provides at best only a partial view of developmental processes (Bruner & Bornstein,

1989; Durkin, 1988; Rogoff, 1991; Strayer & Moss, 1989), and the fact that cognitive developmentalists have started the running does not of course guarantee that they have been heading in the best direction.

Admitting multidetermination, then, at least directs attention to a wider range of considerations than has tended to be the case in recent treatments. This promotes a broadening of the *descriptive* task, raising the possibility that there is more to learning about numbers and their use than the formidable formalities of the number system and mathematical operations. For instance, there are the socio-cultural practices of the community within which numbers are transmitted, the specific strategies of caregivers and teachers, the functions of numerical references within everyday trans-actions. There is also the language within which the number system is encoded, described, operated upon and shared. And, of course, there are the interactions, interdependencies and conflicts among these domains and processes. The goals of this chapter are to consider how examination of these interactions might contribute to understanding of the why and the how of the early development of numerical representation. Developing a description of the various factors involved in the emergence of numeracy is not only a prerequisite to a satisfactory explanation of how normal human achievement in this area is possible, but may also contribute to the broader study of the development of representation by providing infor-mation on a highly specialised domain, yet one with implications for analysis of cognition, socialisation, linguistic development and educational processes. While this chapter makes no pretence towards having com-pleted the explanatory task, it does at least aim to highlight some of the data beyond those of numerical systems themselves, which require account in any theory of the development of numeracy.

The notion of early number representation as *activity* and as a *social* process may seem uncomfortable if mathematics is regarded as an inter-nally regulated domain of transcendental logic—pure knowledge that is independent of the human agent and waiting out there to be discovered. But this Platonic assumption has been seriously undermined by philo-sophers of mathematics and others (MacLane, 1981; Lakoff, 1987) who point out that it is not coincidental that branches of mathematics *work* when applied to human activities. They are *derived from* human attempts to understand those activities. Lakoff, in a succinct exposition of these issues, is led to the conclusion that, 'it is the human capacity to understand experience in terms of basic cognitive concepts that is at the heart of the success of mathematics—that and hard work' (1987, p. 364). Granting this, it could be added that Lakoff overlooks the productive and regulative processes of exchange of ideas and peer review. Again, if representation as a social process seems uncomfortable against traditional depictions of representation as an individual mental activity, then it should be recalled that, 'the meaning of a mental representation can never be intrinsic to it'

(Russell, 1984, p. 179, after Wittgenstein). For young children, as we shall see, the initial meaning of a number representation is that it is part of something done in certain circumstances, with adults.

This chapter will be concerned chiefly with the early stages of numerical representation, from infancy to the early school years. In the following section, I consider *why* children should attempt to represent number, suggesting that they do so because other people with whom they interact introduce them to the practice, and pointing to cross-cultural evidence that variations in how cultures and languages present numbers are associated with differences in how children represent them. Then, we consider *how* children learn to represent numbers. It is acknowledged that prelinguistic infants appear to have abilities to discriminate among small sets, but it is argued that the use of language is integral to early numerical development, and that language introduces discontinuities. This leads to a discussion of how children experience number words and how they understand and use them. Throughout, it is emphasised that progress does not consist simply in the child being exposed to input data and attempting to make sense of and use them, but that these processes are themselves engaged in the context of adult interest and monitoring which in turn lead to adult inter-ventions. The latter parts of the chapter are concerned with the character of the negotiations that result. It is argued that, although parents often exhibit pedagogical goals and sensitivities, the process of learning is not isomorphic with the structures of teaching; indeed, there are many con-tradictions and conflicts inherent in the (multidetermined) interactions, and it is speculated that these are fundamental to development. The chapter concludes with an overview of how the interpersonal and intra-psychological processes bearing upon number use may contribute to development.

WHY REPRESENT NUMBER?

Many studies have addressed the question of *how* young children learn to represent numbers. Before considering these, it is useful to consider *why* children should wish to engage in these forms of numerical discoveries. A natural assumption of developmentalists (shared by the author) is the 'because it is there' syndrome. That is, children are motivated towards cognitive and communicative mastery, and encounter number and mathematics as part of their explorations of the objective environment: 'Available structures are taken to be self-motivating' (Gelman & Massey, 1987, p. 140). This is not particularly controversial, but it is important to consider why it (the task of acquiring numeracy) is there, whether there are any variations in its manifestations, and whether such variations might be associated with differences in development.

In part, this is a phylogenetic question: why have human beings evolved number systems? Most historical accounts concur that the early stages of number development were closely related to agricultural activities (Dilke, 1987; Eves, 1976; Flegg, 1983; Kearins, 1991; Kline, 1964; Menninger, 1969). Early farmers needed to monitor the size of their herds of animals, to measure yields from different sections of their land, to record levels of irrigation and to organise their work calendrically (i.e. taking into account the predictability of the seasons). The need to objectify data, making them available for re-reference over time or amenable to public negotiations (e.g. in trading), seems likely to have provided motivation for the emergence of number words, the sharing of number words within a community and the discovery of ways of recording numerical facts symbolically, at first by means of tallying and eventually by means of numerals (Flegg, 1983). Linguistic evidence indicates that, for a long time, words for number were closely related to bodyparts or directly associated with the particular objects being counted (Flegg, 1983), which is still the case in the languages of several contemporary non-industralised peoples (Flegg, 1983; Hurford, 1987).

Thus, historically, the emergence of number systems seems to have been motivated and refined by adaptive behaviours. Of course, it is important to avoid confusing phylogeny and ontogeny in this context. The establishment of numeral systems and their integration into human life confers a socio-cultural advantage which does not have to be discovered in the same painstaking ways by successive generations. Today's children do not have to invent number: it is an inescapable feature of their environment.

This leads to the obvious but important answer to the question of why children learn about number systems. They are a pervasive and salient aspect of their everyday lives. Young children in our societies encounter references to number extensively. Number words occur often in adult language (Hurford, 1987), including adult language directed to infants and toddlers (Durkin et al., 1986; Fuson, 1988; Saxe, Guberman & Gearhart, 1987; Wagner & Walters, 1982). Number symbols are commonplace in the urban environment. Sinclair (1991) lists speed limits, bus numbers, page numbers, house numbers, telephone numbers, life numbers, TV channel numbers, time references, weight references, prices, contents, winners of races and other examples of uses of numbers that we take for granted and that form part of the backdrop to number learning in the preschool years. Children have to learn something about number because it is there, but *there* is the social milieu in which the child participates.

Importantly, number is not there in the same form for all children, and variations in cultural provisions with respect to number learning opportunities are reliably associated with differences in development.

First, the relevance of the historical sketch above is limited to peoples with agricultural pasts; the circumstances of some communities are quite different. For example, Kearins (1991) points out that the needs of hunter–gathering people, such as Australian Aborigines, were not oriented around keeping animals or growing and storing crops. Time measurements were probably less important to early people living in tropical and temperate zones because the seasons and day length vary less markedly and are less significant for economic activity than in northern Europe. Age knowledge, Kearins suggests, is less salient and perhaps even mysterious to people who do not have a tradition of measurement and whose lives are not oriented around the Western calendar. As a result, reference to number is far less common in Aboriginal languages than in European languages. Some Aboriginal languages have no separate words for numbers (though there are conventional ways of using bodyparts to represent numbers, Dixon, 1980), and most have relatively limited number word systems (Harris, 1987). Not surprisingly, traditions for the teaching of counting to children do not appear to have developed in hunter–gathering groups (Kearins, 1991).

Second, even among cultures which do employ numerical reference ubiquitously, and which have extensive verbal numeral systems, there are differences in the ways in which languages organise numbers. For example, there is a substantial difference between several European languages and several Asian languages in terms of the named-valued systems of number words (Fuson & Kwon, 1991). Asian languages such as Chinese, Japanese, Korean and Thai have a regular named-value system, whereby a number word is said and then the value that it represents is named (e.g. two thousand six hundred seven ten six for 2676). European languages have similar systems for the larger values (i.e. we would name the thousands and hundreds in ways analogous to the Asian languages) but irregular systems for the numbers below 100. Clearly, what is there to be learned varies among learning contexts.

Third, even with communities which share the same language, there are considerable differences in the ways in which adults contribute to young children's number-related experiences. There appear, for example, to be social class differences in this respect: Saxe et al. (1987), studying mother-preschooler dyads from Brooklyn, New York, found that working-class mothers expressed slightly less interest in their children's number activities than did middle-class mothers. The working-class children were found to be engaged at home in less complex number activities than were middle-class children, and in laboratory settings working-class mothers structured number tasks at lower levels of goal complexity than did their middle-class counterparts.

As prefaced above, these differences in environmental opportunities are reflected in differences in numerical/mathematical performance in the children. Aboriginal preschoolers tested by Kearins & Butters (1986) were substantially less likely to be able to report accurately their age in years than were either working-class or middle-class Anglo-Australian peers. The Aboriginal children's counting was not as advanced as their Anglo-Australian peers. Children speaking Asian languages tend to fare much better with tens and units tasks (i.e. consistent with their linguistic advantage in terms of the naming of the former value) than English-speaking peers (Miura, 1987; Miura & Okamoto, 1989), and Asian children learn elementary arithmetical skills more swiftly than US children (Song & Ginsburg, 1987; Fuson & Kwon, 1991). Finally, Saxe *et al.* (1987) found that middle-class 4-year-olds achieved more advanced performances on tasks involving cardinality, numerical reproduction and elementary arithmetic.

This is not merely a matter of disadvantage to a particular group due to lack of opportunity or other barrier. Equally important is the fact that the very activity of acquiring numerical and mathematical knowledge can be qualitatively different according to socio-cultural or linguistic context. For example, Kearins found that Aboriginal children both from remote settlements and urban homes had superior direction judgement skills to those of Anglo-Australian children. Direction finding is presumably much more important to nomadic communities and may even be sustained for at least the early stages of urbanisation, and transmitted to new generations (Kearins, 1991). Fuson & Kwon (1991) review findings that indicate that English-speaking children develop initially a unitary representation of multidigit number words; that is, each number, such as 13, is treated as a single unit, and children are unaware of the components of the number, so that given the task of adding 10 and 3 they have to count up. Their linguistic experience of the number guides them to adopt a rote learning strategy whereby they store the association between each number word and a certain number of countables, in contrast to Asian-speaking children whose languages guide them to a ready apprehension of the incorporation of '10' in each of the teen words.

Cultures vary substantially in terms of the extent to which they promote different number-oriented activities among the young, resulting in intercultural discrepancies and intracultural décalage (see Lancy, 1983). In some societal contexts, children develop numerical and mathematical skills in the course of everyday activities (such as street trading) which they do not exhibit in more conventional settings for mathematical instruction (e.g. school—Carraher, Carraher & Schliemann, 1985). Saxe (1988), like Carraher *et al.*, worked with young Brazilian street vendors and found that although the children were often adept at computations involving large denomination notes (a function of higher inflation in that country) and at naming the bill correctly (e.g. 5000 cruzeres), they were quite poor at reading multidigit numerical volumes (e.g. 5000). Nevertheless they could discriminate bills well, promoting the conclusion that 'unschooled Brazilian children had available a representational means for number that was distinct from the standard orthography' (Saxe, 1988, p. 1424), in this case based on other features of the notes. Again, number is acquired and operated upon because it is there, but *there* is the social context within which the child is developing, and learning involves interactions among child, cognitive domain, language and socio-cultural practices. This view contrasts with the traditional notion of the child discerning an abstract body of knowledge and struggling to work out its intrinsic structures, and emphasises instead the child as needing to make sense of activities in which others enlist her or him, so that 'knowing about number is a question of knowing how and when to use numbers' (Solomon, 1989, p, 159).

HOW DO CHILDREN LEARN TO REPRESENT NUMBER?

So far, it has been proposed that learning about numbers is circumscribed by the functions number serves in the child's socio-cultural context and by the ways in which that context makes number activities available and salient. This does not explain how it is possible to represent number, but emphasises the circumstances which affect the achievements involved. An adequate theory of how children learn to represent number will have to account for the interactions among perceptual, cognitive, linguistic and social-cognitive processes that take place within the learning context. The following sections present an attempt to sketch out some of the ways in which these interactions appear to occur, and to consider how they may promote development. The emphasis will be upon multidetermination, but a focal concern will be the ways in which language is implicated in the representation of number since the latter is inextricably linked to the former which provides the mental apparatus enabling us to access, objectify and operate upon it: 'Without language, no numeracy' (Hurford, 1987, p. 305). As Hurford points out, it is not logically necessary that this be the case, but it is universally observable that the development of numeracy (beyond perhaps the ability to discriminate small sets or make few to many distinctions) is dependent upon the possession of language. This section will be concerned primarily with linguistic activity and the representation of number. However, there is evidence to indicate that prelinguistic infants are able to discriminate among sets based on their numerosities, and it is important to consider what is involved in this ability and how it might relate to subsequent developments.

Early perception of number

Several researchers have provided evidence that human infants can discriminate between small collections containing different numbers of elements. Starkey & Cooper (1980) demonstrated that babies aged 4–6 months who had habituated to an array containing a certain number of dots would dishabituate to an array containing a different number of dots, provided that the number was no more than four. This finding has been replicated with 1-week-old infants by Antell & Keating (1983), and the paradigm extended to demonstrate comparable effects with three-dimensional objects of varying qualities, colours, etc. (Starkey, Spelke & Gelman, 1983; Strauss & Curtis, 1981). Infants of 6–8 months have been shown able to detect numerical correspondence between sets of entities presented in different modalities (Starkey, Spelke & Gelman, 1983, 1990). These are well-designed experiments with careful control of length, density, brightness and configuration cues: the finding seems robust, even if work is continuing on some of the details concerning exactly how many items infants can discriminate among and at what ages. As Starkey and his colleagues have argued (Starkey *et al.*, 1983; Klein & Starkey, 1987), what is important about the findings is that they indicate more than a few to many differentiations (cf. Davis, Albert & Barron, 1985). The differentiations are too precise, occurring only for sets of two, three or four items, and not for sets of four, five and six. Starkey and his colleagues propose that infants possess an elementary type of numerical knowledge which 'might serve as a basis for the acquisition of a particular mathematical system. The child would acquire a particular system with facility because at least some of its underlying characteristics are already in place' (Starkey *et al.*, 1990, p. 99). In their view, this helps to explain 'why counting and other numerical abilities develop so early, so spontaneously, and so universally across human cultures' (p. 124).

However, the relationship between these early abilities and the emergence of later number knowledge and procedures, such as labelling numerosities and counting, is unclear. Klein & Starkey (1987) and Starkey *et al.* (1990) imply a continuity, and it does indeed seem plausible that those abilities involved in the perception of differences between small collections could be useful in the acquisition of counting skills. Others, however, have argued that 'it should be clear that such discriminatory ability has nothing to do with number words, counting, or any kind of number system' (Steffe, Cobb & von Glasersfeld, 1988, p. 13). Part of the difficulty in interpreting the significance of the infant perception studies concerns the representational status of the discrimination, and part concerns the relationship between the representation and number words.

Steffe *et al.*, point out that evidence of built-in neurophysiological sensitivities is not evidence of numerical *concepts*. Indeed, Klein & Starkey (1987) see 'numerosity perception', as they term the discriminations revealed in the infancy experiments, as the most elementary of enumerative processes 'because it is a perceptual process' (p. 6), and in fact one which is also demonstrable among some lower species (in some cases, extending to a greater number of items than human infants can handle;

see Klein & Starkey, 1987, for a review). But exactly what is perceived and what ontological significance it has are not known.

Infants' abilities in this regard are often equated with subitizing (e.g. Klein & Starkey, 1987). However, much depends upon how one defines subitizing. Early work showed that adults exposed to brief ($\frac{1}{5}$ second) exposures of randomly arranged dots could say how many dots there were accurately for up to five or six items (Kaufman et al., 1949). With greater numbers, subjects were more prone to error, and were presumably estimating rather than apprehending directly the numerosities. Kaufman et al. saw subitizing as the ability to recognise and label the cardinality of small sets without counting. Hence, a common description of subitizing is the ability 'to apprehend directly the appropriate cardinal or measure word' (Fuson, 1988, p. 10). Clearly, infants do not apply *words* to their perceptions of numerosities (Fuson, 1988), but even whether they have a conceptual apprehension of cardinality or relative amounts is open to question. At some point in development, these abilities (perceptual, conceptual and verbal) must interrelate (since subitizing is achievable) but there is no empirical basis for an assumption that this is the outcome of natural continuities. It could, in fact, be multidetermined, and the processes of development could be subject to discontinuities and to contextual variations. For example, the involvement of the linguistic system may incur radical changes. Gelman & Gallistel (1978) draw upon Chi & Klahr's (1975) demonstration that the slope of the reaction time (RT) function for small numbers is not flat (RT increases slightly with numerosity) even among adults, and argue that the phenomenon identified in 'subitizing' experiments can itself be explained in terms of rapid, sub-vocal counting. If this, or some other integration of perceptual and verbal knowledge, is involved, then people acquiring different number systems may (have to) learn to subitize in different ways.

Cross-cultural issues are returned to below. For the moment, I will simply conclude that there is good evidence of intriguing number-related perceptual abilities in human infants, and that it is conceivable that these, arguably innate, abilities are implicated in later stages of number acquisition. But they are not representational abilities, and they are non-linguistic. (Riem, 1985, has also pointed out that they are not necessarily spontaneous either. The experimental studies elicit discriminations under ideal laboratory conditions where repetitive exposure to carefully selected stimuli can be controlled rigorously, and we do not know how this relates to everyday perceptual activity.)

Gelman & Gallistel (1978) report that when asked to give the numerosity of small sets (i.e. within the subitizable range), children display a predilection for counting, and perform better when counting is permitted. In order to count, children have (among other things) to learn the count words of their community. This means that learning to count is integrally related to acquiring language, though surprisingly little attention is paid to this consideration in cognitive-developmental accounts. In the next section, we consider some of the linguistic challenges involved and the ways in which these may relate to pre-existing abilities and the basic features of number systems.

Language and learning to count

Consider the challenge to the young language learner attempting to discover the meaning of number words. Note first that children at this stage will have little conscious understanding of numerosity and no *a priori* knowledge that the specific words they encounter in numerical references are a special area of the lexicon. (This holds whether or not one accepts the Starkey & Gelman position that number knowledge is a distinct cognitive domain; no-one has proposed that the number lexicon of a given linguistic community can be known to the learner in advance.) Thus, the children have to discriminate the number words among all the other words that they encounter (and which, of course, are also being discriminated and learned) and determine what functions and meanings they have. To understand how children succeed in this task, we need to take into account what they already know about number, what they already know about language, and how other people affect the structure and processes of the task.

One view might be that there is a convenient and harmonious continuity here: children have an early emerging ability to discriminate among small sets, and caregivers are keen to facilitate and guide discovery. I will argue, however, that this view assumes too ready a continuity between innate perceptual abilities and the social conventions of language use, that it disregards the complexities of number word meanings, and that it fails to accredit the dynamics of interactions among social-cognitive and communicative purposes of adult and child.

The transition from perceptual discrimination of numerosities to number word use

Children discover all sorts of things about their environments and themselves before they begin to speak. Children engage in quite remarkable forms of interaction with their caregivers during the prelinguistic period (Durkin, 1987; Garton, 1992). Many of the things infants discover, and much of the form of their early interactions (or 'conversations'), are analogous to aspects of the content, structures and processes of the linguistic level of communication they will subsequently achieve. Recognition of these analogies has led to a widespread feeling that there is a continuity from prelinguistic to linguistic communication. It is tempting to apply this consensus to account for the transition from pre-linguistic apprehension of numerosity to the use of number words. In such an account, number words would be 'mapped on' to a pre-existing social basis.

I recommend that we avoid this temptation. First, although this is not the place for a full analysis of the credibility of the orthodox transition metaphor, it can be agreed with Gelman (1983, p. 276) that the phase of language acquisition research marked by a commitment to this hypothesis (sometimes called the 'Precursor Hypothesis') has been rich in speculation and correlational reasoning, but modest in terms of empirical evidence. As Gelman points out, there have been no detailed accounts of the 'grammar' of early interactions and no accounts of the translation procedures whereby language is acquired, although there has been acknowledgment from the theorist to whom this view is most often attributed that it is in fact unsatisfactory (Bruner, 1983; and see also Gelman, 1983). In short, not-withstanding the consensus mentioned above, the Precursor Hypothesis does not 'go very far in explaining how the child moves so easily into proper speech' (Bruner, 1983, p. 29). It would seem unduly optimistic to assume that it will serve us any better in explaining how the child moves into the proper use of numbers which is, in any case, integrated with the larger task of acquiring language and, as we have seen, varies from language to language.

Second, while early emerging abilities to discriminate among small sets are presumably common to all normal infants, universals in the structure of number lexicons are difficult to discern. We have already touched upon differences among languages in terms of how the place value system is articulated. But there are differences too, even in the structure of the very basic elements of the system. For example, while most languages have a series of distinct basic terms (usually the words for the numbers 1–10) and then construct subsequent numbers syntactically (combining the basic terms), some have much smaller basic sets, and some have much larger. Hurford (1987) points to a Queensland Aboriginal language which has only two basic terms for number, and in which numbers are constructed thus:

1   ganar
2   burla
3   burla-ganar
4   burla-burla

Expressing higher numbers in such languages is cumbersome, and most do not go beyond about 5 (Hurford, 1987). On the other hand, there are languages, such as Hindi, with very irregular numeral series (Hurford, 1987) wherein it appears the learner would have to acquire by rote memory all of the words up to 100 (or a set of complex rules which generate them).

Other languages reportedly have several different sequences of number words which are dependent upon what is being counted (Flegg, 1983). Particularly important is the fact that some languages do not have any number words (Hurford, 1987). Whatever innate abilities infants have with respect to the perception of number, the ways in which they will hear and refer to numbers will vary according to their linguistic community. Thus, if there is a continuity between perception and vocabulary acquisition in this domain, its manifestations are quite diverse, and the possibility remains latent in some communities.

Third, the continuity assumption does not address the question of how or why children would progress from non-verbal *perception* to verbal *production* of numbers. It is certainly possible to conjecture plausible motives for this progress, but presumably they would allude to inherent desire for cognitive mastery and/or extrinsically prompted attention. But if these are admitted the presence of innate perceptual abilities becomes little more than a forerunner, not a teleological basis.

In sum, assumptions of a continuity between early numerical perception and early numerical lexicons (i) seem merely to echo a metaphor that has failed to account for the details in other areas of language learning, (ii) tend to presuppose a universal pattern of development while cross-linguistic evidence points to considerable diversity in the content of numeral systems, and (iii) would have, in any case, to rely on more general procedures to account for development.

REPRESENTATION OF NUMBER IN EARLY LANGUAGE

Children are exposed to, and use, number words from relatively early in life. These facts raise two closely related questions which are fundamental to the study of the early representation of number: (i) What meanings could number words have for young children? (ii) In what kinds of linguistic activity do they deploy them? Only partial answers are available, but they are important and will be considered in the sub-sections below.

Inferring the meanings of number words

Part of children's task with number words is the same as their task with any other words they acquire—to discriminate them in the speech stream and determine to what they refer. Little is known of how children deal with the first problem, though it is worth noting in passing that there are certainly special challenges here. For example, some of the most frequent number words are homophonous with high frequency function words (e.g. two/ too/ to, four/ for) and the first (and most frequent) number word is also used as a pronoun (one) (Durkin *et al.*, 1986; Wynn, 1990). Given that function words are generally subject to less emphasis in parental speech (Messer, 1981), it is uncertain how readily distinguishable the 'raw data' might be in this area of the language learner's task (we return to parental input below). However, for the present we will focus on the second challenge—to determine what number words refer to.

As is well recognised, the naive listener faces an enormously ambiguous task in inferring the meaning of a single word uttered in evident reference (for example, accompanied by a point or look) to an object (Markman, 1989; Quine, 1960, 1971). The word could be the proper name or the category name of the referent, or it could denote just some part of the referent or any of countless properties, such as colour, texture, age, motion, or perhaps an action, or even, in the case of an animate being, some covert mental state. Philosophers and developmental psychologists have considered at length how it is possible for human beings to surmount this problem. The traditional view is that concept acquisition involves analysing the properties of a referent, generating and testing hypotheses about the defining criteria of the relevant concept, and using these criteria to evaluate future potential members of the category. A contrary view has been advanced by Markman (1989), who holds that children are pre-disposed to place constraints upon possible word meanings which make the task of inferring the meaning of a new category label less onerous. Specifically, Markman proposes that, 'when children hear a novel label, they assume it refers to a whole object, not to its parts, its substance, its colour, and so on (the whole object assumption) and that it refers to objects of this type, not other objects it is thematically related to (the taxonomic assumption)' (p. 219). In an extensive series of experimental studies of children's responses to novel labels (nonsense words), Markman and her colleagues demonstrate considerable support for these claims (see Markman, 1989).

A problem relevant to present concerns is: what are children pre-disposed to do when they hear number words? Markman's argument is that when children hear a new word they look for taxonomic relations, and suppress the tendency to look for thematic relations. A standard context in which children could be most expected to rely upon this strategy is that in which they are exposed to an ostensive definition, i.e. an adult points to an object and labels it. This has been described as the 'core' process through which vocabulary teaching and practice occurs (Ninio, 1983). However, pointing at an object and uttering a word is precisely what adults do when they are using numbers with young children (Fuson, 1988; Riem, 1985). If children are biased to interpret the novel word as a category label, this would predict that early inferences about number words would be woefully astray, based on the assumption that they were names.

There is evidence that children do initially treat number words as though they were denotational. That is, they utter a string of number words in reference to countables, but with no attempt to link the words one-to-one to the items. Often, the recitation is accompanied by a global gesture, such as a sweep of the hand (Durkin *et al.*, 1986; Riem, 1985; Saxe *et al.*, 1987). Clearly, there are some differences between these uses of number words and other early nominal productions, which usually are tied more specifically to particular objects, but the global application of a number word sequence to a given set or actions based upon that set (such as pointing) bears similarities to the pervasive denotational reference of early language (Saxe *et al.*, 1987). Further, even as children begin to use number words in more constrained ways, such as in a one-to-one relationship with the countables, they appear unaware of the cardinal value of the last word of their count. If asked immediately after a count how many items there are in the set, preschoolers often respond with a number other than the last word they have used, or by reciting several of the number words (Fuson, 1988; Saxe *et al.*, 1987; Schaeffer, Eggleston & Scott, 1974; Wilkinson, 1984).

Early uses of number words

It appears that the meaning of early number words is closely tied to the situations in which they are used; like other phenomena in early language acquisition, they are 'event bound' (Barrett, 1986). At certain prompts (usually 'how many' questions and/or points), children learn to engage in a routinised activity (saying their number word sequence and/or pointing) and to orient it towards given collections of objects. Saxe *et al.* (1987) hold that this early use of number words, which they term 'nominal-enumerative', is the initial level of a series of increasingly sophisticated levels of representation of number which develop during the preschool years through an interaction between the child's developing cognitive goals and the socio-cultural context.

Early number productions often take the form of rote units, where a string of words is treated as a single verbal item (Fuson, 1988). This is a familiar occurrence in early language (MacWhinney, 1978, 1982; Peters, 1983). It seems a fortuitous one in number word acquisition since, as noted at the outset, one of the special features of its lexical area is that, when counting, the words must occur in a fixed order. Fuson (1988) has emphasised that children progress from the initial string productions to the use of unbreakable links, where the number word sequence has to be said in its fixed order, and the child is unable to break into it, for example by starting a count at an intermediate place. Insofar as early productions are unanalysed or partially analysed units, they remain open to later activity and decomposition (MacWhinney, 1982; Peters, 1983). This may be influenced by exposure to other, non-string uses of number words, which may lead to periods of development during which children have multiple (or at least dual) representations of some numbers which are in due course, in Karmiloff-Smith's (1979, 1985) terms, implicitly redescribed. One of Karmiloff-Smith's best-known examples of this plurifunctionality of early words concerns a word, which *inter alia*, has a numerical sense—'une'. She proposed that children's early uses of this form serve a plurality of functions, including indefinite reference, nomination and numerical description. In her view, children may initially represent each of these functions separately, and through use they become available to metaprocedures which establish the links among them. Very similar points could be made of the use of 'one' in English, and it appears that for many children 'one' is initially part of other units ('Anotherone' is particularly popular) as well as the number string. More generally, children using numbers in unbroken strings/recitations will elsewhere encounter numbers used independently of the sequence (Durkin *et al.*, 1986).

Note that if children do learn parts of the number sequence initially by rote, and segment them subsequently, this process seems to be discontinuous with early perceptual abilities, and mediated by language and social activity. Language introduces new structure and information. The point is made well by Hurford (1987):

> Before the establishment of the conventional recitation sequence, one could not say of three that it was the word after two in the conventional sequence. Three acquires a new significance as holding a place in the conventional sequence, a significance not at odds with its previous significance, but new nevertheless (p. 113).

Hence, as has already been indicated, the *meaning* and *use* of number words in early development are closely interrelated. Children do not appear to form concepts of numbers and then map number words upon them, but are enjoined in number word activities wherein they discover possibilities and constraints, modelled and imposed by others who in turn are affected by the functions and traditions of number activities in their socio-cultural context. The achievement of number representation is thus located in the interaction of the different understandings of child and adult in the context of social activity.

Early number word activities of the type discussed here are generally prequantitative. One-to-one correspondence is often lacking in children's early productions, and another important characteristic of number words—that the final word in the sequence summarises the number of items in the set—is not yet established. In the course of interpersonal activities, children are provided with many cues and interventions which form the contexts within which they encounter these fundamental principles. In the following sections, the development of one-to-one correspondence and the cardinal use of number words, respectively, are considered.

The development of one-to-one correspondence

Space does not permit a full review of the extensive recent literatures on the development of one-to-one correspondence in early counting (Fuson, 1988; Gelman & Gallistel, 1978; Riem, 1985) and in subsequent development of conservation skills (Brainerd, 1979; Cowan, 1991). Instead, the focus here will be on the ways in which one-to-one correspondence is introduced into early representations of number activity, and how this may contribute to the child redefining the demands of the activity.

So far, we have seen that early number word activity is prequantitative, consisting of the uttering of number words, often accompanied by referential gestures. Parents often coax children to participate in this activity, with 'How many?' questions, and attempt to protract it with 'What comes after *n*?' questions (Riem, 1985). As Riem (1985) points out, the meaning of this situation *for the parent* is that the child is counting. Parents know what number words mean, and are not necessarily aware that the child is ignorant of, say, the cardinal meaning of words. However, parents do detect performance deficiencies in the execution of counting, such as missing or ill-ordered words, and pointing errors, and this leads to intervention in the process.

Young children usually point when responding to 'How many?' instructions, but the correspondences among number words, points and objects are often poor (Fuson, 1988; Riem, 1985). Fuson holds that the child has to coordinate two correspondences in order to perform accurately in counting: the point–word correspondence and point–object correspondence. Riem (1985), in detailed longitudinal observational studies of several mother/toddler dyads engaged in counting activities, found that mothers intervene primarily by trying to get their child to watch where they (mothers) are pointing, presumably because partitioning by pointing is an intuitively straightforward technique for adults who know the mnemonic function of the gesture in this context. Riem found that English, middle-class mothers responded to correspondence errors by prompting with point-cues, requiring the child to produce one number word in association with each of her points. Riem argues that in due course children internalise this joint activity; he offers persuasive evidence for this in the finding that four of his five subjects developed point–word correspondence before point–object correspondence. If Riem's account is correct (and replicable in larger samples from more diverse contexts), then what appears to occur is that parents take advantage of an established prequantitative number word repertoire and attempt to constrain the activity so that it meets their understanding of counting. Children come to represent a familiar activity (reciting number words) in a more refined way, coordinating word and gesture initially, and word–gesture–object eventually. Riem (1985) proposes the interesting possibility that the order of progress here reflects the fact that in point–word correspondence children are pairing two *actions*, while in point–object correspondence, they are pairing action and environment. He stresses that this difference has consequences for maternal feedback.

An important way in which progress is made is through the discovery of the 'count all' rule which is usually developed by around age 3 years (Briars & Siegler, 1984; Fuson & Hall, 1983; Gelman & Meck, 1983). Children learn that another demand of the situation is that they perform the action (saying the number word and pointing *in respect of each object*). Riem (1985) found that parents sometimes allude to this constraint ('Count all of them', 'You missed one', 'What about this one?'). However, the clarity of this feedback is not assured; for example, *one* is being used here as a pronoun rather than a number description, and sometimes the exhortation can be quite imprecise ('Count properly'). Although feedback may draw the child's attention to problems in his or her counts, Riem proposes that the principal means of discovering the all-rule is observational. Mothers generally obey the rule in their demonstration counts, and children, he claims, learn from watching the exhaustiveness of the activity. The child may be internalising a property of the other's behaviour, and developing a representation of the activity accordingly.

Even if the mechanism is debatable, the evidence that the count-all rule is represented relatively early on is strong. This is reflected in an interesting finding by Fuson & Hall (1983; see also Fuson, 1988) concerning children's responses to requests to 'try really hard' after erroneous counts. Fuson and her colleagues found that 3-year-olds reduce skipping errors (i.e. missing an item) when given this instruction, whereas double count errors (i.e. counting the same object twice) still occur, even among 6-year-olds. This suggests that young children infer and then generalise a counting principle, making it available (albeit sometimes neglected) to future counting activity (Wynn, 1990). This conclusion is, of course, quite the opposite of Gelman & Gallistel's (1978, p. 204) conclusion that 'knowledge of counting principles forms the acquisition of counting skill', but then Gelman & Gallistel did not undertake the descriptive step of considering how numbers are made available to children, and make no attempt to explain how social interaction could relate to the genesis of everyday numerical knowledge. These broader issues will be returned to later; in the next section we consider another critical discovery in the acquisition of number words—the significance of the final word in a count.

Cardinal uses of number words

Learning that the final word in a count gives the number of items in the set is a particularly important achievement. Although the exact procedures whereby children attain this level of understanding of number word meaning are subject to controversy, it is clear that 'last word responding' (Fuson, 1988), that is learning that the appropriate response to a 'How many?' question is the last word uttered in a count, involves social, linguistic and cognitive factors. A fundamental consideration is that it is difficult to see how far children could proceed toward the acquisition of cardinal use of number words without anybody else making the task salient to them. It is a moot point how often monadic infants would reflect on the numerosity of their toes, or even how often toddlers would need to invoke numerical accounts to ensure consistency in their cookie requests; by and large, the main reason for worrying about how many there are of anything is that someone else wants to know.

The fact that there is a discrepancy between young children's and older persons' representations of the purposes of counting is illustrated in response to the cardinality task of Schaeffer *et al.* described above. Here, children count when instructed to do so, yet fail to offer the last word when asked, immediately after the count, how many there are in the set. Note that this occurs even with very small sets of two or three items, numerosities within the range of early perceptual discriminatory abilities. Schaeffer *et al.* (1974) proposed that children learn about cardinality by observing the coincidence of outcomes when they subitize a very small set and count that set. They notice that the last word in the count is the same as the subitized word for that set. Subsequently, children come to generalise this discovery, dealing with larger (non-subitizable sets) by counting and then taking the last word to represent the numerosity of the set.

Several other positions on how children achieve cardinality have been advanced (a more thorough outline and critique of some of these is provided by Fuson, 1988). They include Gelman & Gallistel's (1978) influential thesis that children's counting skills depend upon an implicit knowledge of counting principles, including the cardinality principle which accords special status to the final tag in the number word sequence. For Gelman & Gallistel, the ability to count does not depend upon subitizing but on implicit understanding. They argue that this understanding is available to quite young preschoolers. Fuson & Hall (1983) proposed an alternative, two-stage account in which children first learn the relationship, 'Count and then give the last count word' when asked, 'How many Xs are there?'. Fuson (1988) points out that this does not entail that the use of the final word has a cardinal meaning for the child, simply that the child knows that this is the appropriate word to use in such a situation. The second stage of their model is termed by Fuson & Hall the 'count-to-cardinal transition', and in this stage the child mentally reconstructs the situation from one of applying words to separate entities to one in which a final number word is attained which refers to all of the entities. As Fuson (1988) acknowledges, the means whereby the transition is achieved were not elaborated by Fuson & Hall (1983). Further proposals include the possibility that young children do not have the processing space both to count and remember the last word said in counting (see also Fuson, 1988).

Fuson (1988) reports an elaborate experiment designed to test the support for each of these proposals. Among 2- and 3-year-olds, she found that no account fitted all subjects, and concluded that children seem to follow different routes to last-word responding. Importantly, the relationship between subitizing and counting was not consistent. Some children were better at subitizing than counting, and some were better at counting than subitizing; counting and subitizing were independent for sets of two and counting was better than subitizing for sets of three and four. Nevertheless, Fuson did find that many (about half of her sample) children's responses were consistent with Fuson & Hall's (1983) first stage. They used last word responses but did not appreciate the cardinal meaning of the word (for example, when asked after completing a count, 'Are these the n stars?', a high proportion of these subjects would choose the last counted object rather than the set as a whole). Of the children who used last-word responding infrequently or not at all, a majority were able to recall the last word of their count, and half of these showed ability to use last-word responses after minimal instruction. The fact that they did not use last-word responding spontaneously might reflect differences in prior numerical experiences (perhaps they had not been prompted to respond in this way by caregivers) or differences in development (perhaps they were still to grasp this strategy); only extensive longitudinal/observational study could answer these questions. It does seem reasonable to conclude, with Fuson (1988), that last-word responding is, for many children, an important step towards acquiring cardinality because it shows that they are *using* counting.

In sum, little support emerges from Fuson's study for the proposal of a subitizing-cardinality transition. At best, it may be that a minority of children exhibit this progress, but it is difficult to rule out the possibility that other factors may be involved even in their discoveries. There is little support for the Gelman & Gallistel position that children have access to the principle providing the set size is small; there was no effect of set size on last-word responding. There is little evidence that discovery of cardinality is directly dependent upon increasing processing space enabling children to handle the distinct demands of the task. There *is* evidence that many children use last-word responding without cardinal meaning, and it is possible that the routes to the count-to-cardinal transition are varied.

In the course of everyday social interchanges, children's understandings of what is required in number activities develop, and parents' input and expectations change. Having alluded at several points to aspects of the social nature of number activities, it is time now to consider more carefully how this develops.

Goals in the social context of early number use

One of the most extensive analyses of the social processes central to early number development is that of Saxe *et al.* (1987). Saxe *et al.* assume that children acquire numerical competencies through participation in home activities, and part of their work is designed to uncover these activities and characterise their goal structures. Not surprisingly, this leads to careful attention to what mothers do and what their aspirations are with respect to their child's mastery of number. Saxe *et al.*'s findings indicate that variation in the complexity of children's everyday number activities (including the complexity of the tasks mothers involve them in and the level of aspiration of the mother concerning the child's mathematical attainment) is associated with variation in the children's numerical understandings. In common with earlier studies, they found social class differences, with middle-class preschoolers exhibiting more advanced competence than working-class peers.

A crucial feature of Saxe *et al.*'s account is its emphasis on the child's goals in the interactive context. They point out that much work concerned with social factors in development has tended to focus one-sidedly upon the adult's purposes and instructional strategies, or on other variables extrinsic to the child. Although this paradigm exemplifies what is often associated with the term 'social' in developmental work, in fact such approaches are *a*social, unidirectional. Saxe *et al.* focus instead upon the dynamic character of the interactions in which children participate, examining the mutual adjustments of both parties, and elucidating the interplay between social and developmental processes. Central to these is the development of the child's goals. Testing first children's performance in unassisted number tasks, Saxe *et al.* provide evidence that 2-year-olds' goals are at relatively low levels of complexity (typically, nominal-enumerative and occasionally cardinal/ordinal representation), and that their strategies in most number-related tasks are determined by these goals. For example, as already discussed, given a task requiring them to reproduce a set (and thus calling for higher level goals of accuracy and comparing numerosities), young children might recite number words without one-to-one correspondence to items, or count either the model array or the copy but not both, and fail to use counting to determine equality. Four-year-olds generated higher level goals, involving comparison/reproduction and arithmetic, and structured the activities using counting strategies. When the researchers interviewed mothers about the children's everyday involvement in number activities (which was extensive), they found broad correspondences between the levels of activities favoured and the children's levels of understanding, consistent with the view that everyday activities support children's developing competencies in this domain.

Saxe *et al.* depict development as occurring within an interweaving of continuous and discontinuous features of number activities. This context allows new problems to emerge which draw upon but extend children's past attainments, providing opportunities for them to use their competencies to serve new functions and to elaborate and specialise their existing strategies. To give a simple illustration, the familiar routine of counting the stairs allows a child to practise number word sequences; when a parent can take the enumerative competency as established, he or she might intervene ('How many stairs have you climbed then?'), thereby raising the level of the task to one of summation and set representation. Once the child can operate at this level, the parent might extend the task to elementary arithmetical demands: 'One more stair to go. How many will you have climbed then?':

> Thus, children's socially organised experiences with number in everyday number activities are emergent ones; they are not "contained in" social practices or in the minds of the participants but are negotiated in interactions and emerge as a result of the mothers' and children's adjusted efforts to accomplish numerical tasks jointly.
>
> (Saxe *et al.*, 1987, p. 117).

These negotiations may prove a rich source of evidence upon developmental processes in the representation of numbers. Saxe *et al.* demonstrate how analyses of the social context and developmental processes can be united by focus upon levels of activity and by the interactions among the forms of knowledge available to the participants and the functions to which they put them. However, a vital means through which negotiations are conducted is language, but Saxe *et al.* were not concerned with this level of analysis in their monograph. Further, their central experimental studies were concerned with deliberate number activities rather than spontaneous ones. As their work shows, there are many number activities in everyday interactions and these may well repay investigation focused upon the ways in which actions and meanings are negotiated. Although there is relatively little research directed at these issues (e.g. Fuson, 1988), some indications of how the linguistic aspects of numerical activities proceed are available, and these will be considered in the next section.

Language in the social context of early number word use

Durkin *et al.* (1986) examined all uses of number words by mothers and infants in a longitudinal, laboratory-based observational study which followed the children from their ninth month to third birthday. Although the study was laboratory based, the participants were very familiar with the setting and at ease with the procedures; the original purposes of the study did not include investigation of number use, and the participants were not prompted in any way to focus on such activities.

Many uses of number words were obtained, and both mothers and children produced them. Consistent with what is known of parental input to young language learners, number word use tended to be simplified and repetitive. The most frequent number words were the most elementary, *one* to *four*; the numbers *five* and above tended to be rare before the child's second birthday and intermittent thereafter. About 40% of the mothers' number uses were what we termed 'incidental'; that is, a number word was used in an utterance for some descriptive purpose but not as part of a recital of the conventional sequence ('Give me two biscuits'). About 5% were set in nursery rhymes or other traditional songs and routines ('three little pigs', 'Goldilocks and the three bears', 'five currant buns'). The remainder consisted of pedagogical strategies, and we identified four classes of these. (1) *Sequential complements*, in which part of the conventional sequence is embellished with an extra word at a fixed location: 'One, two, three, go', 'One step, two step and a tickley under there'; overall, these accounted for about 10% of the number inputs, although frequency declined with age of child, and at 9 months they accounted for almost 50%. (2) *Repetition and clarification of cardinality*, in which the parent attempted to draw attention to the significance of the final number in a count: 'Look, Four, One, two, three, four', 'One, two, three. Three'. Overall, these accounted for about 19% of the number-related utterances, although they tended to be increasingly common as the children approached their third birthday. (3) *Recitation of the number string*. These were straightforward recitals, usually of the first few numbers, and often preceded by an overt labelling of the activity: 'Let's count. One, two, three', 'Count them. Look, one, two, three, four'. (4) *Alternating strings*. These appear to be related to recitals, but differ in that the emphasis is upon joint production of the string via turn-taking. Mother: 'Count with me, one...', Child: 'One', M: 'Two', C: 'Two'. Recitations accounted for about 12% of the input utterances, and alternating strings accounted for about 16%; recitations tended to decline with age (perhaps reflecting mothers' confidence that their child now knew how to say the basic sequence), while alternations tended to fluctuate and were still very common at 36 months (perhaps indicating parental interest in encouraging the child to work upon, and segment, the string).

Although much of the input to young children concerning number has a transparently pedagogical purpose and is generally couched in simplified structures, the task of learning about numbers is by no means simple. All of the points made earlier, concerning the ambiguity of number words, hold for this early experience. In addition, some of the modifications to the conventional string (as in sequential complements) do not obviously reduce the demands of trying to work out the meanings and functions of these words. For example, as we have seen, part of learning about number words is to learn that they occur in fixed order—*one two three four*—and some (about 12% in our data) of the input examples will exhibit this order clearly. Yet given occasional exposure to strings of the form *one two three go, one two three tickley, one two—got you*, what might the learner induce about the constraints upon the third and fourth places in the sequence? There are no reports in the literature of children using *tickley* (etc.) as a number word, though it is conceivable that some children's early counting routines may include one or more of these decorations; correspondingly, it is possible that some children may use the conventional string in games where the parent might expect a complement (e.g. starting a race with 'One, two, three, four', instead of 'One, two, three, go'). What children have to do is to learn which string is appropriate in which context, and at some point presumably have to discover that one string has higher status than others. The right answer is perfectly obvious to those who already know it, and because children are often mistaken for mini-scientists, the possibility that they could be misled occasionally by noise in the raw data is rarely considered. Speculating, I suggest that errors probably do occur in this area from time to time, and observational data from naturalistic studies may well yield examples. Irrespective of the availability of such illustrations, however, it seems at the very least that sequential complements increase the amount of information the child has to deal with, diversifying the ways and situations in which number words are used.

Further, young children engage in many activities and their parents have many pedagogical and management concerns. Even though certain activities may be signalled (for example, number word teaching and games are sometimes prefaced with 'Let's count' instructions), the behaviours and strategies of each participant will not always be unique to a given domain. Thus, the possibilities arise that a technique used for one purpose may solicit inappropriate responses when it is applied to another. Evidence that this is the case is abundant if we look carefully at the transcripts of parent–child interactions about number. For example, the alternating string routine, in which participants take turns to produce number words, building the sequence between them, frequently leads to mismatches. Sometimes the exercise can solicit a response from the child which is accepted and explicitly or implicitly rewarded, leading the child to infer that the response is a good one which should be used again in this situation. However, the parent expects a different response on the next stage of the game:

Mother: Count them.
Child: One
Mother: Two

Child: One
Mother: No, two

Sometimes, the participants differ over whether the child is to imitate or to extend:

M: One
C: One
M: No, two

Sometimes, the child misreads a request to repeat as a prompt to recite:

M: What happened to number one? One, say one
C: Two
M: I know two comes after one. Say one, One

Sometimes, the child seems to read the activity as, 'Copy what I say' (presumably a common enough routine in everyday interactions), and includes too much of the stimulus string:

M: That's one
C: That's one
M: That's two
C: That's two
M: Three
C: Three

Elsewhere, mothers inadvertently cue children with a reference to the wrong superordinate domain:

M: Pretty colours, One, two, three, four

In this case the child did not respond verbally; it is an open question whether this information would lead the naive to categorise the words as colour terms or count words. In a related example from a different dyad, the child certainly seemed to perceive the weight of the cues differently from that intended by her mother:

M: Shall we count them? One yellow one
C: Yellow

In the following example, the mother wanted a count while the child interpreted the 'How many?' cue as a prompt to recite:

M: Tell Mummy, how many eyes has Mummy got? How many eyes?
C: Mm, er
M: One
C: Doo, fwee
M: Two, three? Oh, poor mum

What seems to occur quite often is a mismatch which is then dealt with by the mother. This is similar to children struggling with aspects of an activity and receiving maternal assistance, as in Saxe and others' experiments. It is important to acknowledge, however, that in both cases we are unlikely to have observed the dénouement of the process—the child's representation of a concept or principle that concurs with the adult understanding. What we do observe is a maternal adjustment of the activity to which the child sometimes responds as required. Any change of representation by the child, if it occurs, could well be a compromise between previous understanding and what is perceived as being recommended. Presumably, such developments are not instantaneous, nor invariably progressive; if they were, they would be very hard to pick up, because every time a parent spotted a problem, he or she would cure it, and mismatches would be rare events. I have argued elsewhere (Durkin, 1987) that mismatches are rare events in the developmental *literature*, because of commitments to theories of development which presuppose harmony between parent and child or models of the child as an isolated investigator, but that they are rife in everyday interactions if we care to look for them. Certainly, in Durkin *et al.* (1986) we found that interactions of the type described above were ubiquitous, and it was very difficult to find an example of a number-related exchange which ran perfectly smoothly.

Correspondingly, while Saxe *et al.*'s studies show that children can attain higher performance in number activities when these are pursued jointly with their mothers, the fact is that the children had already had many everyday interactions with their mothers, including much number activity at various levels of complexity, before Saxe *et al.* tested their performance alone. Yet the benefits demonstrable in experimental studies of joint activity were not manifest in the independent performances. The seeming paradox here can be avoided without denying that joint activity makes a central contribution to the child's progress. What becomes clear is that the mere presence of teaching does not explain or even describe the remarkable achievement of learning. The fact that the parent structures an activity in a way which makes sense to those who know the rules does not mean that the child's understanding is isomorphic with the lesson offered.

A similar point is illustrated in a quite different context in an interesting experiment by Keil (1989). Keil had parents teach the meaning of novel concepts to their children, aged 3–7 years. He reports that clear definitions did not guarantee that the child would learn the concept (the purpose of definitions was sometimes misunderstood, or they were simply ignored). This is not simply a matter of conceptual readiness but one of how children perceive the requirements of the current interaction. Children may make use of the parental input, but this use may well have characteristics that are not evident in the overt behaviours of particular responses to particular instructions.

At the risk of labouring the obvious, the point is that we cannot be sure from observing, say, a teach-error-correction episode that the child has interpreted the activity in the same way as the adult. Indeed, even some exchanges which appear to be problem-free may nonetheless reflect quite different meanings for the participants. For example, Riem (1985) found that parents were often unaware that their young children did not have cardinal meanings for number words, and they were surprised when their children failed cardinality activities in these dyads:

Mother: See how many chairs there are.
Child: One, two, three, four, five (bangs each chair).
Mother: Well done! That's brilliant!   (Riem, 1985, p. 198)

Parents and some horse owners are known to be somewhat generous in these circumstances, but of course it behoves psychologists to be more cautious in imputing learning. What should be acknowledged is that cardinality *is* present in the interaction because the parent assumes it (Riem, 1985). In due course, through attempts to organise information gleaned from a variety of social activities, the child will also assume it.

IMPLICATIONS AND CONCLUSIONS

Perner (1991) observes that the hallmark of a representation is that it stands for something else. He finds it ironical that cognitive psychology's embrace of the notion of representation has largely neglected this defining feature. There is a risk that cognitive developmental approaches to the study of number development could sustain the same oversight. In this field, the exciting search for the principles governing counting activity has often been conducted with scant regard for the very mode of representation that human beings use to encode and share numerical knowledge. Perhaps this is because language is transparent to those who have it, or perhaps it reflects the cognitivist's premise that language is (simply) mapped onto something else.

In this chapter, it has been argued that number words are central to the developmental achievement of number representation. Number words have been taken here not as linguistic symbols mapped onto innate percepts or nascent concepts, but as components of multifaceted social activities (with linguistic, perceptual and cognitive dimensions) taking place between child and parent. The courses of these activities are determined by the expectations of each participant concerning the meanings and goals of the behaviours involved, and their respective competencies, as well as the constraints of the particular linguistic system being used and the logic of the culture's number system.

As we have seen, children may be endowed with specific discriminatory abilities that enable them to distinguish among very small sets of different numerosities. This facility may well relate to later numerical abilities in ways that are not yet understood. However, to suppose that the relationship is one whereby children detect correspondence between their perceptual knowledge and the counting behaviour of more skilled members of their community attributes metarepresentational ability to the infant (coincidentally akin to that of the adult scientist) and at the same time neglects the medium of representation that the child has to operate upon. Part of a child's task is to discover that number words stand for something.

The child encounters number activities as part of everyday life (Riem, 1985; Saxe et al., 1987). The child is enlisted in these activities and has to discover what role he or she is expected to play; parts of this information are modelled and directed by caregivers. In due course, the child forms a representation of what to do in these situations, and learns to recognise cues that signal which routine is in play. For example, I have noted that many parents use the 'How many?' prompt frequently, and that their children often respond with a recitation of part of all of their number word sequence. The parent's understanding of the situation seems to be that the child should practise counting; the child's understanding seems to be that he or she should produce a particular string of sounds. Often, there is only a vague referential connection between the number words thus elicited and the countables. Sometimes, the child recites to a number which exceeds the number of countables, and sometimes the child skips one or more of the countables. Incidents like these sometimes lead parents to intervene; for example, they emphasise cardinality or challenge a cardinal reference. In so doing they present examples which clarify the situation *for the adult*, such as emphasising the importance of the final number word ('One, two, three, four, FOUR'), though they happen to conflict with one of the basic principles of counting (that each tag should be said once and only once). It was noted that other prompting techniques sometimes used by parents often initiate mismatches, due to the child imitating when the parent wants the next word, or producing the next word (or something related to another routine) when the parent wants an imitation.

Thus, early representations of number word activities are located in the partly complementary, partly conflicting goals of adult and child, and the very processes of engaging the activities incur complements and conflicts among systems of knowledge—linguistic and number—which are at different levels of sophistication in each participant. The dynamics of the interchange involve discrepancies at both the interpersonal and intra-psychological levels. Importantly, the child will sometimes be told, shown or indirectly advised of a parental requirement distinct from actual performance, and sometimes will not.

Of course, it is relatively easy to suggest, and perhaps even to demonstrate, that the world is a complex place and development a multifaceted phenomenon (it is also relatively easy to disregard these considerations, though I am not sure that theoretical advance is guaranteed by doing so). It may appear that simply to propose that there are complementarities and conflicts among systems of behaviour and knowledge leads only to a prognosis of undirected change within chaos—not a basis for a particularly powerful account. However, the present account actually enables us to explain parsimoniously various well-established characteristics of children's problems in relation to numerical and mathematical tasks, to identify the causes underlying widely reported difficulties and at least to sketch the bases for development. Specifically, it leads to the claim that problems will arise in relation to two overlapping areas: divergent representations of contextual demands, and conflicts between meanings. If we look ahead, to later aspects of number representation, we find very similar dynamics.

There is an abundance of evidence to show that mismatches between adults' and children's understandings of what is involved in the context of doing mathematical activities lead to outcomes in children's behaviour which are usually construed by adults as errors or failures. Donaldson (1978) drew attention to the misleading conclusions that can be made about young children's competencies by testing them in contexts which they understand differently from the investigator. Hughes (1986) provides many illustrations of discrepancies between children's abilities to handle elementary arithmetical operations adequately in contexts which make sense whilst stumbling with the same tasks presented in 'disembedded' code. Demonstrating also that preschool children tend to represent number iconically when encouraged to put it on paper, Hughes highlights 'a serious mismatch between the system of symbols which children are required to learn, and their own spontaneous conceptualisations' (1986, p. 78).

Solomon (1989) shows, in reanalyses of transcripts of adult–child interactions around addition and subtraction tasks, that children may sometimes perceive what the adult intends as a concrete representation of a hypothetical arithmetical problem *as the very content* of the problem. For example, experimenters provided children with a set of, say, ten buttons and then asked them to work through seemingly simple problems such as imagining Jane has eight buttons in a bag and removes two to sew on a dress: how many buttons are left in the bag? Solomon shows that the children's 'errors' are consistent with them failing to understand that the context is one in which the buttons are supposed to *represent* the ones talked about and are not the *actual* buttons talked about. Not grasping this, a child is unaware of the requirement that some of the buttons be used to set up the task, and attempts to use them all. As a result, even familiar strategies become unreliable (counting results in the number ten, but the adult has said that there are eight). Divergent representations of contextual demands lead to divergent outcomes.

Closely related problems are prevalent with respect to the meanings of words and statements made in the course of number activities. Ambiguity is inherent in the very application of everyday language to the mathematical domain (Adda, 1982; Durkin & Shire, 1991a,b; Hughes, 1986; Pimm, 1987). Many words which are used in mathematics have everyday meanings which are subtly or radically different, and the everyday meaning is generally the one which is acquired first. For example, most children are likely to regard a *table* as a piece of furniture before they encounter reference to mathematical tables, *odd* means peculiar before it is applied to numbers, *volume* is something to do with the scale of noise emerging from stereos and TV sets before it gets silently into containers in maths lessons. In each of these cases, there is evidence that children attempt to interpret mathematical uses of the terms in their more familiar, basic senses (Durkin & Shire, 1991b; Pimm, 1987). Difficulties result from interpersonal differences in what the words are intended to represent, leading to intrapsychological tensions that the child must resolve if he or she is to become proficient in the use of polysemous vocabulary.

Development in the representation of number, then, is not at its core a matter of increasingly sophisticated reasoning about abstract problems and rules by an isolated discoverer. It is a social process in which the learner has to discover what other people mean. Other people convey their meanings in complex and sometimes confusing ways. Although there are patterns and consistencies within these processes, they are not readily apparent to the learner, who has to act on the basis of his or her current level of understanding. This understanding does not demarcate (as reliably as proficient performers) those aspects of the context which are domain specific and those which are not: the child does not always know that a current situation is intended as a representation of an absent procedure or that a familiar everyday expression denotes a novel mathematical meaning. Progress consists of resolving these tensions, which I have stressed have both interpersonal and intrapsychological dimensions. If this is correct, then progress is dependent upon social achievements and conceptual-linguistic reorganisation. The assumption in the present chapter has been that other people serve to make the discrepancies available to the child, who has ultimately to resolve them. This is not to deny that other people may with varying degrees of proficiency offer solutions, too; parents spend a lot of time doing this, and teachers are paid to do so. However, a social account of progress presupposes that the child's contributions are integral. People represent number to children, children form representations of what adults want them to do, and these representations form the basis of protracted discourse in which children shift their representations increasingly in the direction of those of their community. Their motive is not to discover essences, but to keep on speaking terms.

REFERENCES

Adda, J. (1982). Difficulties with mathematical symbolism: synonymy and homonymy, *Visible Language*, **16**, 205–214.

Antell, S.E. and Keating, D. (1983). Perception of numerical invariance by neonates, *Child Development*, **54**, 695–701.

Barrett, M.D. (1986). Early semantic representation and early word-usage. In S.A. Kuczaj and M.D. Barrett (eds), *The Development of Word Meaning*. New York: Springer Verlag.

Brainerd, C.J. (1979). *The Origins of the Number Concept*. New York: Praeger.

Briars, D. and Siegler, R.S. (1984). A featural analysis of preschoolers' counting knowledge, *Developmental Psychology*, **20**, 607–618.

Bruner, J. (1983). The acquisition of pragmatic commitments. In R.M. Golinkoff (ed.), *The Transition from Prelinguistic to Linguistic Communication*. Hillsdale, New Jersey: Lawrence Erlbaum.

Bruner, J.S. and Bornstein, M.H. (1989). On interaction. In M.H. Bornstein and J.S. Bruner (eds), *Interaction in Human Development*. Hillsdale, New Jersey: Lawrence Erlbaum.

Carraher, T.N., Carraher, D.W. and Schliemann, A.D. (1985). Mathematics in the streets and schools, *British Journal of Developmental Psychology*, **3**, 21–29.

Chi, M.T.H. and Klahr, D. (1975). Span and rate of apprehension in children and adults, *Journal of Experimental Child Psychology*, **19**, 434–439.

Cowan, R. (1991). The same number. In K. Durkin and B. Shire (eds), *Language in Mathematical Education. Research and Practice*. Milton Keynes and Philadelphia: Open University Press.

Davis, H., Albert, M. and Barron, R.W. (1985). Detection of number or numerousness by human infants, *Science*, **228**, 1222.

Dilke, O.A.W. (1987). *Reading the Part. Mathematics and Measurement*. London: British Museum Publication.

Dixon, R.M.W. (1980). *The Languages of Australia*. Cambridge: Cambridge University Press.

Donaldson, M. (1978). *Children's Minds*. Fontana.

Durkin, K. (1987). Minds and language: social cognition, social interaction and the acquisition of language, *Mind and Language*, **2**, 105–140.

Durkin, K. (1988). The social nature of social development. In M. Hewstone *et al.* (eds), *Introduction to Social Psychology: A European Perspective*. Oxford: Blackwell.

Durkin, K. and Shire, B. (1991a). Primary school children's interpretations of lexical ambiguity in mathematical descriptions, *Journal of Research in Reading*, **14**, 46–55.

Durkin, K. and Shire, B. (1991b). Lexical ambiguity in mathematical contexts. In K. Durkin and B. Shire (eds), *Language in Mathematical Education. Research and Practice*. Milton Keynes and Philadelphia: Open University Press.

Durkin, K., Shire, B., Riem, R., Crowther, R. and Rutter, D. (1986). The social and linguistic context of early number word use, *British Journal of Developmental Psychology*, **4**, 269–288.

Eves, H. (1976). *An Introduction to the History of Mathematics*. New York: Holt, Rinehart and Winston.

Flegg, G. (1983). *Numbers, Their History and Meaning*, New York: Schocken.

Fuson, K.C. (1988). *Children's Counting and Concepts of Number*. New York: Springer Verlag.

Fuson, K.C. (1991). Children's early counting: saying the number-word sequence, counting objects, and understanding cardinality. In K. Durkin and B. Shire (eds), *Language in Mathematical Education. Research and Practice*. Milton Keynes and Philadelphia: Open University Press.

Fuson, K.C. and Hall, J.W. (1983). The acquisition of early number word meanings. In H. Ginsburg (ed.), *The Development of Children's Mathematical Thinking*. New York: Academic Press.

Fuson, K.C. and Kwon, Y. (1991). Chinese-based regular and European irregular systems of number words: the disadvantages for English-speaking children. In K. Durkin and B. Shire (eds), *Language in Mathematical Education, Research and Practice*. Milton Keynes and Philadelphia: Open University Press.

Garton, A.F. (1992). *Social Interaction and the Development of Language and Cognition*. Hillsdale, New Jersey: Lawrence Erlbaum.

Gelman, R. (1983). Reconsidering the transition from prelinguistic to linguistic communication. In R.M. Golinkoff (ed.), *The Transition from Prelinguistic to Linguistic Communication*. (pp. 275–279). Hillsdale, New Jersey: Lawrence Erlbaum.

Gelman, R. and Gallistel, C.R. (1978). *The Child's Understanding of Number*. Cambridge, Massachusetts: Harvard University Press.

Gelman, R. and Massey, C.M. (1987). The cultural unconscious as contributor to the supporting environments for cognitive development. Commentary in G.B. Saxe, S.R. Guberman and M. Gearhart, (eds), *Social Process in Early Number Development*. Monographs of the Society for Research in Child Development, No. 216 (pp. 136–152).

Gelman, R. and Meck, E. (1983). Preschoolers' counting: principles before skill, *Cognition*, **13**, 343–359.

Harris, J. (1987). Australian Aboriginal and Islander mathematics, *Australian Aboriginal Studies*, **2**, 29–37.

Hughes, M. (1986). *Children and Number: Difficulties in Learning Mathematics*. Oxford: Blackwell.

Hurford, J.R. (1987). *Language and Number: The Emergence of a Cognitive System*. Oxford: Blackwell.

Karmiloff-Smith, A. (1979). *A Functional Approach to Child Language: A Study of Determiners and Reference*. Cambridge: Cambridge University Press.

Karmiloff-Smith, A. (1985). Language and cognitive processes from a developmental perspective, *Language and Cognitive Processes*, **1**, 61–85.

Kaufman, E.L., Lord, M.W., Reese, T.W. and Volmann, J. (1949). The discrimination of visual number, *American Journal of Psychology*, **62**, 498–525.

Kearins, J. (1991). Number experience and performance in Australian Aboriginal and Western children. In K. Durkin and B. Shire (eds), *Language in Mathematical Education, Research and Practice*. Milton Keynes and Philadelphia: Open University Press.

Kearins, J. and Butters, J. (1986). Cultural number learning and school expectation. Conference paper: 8th International Congress of Cross-Cultural Psychology, Istanbul, Turkey.

Keil, F.C. (1989). *Concepts, Kinds and Cognitive Development*. Cambridge, Massachusetts: MIT Press.

Klein, A. and Starkey, P. (1987). The origins and development of numerical cognition: a comparative analysis. In J.A. Sloboda and D. Rogers (eds), *Cognitive Processes in Mathematics*. Oxford: Clarendon Press.

Kline, M. (1964). *Mathematics in Western Culture*. London: Penguin.

Lakoff, G. (1987). *Women, Fire and Dangerous Things. What Categories Reveal about the Mind*. Chicago: University of Chicago Press.

Lancy, D.F. (ed.) (1983). *Cross-Cultural Studies in Cognition and Mathematics*. New York: Academic Press.

MacLane, S. (1981). Mathematical models: a sketch for the philosophy of mathematics, *American Mathematical Monthly*, Aug./Sept., 462–472.

MacWhinney, B. (1978). The acquisition of morphophonology, *Monographs of the Society for Research in Child Development*, **43**, (1–2).

MacWhinney, B. (1982). Basic syntactic processes. In S. Kuczaj, II (ed.), *Language Development, Vol. 1: Syntax and Semantics* (pp. 73–136). Hillsdale, New Jersey: Lawrence Erlbaum.

Markman, E.M. (1989). *Categorization and Naming in Children: Problems of Induction*. Cambridge, Massachusetts: MIT Press.

Menninger, K. (1969). *Number Words and Number Symbols: A Cultural History of Numbers* (P. Broneer, trans.). Cambridge, Massachusetts: MIT Press (translated from original publication, *Zahlwort und ziffer*, 1958, Vanderhoeck & Ruprecht).

Messer, D.J. (1981). Non-linguistic information which would assist the young child's interpretation of adults' speech. In W.P. Robinson (ed.), *Communication in Development*. London: Academic Press.

Miura, I.T. (1987). Mathematics achievement as a function of language, *Journal of Educational Psychology*, **79**, 79–82.

Miura, I.T. and Okamoto, Y. (1989). Comparisons of US and Japanese first graders' cognitive representation of number and understanding place value, *Journal of Educational Psychology*, **81**, 109–113.

Ninio, A. (1983). Joint book reading as a multiple vocabulary acquisition device, *Development Psychology*, **19**, 445–451.

Perner, J. (1991). *Understanding the Representational Mind*. Cambridge, Massachusetts: MIT Press.

Peters, A.M. (1983). *The Units of Language Acquisition*. Cambridge: Cambridge University Press.

Piaget, J. (1952). *The Child's Conception of Number*. London: Routledge and Kegan Paul.

Pimm, D. (1987). *Speaking Mathematically: Communication in Mathematics Classrooms*. London: Routledge and Kegan Paul.

Putnam, H. (1989). *Representation and Reality*. Cambridge, Massachusetts: MIT Press.

Quine, W.V. (1960). *Word and Object*. Cambridge, Massachusetts: MIT Press.

Quine, W.V. (1971). The inscrutability of reference. In D.D. Steinberg and L.A. Jakobovits (eds), *Semantics*. Cambridge: Cambridge University Press.

Riem, R. (1985). Children learning to count: a social psychological reappraisal of cognitive theory. Unpublished PhD dissertation, University of Kent at Canterbury.

Rogoff, B. (1991). The joint socialization of development by young children and adults. In M. Lewis and S. Feinman (eds), *Social Influences and Socialization in Infancy*. New York: Plenum Press.

Russell, J. (1984). *Explaining Mental life. Some Philosophical Issues in Psychology*. London: Macmillan.

Saxe, G.B. (1988). The mathematics of child stress vendors, *Child Development*, **59**, 1414–1425.

Saxe, G.B., Guberman, S.R. and Gearhart, M. (1987). Social and developmental processes in children's understanding of number, *Monographs of the Society for Research in Child Development*, **52**(2).

Schaeffer, B., Eggleston, V.H. and Scott, J.L. (1974). Number development in young children, *Cognitive Psychology*, **6**, 357–379.

Sinclair, A. (1991). Children's production and comprehension of written numerical representations. In K. Durkin and B. Shire (eds), *Language in Mathematical Education, Research and Practice*. Milton Keynes and Philadelphia: Open University Press.

Solomon, Y. (1989). *The Practice of Mathematics*. London: Routledge and Kegan Paul.

Song, M. and Ginsburg, H.P. (1987). The development of informal and formal mathematical thinking in Korean and U.S. children, *Child Development*, **57**, 1286–1296.

Starkey, P. and Cooper, R.G. Jr. (1980). Perception of number by human infants, *Science*, **210**, 1033–1035.

Starkey, P., Spelke, E.S. and Gelman, R. (1983). Detection of intermodal numerical correspondences by human infants, *Science*, **222**, 179–181.

Starkey, P., Spelke, E.S. and Gelman, R. (1990). Numerical abstraction by human infants. *Cognition*, **36**, 97–127.

Steffe, L.P., Cobb, P. and von Glasersfeld, E. (1988). *Construction of Arithmetical Meanings and Strategies*. New York: Springer Verlag.

Strauss, M.S. and Curtis, L.E. (1981). Infant perception of numerosity, *Child Development*, **52**, 1146–1152.

Strayer, F.F. and Moss E. (1989). The co-construction of representational activity during social interaction. In M.H. Bornstein and J.S. Bruner (eds), *Interaction in Human Development*. Hillsdale, New Jersey: Lawrence Erlbaum.

Wagner, S.H. and Walters, J. (1982). A longitudinal analysis of early number concepts: from numbers to number. In G.E. Foreman (ed.), *Action and Thought: From Sensorimotor Schemes to Symbolic Operations*. New York: Academic Press.

Wilkinson, A.C. (1984). Children's partial knowledge of the cognitive skill of counting, *Cognitive Psychology*, **16**, 28–64.

Wynn, K. (1990). Children's understanding of counting, *Cognition*, **36**, 185–193.

9 The Development of Social Representations

BARBARA LLOYD
University of Sussex

GERARD DUVEEN
University of Cambridge

We begin this chapter by discussing Moscovici's theory of social represen-tations. Next we consider developmental aspects of the theory. Finally, we describe the ontogenesis of social representations of gender.

MOSCOVICI'S CONCEPT OF SOCIAL REPRESENTATIONS

The concept of social representations introduced into social psychology by Moscovici and his collaborators has had a chequered reception in the English-speaking world. Moscovici (1976a) elaborated the concept of social representation most fully in *La Psychoanalyse, son image et son public*, but in the absence of a translation, even his own English presentations have an abstract, general or programmatic character. They introduce a theoretical perspective without the benefit of a clear demonstration of its value for empirical research (cf. Moscovici, 1973, 1981, 1983, 1984, 1988; Moscovici & Hewstone, 1983). Moscovici defines social representations as:

> system(s) of values, ideas and practices with a twofold function; first, to establish an order which will enable individuals to orient themselves in their material and social world and to master it; and secondly to enable commu-nication to take place among the members of a community by providing them with a code for social exchange and a code for naming and classifying unambiguously the various aspects of their world and their individual and group history. (Moscovici, 1973, p. xiii)

This definition establishes social representations as particular kinds of structures which function to provide collectivities with intersubjectively shared means for understanding and communicating. Moscovici also uses the term to designate the process through which these structures are con-structed and transformed. As a process, social representation is not bound by the canons of logical discourse, nor is it regulated by procedures of empirical verification or falsification. Rather, social representation is

Systems of Representation in Children: Development and Use. Edited by C. Pratt and A.F. Garton
© 1993 John Wiley & Sons Ltd

168 SYSTEMS OF REPRESENTATION IN CHILDREN

construed as being composed of two complementary functions, anchoring (whereby the unfamiliar or remote is absorbed into the familiar categories of everyday cognition) and objectification (whereby representations are projected into the world, so that what was abstract is transformed into something concrete). These two functions are interdependent in the sense that a representation can become securely anchored to the extent that it is also objectified and, vice versa, that objectification would be impossible unless a representation were anchored. Nevertheless, they can be distinguished analytically as two moments in the process of social representation.

Moscovici's conceptualisation of the process of social representation is related to his distinction between the consensual universe of social representations and the reified universe of scientific discourse which respects the laws of logic and whose products are open to empirical investigation (Moscovici, 1981). His purpose in making this distinction is not to propose a particular philosophy of science, but to point to a central phenomenon of our own society whereby the category of scientific understanding is distinguished from the category of everyday or common sense understanding. What is proposed, then, is that these two universes, the reified and the consensual, correspond to a particular social representation in which the realm of the scientific is distinguished from that of commonsense. The distinction is, nevertheless, a powerful one as science, Moscovici notes,

> attempts to construct a map of the forces, objects and events unaffected by our desires and consciousness. [Social representation] stimulates and shapes our collective consciousness, explaining things and events so as to be accessible to each of us and relevant to our immediate concerns.
> (Moscovici, 1981, p. 187)

Social representations thus provide the central, integrative concept for a distinct perspective on social psychology. This perspective shares with Piagetian theory and other constructivist trends in psychology and the social sciences an epistemology which treats the subject and object of knowledge as correlative and co-constitutive and which rejects the view that these terms designate independent entities. The ontological corollary to this position is that social representations are constitutive of the realities represented, a constitution (or construction) effected through anchoring and objectification. Thus the *content* of what is constructed is accorded the same significance as the process of construction, and hence Moscovici's dictum that social representations are always the representation of *something* (Moscovici, 1976a, 1984).

As well as being the representation of something, social representations are also representations of *someone or some collective* (Moscovici, 1976a,

1984). The interdependence between social representations and the collectives for which they function means that social life is always considered as a construction rather than being taken as a given.

The duality of social representations in constructing both the order of social life and an understanding of it recalls a similar duality in Piaget's conceptualisation of operational knowing. Piaget's empirical task was facilitated by the availability of scientific knowledge, i.e. the structured domains of physics, mathematics and logic. They provided him with a perspective from which to understand and interpret the behaviour of subjects at different levels of development. The logic of class inclusion served as a tool in understanding children's answers to such questions as whether there were more flowers or more roses in a given collection.

In the consensual universe of social life there is no privileged vantage point offering an objective perspective from which to orient an investigation. In some circumstances it is possible to locate a point of reference comparable to the 'objectified' perspective available to Piaget. In Moscovici's (1976a) study of psychoanalysis, he took the body of psychoanalytic theory originating in Freud's work as an objectified point of reference from which to compare and contrast the social representations of psychoanalysis constructed by different social groups. He observed the transformation of this body of knowledge as it was re-constituted in the network of representations held by different groups.

But not all social representations have such well-defined origins. As well as describing the reconstruction of scientific knowledge in the consensual realm, social representation also refers to the construction and transformation of knowledge within the consensual realm. For example, in the case of gender, current representations cannot be traced back to any original source in scientific discourse. There is a methodological issue here which concerns the relation of an epistemological position to empirical investigation. It is a strategic problem for research on social representations rather than a question of specific techniques. The researcher has to proceed by identifying what Goldmann described as a *significant structure* (Goldmann, 1976, 1980), that is a structure which has a functional necessity for a particular group. Social representations as significant structures identify both the group which constructs a representation as well as the content which is represented.

SOCIAL REPRESENTATIONS AS A GENETIC THEORY

A genetic perspective is implied in the conception of social representations in the sense that the structure of any particular social representation is a construction and thus the outcome of some developmental process. The works of Piaget and Goldmann again offer a comparable point of view as both described their approach as a *genetic* structuralism in which a structure is always viewed as a particular moment in development. A structure is the relatively enduring organisation of a function, while the realisation of a function implies its organisation in a structure. Even if social representations as structures do not meet the strict formal criteria proposed by Piaget (1971), they nonetheless constitute organised wholes with the specific function of making communication and understanding possible.

From a developmental perspective it is useful to distinguish three types of transformations associated with social representation. These are *sociogenesis*, which concerns the construction and transformation of the social representations of social groups about specific objects, *ontogenesis*, which concerns the development of individuals in relation to social representations, and *microgenesis*, which concerns the evocation and transformation of social representations in social interaction.

Sociogenesis

Sociogenesis refers to the elaboration of social representations themselves. Moscovici's (1976a) study of psychoanalysis is an example of the diffusion of scientific knowledge through the community as it is reconstructed by different social groups. But, as we noted above, it is not only knowledge originating in scientific discourses which gives rise to social representations; other themes also circulate in society through the medium of social representations. In recent years social representations of gender have been in transformation as different groups have re-examined this domain.

Sociogenesis takes place in time. Thus, when social representations are investigated at a particular moment the resulting description needs to be viewed in a diachronic perspective. Moscovici's study, for instance, was originally published in 1961, and describes the structure of social representations of psychoanalysis at that time. The sociogenesis of these representations had taken place over the years since Freud's work first appeared. In the intervening years since Moscovici's study, the theory of psychoanalysis has itself evolved and the characteristics of many social groups have also changed. A comparable study undertaken today would reveal transformations in the social representations of psychoanalysis.

Ontogenesis

Human infants are born into a social world constructed in terms of the social representations of their parents, siblings, teachers, etc., representations which also structure the interactions of these others with the child. If, as Moscovici asserts, the society into which children are born is a 'thinking society', it is social representations which constitute the 'thinking environment' for the child. Developing the competence to participate as actors in this thinking society implies that children gain access to the social representations of their community. We describe this process as the ontogenesis of social representations. It is not restricted to childhood but occurs whenever individuals, children or adults engage with novel social representations in order to participate in the life of a group.

An adequate account of ontogenesis needs to describe how social representations become psychologically active for individuals. Elsewhere (Duveen & Lloyd, 1986) we have suggested that ontogenesis is a process through which individuals reconstruct social representations, and that in doing so they elaborate particular social identities. It is as social identities that social representations become psychologically active for individuals, and in expressing a social identity individuals draw on resources made available through social representations. Although it is subtle, the distinction between social representations and social identities is nevertheless important. As we report below, for example, boys and girls develop similar representations of gender, but they express distinct social identities.

The influence exercised by social representations on individuals can take different forms (Duveen & Lloyd, 1990). Some social representations impose an imperative obligation on individuals to adopt a particular social identity. This is the case, for example, with representations of gender or ethnicity where individuals are constrained to construct the corresponding social identity. In these domains there is an external obligation which derives from the ways in which others identify an individual in terms of gender and ethnicity. In other instances the influence of social representations is exercised through a contractual obligation rather than an imperative one. In these cases an individual joining a social group contracts to adopt a particular social identity. Social representations of psychoanalysis provide an example of a contractual obligation. As a body of knowledge psychoanalysis exercises no external obligation on individuals to interiorise the categories of analytic thinking as psychologically active constructions. But entry to some social groups (principally that of psychoanalysts themselves, but also other social groups for whom an analytic perspective forms part of their world-view) is dependent upon individuals contracting to construe the world in terms of psychoanalytic categories.

Microgenesis

The third aspect of social representations occurs in interpersonal communications as they are evoked by the social identities asserted in the activity of the participants. Social identities may be relatively stable but need not remain invariant through the course of interaction. There is a genetic process in all social interaction in which aspects of social identities and the social representations on which they are based are elaborated and negotiated. We describe this process as the microgenesis of social representations.

The evocation of social representations in social interaction occurs as individuals construct an understanding of the situation and locate themselves and their interlocutors as social subjects. In many circumstances there will be a mutuality in the understanding constructed by different participants which will obviate the need for any explicit specification or negotiation of social identities. But where the mutuality of understanding cannot be taken for granted, or where an assumed mutuality breaks down, the negotiation of social identities becomes an explicit and identifiable feature of social interaction. In these circumstances the negotiation of social identities may involve the coordination of different points of view and the resolution of conflicts.

Language is, of course, a central medium through which social interactions are conducted, and studies in sociolinguistics have emphasised the construction of social identities in discourse (Gumperz, 1982) as well as the role of social representations (Rommetveit, 1974, 1984). Through the course of social interaction, participants come to adopt positions distinct from those with which they entered the interaction. In this sense microgenesis is always a process of change although many changes are transitory rather than structural as individuals adopt particular social identities in order to pursue specific goals or accomplish specific tasks. Nonetheless, social interaction is also the field in which social influence processes are most directly engaged (cf. Moscovici, 1976b), and social interaction may lead to structural change in the representations of participants. These changes may be ontogenetic transformations in the development of social representations in individual subjects (cf. Doise & Mugny, 1984), but they may also involve sociogenetic transformations.

Some examples may help to illustrate the possible relationships between these three types of genetic transformation. Consider first of all the scientist who proposes a new theory, and let us assume that we are dealing with an Einstein or a Freud proposing a radical new interpretation of the human situation or human experience. Through various forms of social interaction (publications or lectures) the scientist tries to communicate his theory to colleagues. The communication is successful to the extent that other scientists understand the concepts being proposed and also accept that these concepts are well-founded and themselves begin to use them. The outcome will be ontogenetic transformations in the representations held by these scientists as individuals, as well as a sociogenetic transformation in the representation held by the scientific community as a social group.

By contrast, consider children as they grasp some social representation of their community—gender or ethnicity for example. For this development to occur, children need to receive some communication, whether through interaction with other children or adults or from the public representations presented in the media. These microgenetic processes may lead to ontogenetic transformations in the child's representation of the world, but the social representations of their community are unlikely to be influenced by these particular microgenetic processes. In this case there is ontogenesis without sociogenesis, a state of affairs which is a characteristic feature of childhood given the negligible influence which children are able to exert on the representations held by their community.

As these examples indicate, social interaction is a creative process. Microgenesis leads to sociogenetic changes when cultural representations are altered and to ontogenetic changes when the representations of individuals undergo development.

SOCIAL REPRESENTATIONS AND THE DEVELOPMENT OF SEMIOTIC SYSTEMS

We have used the concept of social representations to explore social psychological aspects of gender (Lloyd, 1987; Lloyd & Duveen, 1989). Here we analyse representations of gender as a semiotic system in order to clarify our presentation of the ontogenesis of social representations of gender. Semiotic systems function as a means of communication for social groups, and their operation is dependent on the intersubjectively shared representations of group members. In this sense semiotic systems can be seen as an expression of social representations. A detailed consideration of the nature of semiotic relations provides a framework in which to examine developmental changes in the construction of social gender identities.

When someone describes a doll as a toy for girls, or a gun as a toy for boys, they are not describing characteristics which are physically inscribed in these toys, but the social markings of these objects. Mugny, De Paolis & Carugati have observed that social marking 'connects relations of a cognitive order with those of a social order' (1984, p. 137). This connection arises through the use of the same social representation to mark objects as well as to structure the cognitive processes required to comprehend the markings. On the one hand, social representations of gender are objectified in the markings of toys as suitable for girls or for boys, while, on the other hand, the comprehension of these markings is made possible through social representations of gender. These are really two sides of the same coin. Social representations establish a common semiotic code for both the marking of objects and the mediation of cognitive processes, and thus provide the connection between the social order and the cognitive order.

The relationship between social representations and social marking emphasises the fact that social representation always involves processes of signification. While the semiotic character of social representations has long been recognised in theoretical accounts (Moscovici, 1976b; Jodelet, 1984), analyses of social representations have stressed the processes of anchoring and objectification rather than the nature of signification. For adults and older children this issue may be relatively unimportant, since it can be assumed that they have developed all the cognitive instruments necessary for handling different types of signification (signals, symbols, signs). But in early childhood this assumption cannot be made since these cognitive instruments develop through the first years of childhood. Indeed, distinguishing between types of semiotic relations is essential for a developmental analysis of the genesis of representation (Piaget, 1951; Wallon, 1970).

We propose to use three terms—signal, symbol, sign—to mark two distinctions between types of semiotic relations. First, we distinguish semiotic relations in which signifiers and signifieds are undifferentiated (signals) from those where they are differentiated (symbols and signs), and second, within the class of differentiated signifiers we distinguish those in which the relation of signifier to signified is motivated (symbol) from those in which there is an 'arbitrary' relation between signifier and signified (sign). These distinctions correspond to the major divisions in the genetic psychologies of Piaget (1951) and Wallon (1970).

Signification is undifferentiated when there is an immediate relation between signifier and signified. In Piaget's words a signifier 'is not differentiated from its *signifié* (signified)...in that it constitutes a part, an aspect or a causal result of that *signifié* (Piaget, 1970, p. 53). Thus a signal may be a part which signifies a whole, as in the case of the branches of a tree overhanging a fence which signify the presence of the remainder of the tree occluded by the fence. Signals are always embedded within the context of the subject's immediate field of practical action. In Piaget's terms signals correspond to the sensori-motor level of psychological organisation; a signal is recognised when it is assimilated to a scheme of action, and this knowledge is realised in the execution of the scheme. An adult's finger or a pencil may signal the scheme of grasping for an infant, and once recognised as a signal, the grasping follows immediately.

'Representation', Piaget writes, 'begins when there is simultaneous differentiation and co-ordination between signifiers and signifieds' (Piaget, 1951, p. 3). The immediacy characterising the relations between sensory event and action is broken in differentiated signification. Events can be assimilated to 'internal schemes' or concepts; the child can know an object as a finger or a pencil without having to act out this knowledge. Equally, past events can be evoked through internal signifiers (images). One object can now be used as an external signifier, to signify another object. But, as Piaget makes clear, one thing can signify another only on the grounds that it can be assimilated to the same operatory structures. We infer that a child using a pencil to signify an aeroplane has assimilated the pencil to the concept 'aeroplane' and that the pencil has become a symbol for the aeroplane. In symbols there is always a *motivated* relationship between signifier and signified; here it is the analogy of shape between the pencil as signifier and the aeroplane signified. The motivation relating a symbolic signifier to its signified is always some knowledge held by the subject. The defining characteristic of symbolic signification is that the motivated relationships between signifiers and signifieds are not regulated by a public or conventional semiotic code, but remain private and personal.

The third category of semiotic relations we consider is signs, where signifier and signified have what Saussure (1974) described as a purely arbitrary relation to one another. For Saussure the signifier in a linguistic sign is a 'sound-image' and the signified a 'concept', but between the signifier 'tree' and the concept 'tree' there is no necessary relationship. Returning to the example of the gender marking of toys, there is no necessity in associating girls with dolls or boys with guns, but social representations of gender establish a necessary association. Since the conventions of a community create the necessary relations between signifiers and signifieds in signs, these semiotic relations are always public and communicable.

A second characteristic of signs follows upon the conventionality of the relations between signifiers and signifieds. Signs do not have meaning when taken singly in isolation, but only in so far as they can be differentiated from other signs. Therefore, signs always appear in systems in which conventions regulate the relations between signifiers and signifieds. Language is the usual example of a system of signs capable of expressing ideas, but other systems have also been considered as signs, such as the food system or the fashion system (cf. Barthes, 1967), and, in our studies, we have considered toys as signs in the semiotic system of gender.

The two modes of differentiated signification, symbols and signs, are distinct from undifferentiated signals in that they are no longer completely embedded in the context of the subject's field of practical action. Both symbols and signs pertain to the field of representation and, from a developmental point of view, demand a higher level of psychological organisation than the sensori-motor coordinations appropriate for signals. While there is a developmental process involved in the passage from undifferentiated to differentiated signification, both Piaget and Wallon note that the use of signs and symbols emerges contemporaneously in the child. It is not possible to mark any developmental difference in the psychological organisation required for symbol or sign use (cf. Furth, 1981); both depend on the same cognitive instruments. In this context our interest lies in the development of sign functioning.

We can now consider the framework which developmental semiotics provides for an analysis of the development of social representations. Social representations establish systematic social markings of objects, events and activities, markings which function as signs. In the field of gender, for instance, not only is the material culture marked in this way, but also behavioural styles as well as other aspects of social interaction. As a semiotic field, social representations of gender encompass a wide range of linguistic and non-linguistic signifiers. The development of social representations of gender provides children with the resources both to comprehend these diverse signifiers as signs of gender, as well as to produce signs of gender in their interactions and communications with others.

Our semiotic approach highlights two issues: the first is the need to distinguish between undifferentiated (signal) and differentiated (sign) signification in children's activity, and the second concerns the use of signs *per se*. Signals always elicit responses from children. So long as signification remains undifferentiated, children are not independently active in the field of gender, but reactive to events and the activities of others. Actively marking gender rather than reacting to gender markings is an indication of differentiated signification.

The development of differentiated signification corresponds to the progressive internalisation of social representations. However, the emergence of differentiated signification is not a sudden, all-or-nothing event, but a gradual process. Initially, differentiated signification remains tied to particular contexts of activity, and only later becomes independent of context (a process which Vygotsky refers to as the decontextualisation of semiotic means, cf. Wertsch, 1985). Differentiated signification emerges first of all in contexts which offer the child some scaffolding (Wood, Bruner & Ross, 1976). An ability to use signs independently of context is a later development.

The development of a social representation can be traced empirically through an analysis of children's capacity to use signs in accordance with the conventions of their community. Such evidence of sign use in children's activity can be construed as indicative of their internalisation of the social representations of their community. We seek to demonstrate children's emergence as semiotic actors capable of differentiated rather than undifferentiated signification, and to show the range of signifiers which they comprehend as signs in different contexts.

In the following section two kinds of studies are reviewed. First, there are studies of the interactions between infants and mothers examining the emergence of children as semiotic actors in the field of gender. Second, there are studies of children aged $1\frac{1}{2}$–4 years which consider the development of gender signification in a variety of contexts. In these investigations the gender meanings current in the child's community have been determined independently of the observations of the child's action, and, subsequently, these consensual gender meanings have been employed as independent variables in analyses of the development of children's ability to control the signification of these meanings. In both cases our focus is on the processes through which signification is achieved. In reporting these studies we seek to describe the function of children's behaviour and to record the means which become available to them; we are not attributing intention or awareness. In this strategy we are following Bruner's (1975) analysis of early communication.

DEVELOPMENTAL CHANGES IN SEMIOTIC FIELDS OF GENDER

Entering the gender system

Infants are born into a world where there is already a highly structured semiotic field, defined in terms of their society's social representations of gender. The initial contribution of the infant to the process of gender signification is limited to the presence of biological characteristics, usually external genitalia, which function *for others* in the community as signifiers of membership in a gender category, feminine or masculine. The clarity of genitals and the verbal labels 'girl'/'boy' as signs of gender is attested by the different descriptions of female and male infants given by parents on initially viewing their first born, even when there are no differences in birth weight, birth length or Apgar scores (Rubin, Provenzano & Luria, 1974). Newborns function as signifiers for others but the rarity of gender differentiation in non-elicited behaviour (Feldman, Brody & Miller, 1980) indicates that infants do not take an active role in gender signification.

We explored the function of conventional signs of gender by observing the behaviour of mothers of firstborn infants playing with an unfamiliar 6-month-old infant whose biological sex was either congruent or incongruent with the infant's dress and name (Smith & Lloyd, 1978). A selection of infant toys independently rated as masculine and feminine was available. Regardless of the biological sex of the infant, when the child was presented as a girl the infant was usually offered the doll first, but when the same infant was presented as a boy the hammer or rattle was offered first. The importance of dress and name was also seen in responses to the infant's activity. Gross motor behaviour provided no means for distinguishing between female and male infants; it is a feature of the behavioural repertoire of human infants. But the social representations of gender evoked by our manipulation of dress and name enabled gross motor behaviour to be comprehended as a sign of gender. When the infant was identified as a boy, mothers offered verbal encouragement to the infant's gross motor activity and responded with further motor stimulation. Yet the gross motor activity of the same infant when presented as a girl elicited soothing and calming.

At 6 months the behaviour of infants is not differentiated according to sex group membership and infants are not yet actors in the semiotic field of gender. Reports of 13-month-old girls spending significantly more time in sedentary and fine motor manipulative play with blocks, a peg board and two toys with faces, and the great vigour of boys, provide some of the earliest evidence that children have entered the semiotic field of gender as actors and have begun to internalise gender as a system of signs (Goldberg & Lewis, 1969). In two partial replications we found little evidence that 13-month-olds were able to use toy preferences as signs of gender but there were systematic gender differences in styles of play, with boys engaging in significantly more gross motor activity, such as banging, shaking, throwing and pushing, and girls showing a trend to engage in more manipulative play, fitting, placing and handling objects (Smith, 1982). Since gross motor play was five times as frequent as manipulative activity and girls and boys both played with the mallet, we believe that object and action are not yet differentiated for these children. The entry of their mothers sharpened the congruent marking of gender in children's activity; the gross motor activity of boys increased significantly though the corresponding increase in girls' manipulative play was not statistically significant.

At 13 months the activity of children begins to appear congruent with membership in a gender category. The importance of adults in structuring the semiotic field of gender is seen in the increased symmetry between social category membership and behavioural style in the presence of mothers. At 13 months there is little evidence that toys function as signs of gender for young children; activity and object are just beginning to emerge as signs of gender. The presence of an *adult other* strengthens the signifying chain and suggests that mothers are amplifying in some way gender resources available to children; interaction between mother and child is an important vehicle for the internalisation of social representations of gender.

Participating in the gender system

By the middle of the second year, with the developing use of language, children begin to make rapid progress in the internalisation of gender as a system of signs. In two studies of children aged $1\frac{1}{2}$–4 years we investigated the developing participation of children in the semiotic field of gender by examining play, language and problem solving. In the first study children were observed playing in pairs, either two girls, two boys or a mixed gender pair, but in the second study a target child was observed playing both in a same and mixed gender pair (Lloyd, 1987; Lloyd & Duveen, 1989, 1990).

In the first study, analysis of duration of play with masculine and feminine toys showed that boys played more with masculine toys, particularly in boy/boy pairs, but that girls did not display a preference in their use of toys. Further analyses indicated that this pattern of preferences was strongest in the older children ($2\frac{1}{2}$–$3\frac{1}{2}$ years). These results suggest that children emerge as independent semiotic actors at about $2\frac{1}{2}$ years.

Results from the second study, restricted to children in their fourth year, showed that boys' toys were played with more frequently than girls' toys and that this difference in toy use arose primarily through patterns in boys' play. Boys used boys' toys significantly more than girls' toys but again there was no significant difference between girls' use of girls' toys and boys' toys.

We also calculated the number of toy choices made by each child which were *congruent* with their gender, and the number which were *incongruent* with their own gender, to avoid the crudeness of our duration measure. It recorded the total time a child maintained any contact with a toy. Congruent choices were more frequent than incongruent ones in children of all ages. This analysis lent further support to the findings based upon duration. Boys playing with boy partners made more congruent than incongruent choices and when playing with girl partners made fewer incongruent choices than did girls. Nonetheless, both girls and boys made fewer congruent choices in mixed pairs, and both boys and girls made more incongruent choices in mixed pairs. Both modes of analysis show that girls and boys have different orientations in their use of toys.

In the second study congruent choices were also significantly more frequent than incongruent choices and boys made more congruent choices and fewer incongruent choices than girls. Again, both girls and boys made fewer congruent choices in mixed pairs while making more incongruent choices in mixed pairs. In this study the congruent and incongruent choices of target girls with girls and with boys are less distinctive than in the first study. In both studies boys differentiate more markedly than girls between congruent and incongruent choices.

Overall the results from the two studies support the conclusion that boys use masculine toys consistently, thus signifying their gender identity, while girls do not employ feminine toys in a similar manner. Boys' assertion of a gender identity is moderated by the gender of their partner; they make more incongruent choices when interacting with girls than when interacting with boys.

We also investigated the capacity of these children to control gender signification across different representational modalities using a series of individual linguistic and cognitive tasks. In the first linguistic task children were presented with pairs of photographs and gender-marked linguistic signs (such as 'LADY' or 'MAN') and asked to match the graphic and linguistic signs (a recognition task), and in the second, to produce an appropriate linguistic sign for the alternative photograph. Sorting tasks assessed children's comprehension of chains of signification. They were presented with an array of signs within a single modality—photographs of people or toys—and asked to partition the signs according to a particular rule, for example, male here and female there.

Performance improved with age and there was consistency in the order of task difficulty. Recognition was easiest followed by production and then sorting. Gender-marked nouns were easier for children to use in signifying gender than were the pronouns used in the recognition and production tasks. Children found it easier to sort photographs of people than to assign photographs of toys according to gender. The performances of even the youngest children offered some evidence of gender marking. Improving performance on all tasks was interpreted as reflecting both increasing cognitive capacities as well as the increasing influence of social representations of gender.

It is instructive to compare children's performances across these tasks. For the linguistic tasks the marking of gender is embedded as a semantic feature of language, so that the use of contrasting terms (such as 'woman' and 'man' or 'girl' and 'boy') provides scaffolding for children. In the sorting tasks children were provided with a photograph of a woman/girl or man/boy but they were not consistently supplied with a linguistic term which would facilitate semiotic mediation. All the children found it easier to assign photographs of people to gender categories than to assign photographs of the toys they later used in play. Toys offer little perceptual and no linguistic support for the social representations of gender which determine their gender marking, and even 4-year-olds perform little better than chance. Without some scaffolding, semiotic mediation is difficult and young children are unable to invoke the social representations available to adults.

These linguistic and cognitive results present a very different picture from the analyses of toy choice in play. In play, children encounter the gender markings of toys in the context of practical activity, while in these tasks the gender markings of materials are no longer embedded in a practical context. The difference between the social identities displayed by girls and boys in their play cannot be ascribed to a difference in their knowledge of gender markings: girls and boys have a similar knowledge. Rather, it seems that the arena of play is one in which boys use their knowledge to mark a difference, but one in which girls do not.

SOCIAL IDENTITIES AND SOCIAL REPRESENTATIONS

The semiotic approach adopted here has helped to clarify two issues in the development of social representations: (1) processes in the internalisation of social representations, and (2) relations between social identities and social representations.

The distinction between signals and signs as types of signification corresponds to two kinds of knowledge which support social identities.

Signals correspond to sensori-motor, practical knowing and a social identity which is always reactive to events. Children whose cognitive instruments only allow them to use signals are always dependent upon others for a social identity. A child's social identity is held by their community, and in this sense is always an externalised social identity. By contrast, signs are always associated with internalised knowing, that is with representation, and a social identity which can be autonomously asserted. An internalised social identity enables the child to participate as an independent actor in the social order.

Both Piaget and Wallon recognised a developmental relation between signals and signs as forms of signification requiring qualitatively different cognitive instruments. Our results support this distinction; externalised social identities associated with signals precede the emergence of internalised social identities associated with signs. In the realm of gender, internalised social identities become visible at about the age of $2-2\frac{1}{2}$ years. However, while it is possible to assert that a qualitative developmental difference exists between these two forms of social identity, this does not mean that the earlier form simply disappears, to be replaced completely by the later form. In psychological development sensori-motor coordinations do not vanish with the development of operatory structures (Furth, 1981). Similarly, it is likely that many of the behaviours acquired through signal use will persist after the development of the semiotic function so that aspects of externalised social identities may coexist with internalised social identities. An individual may come to operate with a combination of both internalised and externalised elements.

The code relating signifiers and signifieds in sign systems is furnished by social representations. While a knowledge of this code is necessary to become an actor in the sign system, such knowledge alone is not a sufficient condition for the development of an internalised social identity. Girls and boys appear to have similar knowledge of the semiotic code of gender, but they use this knowledge in different ways in their play. Boys play with toys in a way which maximises the differentiation between masculine and feminine marked toys, while girls minimise this difference. On the basis of the same knowledge, boys and girls adopt different positions in relation to it. Thus the expression of an internalised social identity depends upon both a knowledge of the appropriate semiotic code as well as the assumption of a position in relation to it.

Social representations furnish a semiotic code, as well as marking out the positions which can be adopted towards it. In this sense the same social representations contain material for the construction of different social identities. Distinguishing between codes and positions as components of social identities allows us to elaborate Mugny et al.'s (1984) proposition concerning social marking. While social marking does indeed connect relations of a cognitive order with those of a social order, it is a connection which is mediated by social identities. In circumstances where children are only asked about their knowledge of the semiotic code of gender, girls and boys display a similar competence. Investigations of activities which draw on both code and position reveal the different social identities of girls and boys, social identities which mobilise different resources available within the same social representation of gender.

ACKNOWLEDGMENT

The research was supported by grant no. HR5871 from the Social Science Research Council and grant no. C00232113 from the Economic and Social Research Council to the first author.

REFERENCES

Barthes, R. (1967). *Elements of Semiology*. London: Jonathon Cape.
Bruner, J.S. (1975). From communication to language—a psychological perspective, *Cognition*, **3**, 255–267.
Doise, W. and Mugny, G. (1984). *The Social Development of the Intellect*. Oxford: Pergamon Press.
Duveen, G. and Lloyd, B. (1986). The significance of social identities, *British Journal of Social Psychology*, **25**, 219–230.
Duveen, G. and Lloyd, B. (1990). Introduction. In G. Duveen and B. Lloyd (eds), *Social Representations and the Development of Knowledge*. Cambridge: Cambridge University Press.
Feldman, J.F., Brody, N. and Miller, S. (1980). Sex differences in non-elicited behavior, *Merrill-Palmer Quarterly*, **26**, 63–73.
Furth, H. (1981). *Piaget and Knowledge*. Englewood Cliffs, New Jersey: Prentice-Hall.
Goldberg, S. and Lewis, M. (1969). Play behaviour in the year old infant: early sex differences, *Child Development*, **40**, 21–31.
Goldmann, L. (1976). *Cultural Creation in Modern Society*. Saint Louis: Telos Press.
Goldmann, L. (1980). *Method in the Sociology of Literature*. Saint Louis: Telos Press.
Gumperz, J. (1982) (ed.). *Language and Social Identity*. Cambridge: Cambridge University Press.
Jodelet, D. (1984). Representation sociale: phenomones, concept et theorie. In S. Moscovici (ed.), *Psychologie sociale*. Paris: Presses Universitaires de France.
Lloyd, B. (1987). Social representations of gender. In J. Bruner and H. Haste (eds), *Making Sense: The Child's Construction of the World*. London and New York: Methuen.
Lloyd, B. and Duveen, G. (1989). The re-construction of social knowledge in the transition from sensorimotor to conceptual activity: the gender system. In A. Gellatly, D. Rogers and J. Sloboda (eds), *Cognition and Social Worlds*. Oxford: Oxford University Press.
Lloyd, B. and Duveen, G. (1990). A semiotic analysis of the development of social representations of gender. In G. Duveen and B. Lloyd (eds), *Social Representations and the Development of Knowledge*. Cambridge: Cambridge University Press.
Moscovici, S. (1973). Foreword. In C. Herzlich, *Health and Illness*. London: Academic Press.

Moscovici, S. (1976a). *La Psychanalyse, son image et son public*. Paris: Presses Universitaires de France.

Moscovici, S. (1976b). *Social Influence and Social Change*. London: Academic Press.

Moscovici, S. (1981). On social representations. In J. Forgas (ed.), *Social Cognition*. London: Academic Press.

Moscovici, S. (1983). The coming era of social representations. In J. P. Codol and J.P. Leyens (eds), *Cognitive Analysis of Social Behaviour*. The Hague: Martinus Nijhoff.

Moscovici, S. (1984). The phenomenon of social representations. In R. Farr and S. Moscovici (eds), *Social Representations*. Cambridge: Cambridge University Press.

Moscovici, S. (1988). Notes towards a description of social representations, *European Journal of Social Psychology*, **18**, 211–250.

Moscovici, S. and Hewstone, M. (1983). Social representations and social explanations: from the 'Naive' to the 'Amateur' scientist. In M. Hewstone (ed.), *Attribution Theory*. Oxford: Blackwell.

Mugny, G., De Paolis, P. and Carugati, F. (1984). Social regulation in cognitive development. In W. Doise and A. Palmonari (eds), *Social Interaction in Individual Development*. Cambridge: Cambridge University Press.

Piaget, J. (1951). *Play, Dreams and Imitation in Childhood*. London: Routledge and Kegan Paul (original edition: 1946).

Piaget, J. (1970). *Main Trends in Interdisciplinary Research*. London: George Allen and Unwin.

Piaget, J. (1971). *Biology and Knowledge*. Edinburgh: Edinburgh University Press.

Rommetveit, R. (1974). *On Message Structure*. London: Wiley.

Rommetveit, R. (1984). The role of language in the creation and transmission of social representations. In R. Farr and S. Moscovici (eds), *Social Representations*. Cambridge: Cambridge University Press.

Rubin, J.Z., Provenzano, F.J. and Luria, Z. (1974). The eye of the beholder: parents' views on the sex of new borns, *American Journal of Orthopsychiatry*, **44**, 512–519.

Saussure, F. (1974). *Course in General Linguistics*. London: Fontana.

Smith, C. (1982). Mothers' attitudes and behaviour with babies and the development of sex-typed play. Unpublished D.Phil. thesis, University of Sussex.

Smith, C. and Lloyd, B. (1978). Maternal behaviour and perceived sex of infant: revisited, *Child Development*, **49**, 1263–1265.

Wallon, H. (1970). *De l'acte à pensée*. Paris: Flammarion (original edition: 1942).

Wertsch, J. (1985). *Vygotsky and the Social Formation of Mind*. Cambridge, Massachusetts: Harvard University Press.

Wood, D., Bruner, J.S. and Ross, G. (1976). The role of tutoring in problem solving, *Journal of Child Psychology and Psychiatry*, **17**, 89–100.

10 Children's Representation of Emotions

ANTONY S.R. MANSTEAD
University of Manchester

What do children know about emotion? As with any aspect of children's knowledge, how one answers this question depends critically on the age of the children in question. At any given age, however, children's knowledge of emotion tends to be more extensive than one might suppose. For example, by the age of 12 months children are able not only to recognise facial expressions of emotion but are also able to respond to such expressions in ways that make it clear that they understand what these expressions signify (Sorce *et al.*, 1985). At 30 months, children not only use emotion terms frequently in their everyday speech, but they also often use these terms in a causal context, suggesting that by this age children understand that emotions have causes and consequences (Bretherton & Beeghly, 1982). By the age of 5 years, children are able to differentiate between the causes and consequences of at least some 'basic' emotions and are also able to specify different causes and consequences for different emotions (Russell, 1990). By the time they are 10 years old children have acquired an ability to recognise facial expressions that does not fall far short of adult standards (Izard, 1971).

What accounts for this early emergence and rapid increase in children's knowledge of the expressive correlates of emotion and of the causes and consequences of emotion? This chapter will attempt to answer this question first by reviewing research on children's knowledge of emotion, and then by discussing different theoretical accounts of the processes mediating the growth of children's knowledge.

THE GROWTH OF EMOTION KNOWLEDGE

Research on children's awareness and understanding of emotion has used a variety of methods to access that awareness and understanding, and this overview of the research literature will be subdivided according to these different methodologies: (a) research on children's ability to label or recognise facial expressions of emotion; (b) research on children's ability to respond appropriately to verbal descriptions of situations that elicit emotions; and (c) research on children's awareness of the causes and

Systems of Representation in Children: Development and Use. Edited by C. Pratt and A.F. Garton
© 1993 John Wiley & Sons Ltd

consequences of emotion. The objective is to provide a representative, rather than exhaustive, review of the literature within each of these subcategories.

Labelling or recognising facial expressions of emotion

Examining children's ability to recognise facial expressions of emotion permits the investigator to study emotional understanding in preverbal children. Indeed, some researchers have studied neonates' responses to facial expressions of emotion and have found that their responses are sufficiently imitative of an adult model's expressions for observers (who could see the neonate's face but not the adult's) to infer the nature of the adult's facial expression with above-chance accuracy (Field *et al.*, 1982; Field *et al.*, 1983). In Field *et al.*'s (1983) research, neonates with a mean age of 36 hours were held at a distance of approximately 15 cm away from an adult female model's face. This adult posed happy, surprised or sad expressions. An observer standing behind the adult model made a number of judgements on the basis of the neonate's facial behaviour, the most important for present purposes being that they had to guess which of the three expressions the model was posing on a given trial. These guesses were significantly more accurate than would have been expected by chance. However, other researchers have failed to replicate these findings (Kaitz *et al.*, 1988), and the limitations of the neonate visual perception system make it rather unlikely that such young infants can access the expressive information in a stimulus face (Nelson, 1985, 1987).

Less controversial are the findings reported for 2- to 6-month-old infants (e.g. Barrera & Maurer, 1981; LaBarbera *et al.*, 1976; Nelson & Horowitz, 1983; Young-Browne, Rosenfeld & Horowitz, 1977). For example, Barrera & Maurer (1981) used a habituation procedure to investigate 3-month-olds' abilities to discriminate and recognise smiling and frowning expressions. Each infant was habituated to a happy or angry facial expression by repeatedly showing that expression until on three consecutive trials the subject looked at the expression for less than half as long as on the first three trials. Then the infant was tested twice with the habituated expression and twice with the novel expression, the order being counterbalanced across subjects. In one experiment, 23 out of 24 infants looked longer at the novel expression than at the habituated one when the expressions were posed by the subject's mother; in a second experiment, 21 out of 28 infants looked longer at the novel than at the habituated expression when these expressions were posed by an adult female stranger.

These results strongly suggest that, by the age of 3 months, most infants are able to process the expressive information in a face sufficiently well to be able to discriminate between happy and angry expressions and to recognise a habituated expression as one that has been seen before, for it is difficult to see on what other basis the subjects preferred the novel expression to the habituated one. Moreover, it appears that by the age of 7 months infants are able to integrate expressive information across sensory modalities, for Walker-Andrews (1986) found that when she presented two films to infants of that age, one showing a happy expression and the other an angry expression, together with a soundtrack of either a happy voice or an angry voice, the infants looked more at the face which corresponded to the emotion they could hear on the soundtrack. By this age, then, infants are able to do more than discriminate between two expressions, recognise which of them has recently been seen, and express a preference for the new expression; to know which expression goes with which tone of voice implies that infants have a representation of 'emotional' expression that includes more than one modality of expressive information. However, the possession of such a representation of expression does not imply that these infants know what these expressions connote, in terms of emotional meaning.

Evidence that infants are capable of extracting meaning from facial expressions comes from studies of 'social referencing'. This term refers to the tendency of infants aged about 12 months to look to their mother for reassurance or guidance when they are confronted with a situation in which they are uncertain about how to act. Some of the best-known studies of social referencing are those reported by Sorce et al. (1985). The 'uncertain' situation with which they confronted their subjects was the visual cliff. When the apparent drop is of intermediate height, most 12-month-olds are unsure about crossing the cliff. The investigators asked the subject's mother to stand on the far side of the cliff and either to smile or to look afraid when her child approached the edge of the cliff. When the mother posed fear, none of the 17 infants crossed to the deep side; when she posed happiness, 14 out of 19 infants crossed to the deep side. In a follow-up study, only 2 out of 18 infants crossed to the deep side when the mother posed anger, but 11 out of 15 infants crossed when she posed interest.

These results show that 12-month-olds can distinguish between positive and negative facial expressions and respond appropriately to the meaning conveyed by these two general classes of expression. What these results do not show is that 12-month-olds are able to attach specific meanings to specific types of facial expression within the general classes of positive and negative emotion; angry and afraid expressions had the same inhibiting effect, while happy and interested expressions had the same encouraging effect.

Harris (1989) has drawn attention to the fact that an important change in the child's emotional repertoire takes place during the second year of life. While the studies of social referencing show that 12-month-olds are capable of responding appropriately to facial expressions, there is no evidence that the child regards the other's emotion as something that can be—or should be—modified. Yet during the second year children begin to make efforts to comfort others who appear to be distressed, which suggests that they are beginning to appreciate: (a) that other people's overt signs of distress are experienced by them as subjectively unpleasant, and (b) that steps can be taken to modify their distress.

Although studies of children's responses to another's distress are not, formally speaking, studies of their reactions to facial expressions, it seems reasonable to assume that expressive information in the face must play a key role in mediating the children's responses. Dunn, Kendrick & MacNamee (1981) asked mothers to keep a record of the behaviour of their oldest child, who was between 2 and 4 years old, towards a younger brother or sister, who was either 8 or 14 months old. Most older siblings helped the younger child if he or she was upset, although there were large individual differences in helping. Almost one-third of the 14-month-old younger siblings sought out the older child for comfort when distressed. Furthermore, by this age some of the younger children had started to comfort their older siblings when the latter became distressed.

Complementary findings emerge from a longitudinal study reported by Zahn-Waxler & Radke-Yarrow (1982). Children aged between 10 and 12 months responded to another person's distress either by becoming distressed themselves or by simply watching or remaining unresponsive. There were few maternal reports of children at this age trying to comfort the distressed person. Over the next 12 months, children were less likely to react to distress by becoming distressed, and were more likely to try to intervene in a comforting way (for example, by approaching and touching or patting the distressed person). With increasing age, these interventions became more focused: children would bring objects to the distressed person, make verbal expressions of sympathy, or seek someone else's help. By the time they were 20–24 months old, the children in this study were reported as intervening in a helpful way in about one-third of the situations in which another became distressed, although there were large individual differences in their reactions (Zahn-Waxler, Radke-Yarrow & King, 1979).

As with the research on social referencing, studies of children's reactions to another person's emotional distress do not establish whether they can infer the meaning of different specific emotions. However, the fact that they make some attempt to comfort a distressed other shows that they can do more than simply use another's expressive information to guide their own behaviour under conditions of uncertainty; by the age of 24 months, many children are implicitly aware that other people's overt expressions of distress are informative about their negative internal states, and that these states can be alleviated by certain kinds of comforting intervention.

Evidence that young children respond differently to specific facial expressions of emotion, rather than general categories of positive or negative expression, comes from research in which they are asked to categorise facial expressions of emotion, to match emotional expressions to a provided verbal label, or to provide their own verbal label for each of a series of facial expressions. Possibly the earliest systematic study is the one reported by Gates (1923), who asked children whose ages ranged from 3 to 14 years to name the emotions shown in various facial expressions. The only expression identified accurately by 3-, 4- and 5-year-olds was that of happiness; anger was not labelled correctly by a majority of children until 7 years of age, fear until 10 years, and surprise until 11 years. Overall, there was 'a gradual increase in ability to interpret each picture as we pass from the youngest to the oldest children' (p. 453).

A large study by Izard (1971) reached broadly similar conclusions. He used carefully selected photographs of 'prototypical' facial expressions of emotion, and asked more than 400 American and French children aged between 2 and 9 years: (a) to produce a verbal label for each photograph, and (b) to select from groups of three the one that matched a provided verbal label. Accuracy on both tasks increased with age. On the labelling task, 4-year-olds averaged about four correct labels out of a total possible of 18; only 9-year-olds achieved an average score of over 50%. Although their performance was better on the recognition task, children's accuracy did not begin to exceed twice the level expected by chance until they were 6 years old.

Odom & Lemond (1972) used 32 photographs from the set developed by Izard (1971). There were four photographs for each of the following categories: joy, distress, anger, fear, surprise, disgust, interest and shame. On each trial of the task, kindergarteners (5-year-olds) and fifth graders (10-year-olds) were shown a set of four photographs, each showing a different expression, and were asked to select from that set one that matched an expression selected by the experimenter (e.g. 'Point to the picture of the person who feels the same way as this one'). The responses of 10-year-olds were consistently more accurate than those of 5-year-olds; responses to certain expressions (e.g. joy) were consistently more accurate than those to other expressions (e.g. fear).

Harrigan (1984) investigated the ability of 3-, 6-, 9- and 12-year-olds to recognise and label facial expressions of happiness, sadness, fear, anger, surprise and disgust. In the labelling task, children were shown a photograph and asked to identify the emotion being expressed. In the recognition task, children were shown three photographs and asked to select a photograph in response to the instructions, 'Point to the person who is x', where x was one of the six emotion terms. As expected, older children performed better than younger children on both tasks. Accuracy scores on both tasks were greater for happy and sad expressions than for other expressions.

Several other examples of research on children's ability to produce labels for or recognise facial expressions could be described (e.g. Felleman *et al.*, 1983; Stifter & Fox, 1987), but the general pattern is consistent across studies. Children's responses on such tasks become significantly more accurate as they grow older, and happy and sad expressions often elicit more accurate responses than do other expressions. Further progress in understanding children's representation of emotion by studying their ability to match, label or recognise facial expressions of emotion requires an approach that goes beyond the assessment of response accuracy at different ages and for different expressions.

One promising approach is that developed by Russell & Bullock (1985, 1986a, 1986b; Bullock & Russell, 1984, 1985, 1986). On the basis of a theoretical approach to emotions that will be discussed in greater detail below, these researchers argued that an analysis of the errors that children make on facial expression tasks would be more revealing than simply scoring responses as 'correct' or 'incorrect'. In a series of studies, they have established that when children are asked to choose a photograph in response to the question, 'Which person is happy (excited, surprised, afraid, scared, angry, mad, disgusted, sad and calm)?', either from an array of 10 (Bullock & Russell, 1984) or simply from a pair (Bullock & Russell, 1985), the errors they make are quite systematic. For example, when the target expression was *happy* and children were choosing from an array of 10 expressions, 89% of the errors made by 3-year-olds were either *calm* or *excited*; likewise, when the target expression was *mad* (meaning angry), 90% of the errors made by 3-year-olds were either *scared* or *disgusted*.

These errors conform to what Bullock & Russell predicted on the basis of a 'structural model' of emotions, in which emotions are organised in circular fashion in two-dimensional space (see Figure 10.1; cf. Schlosberg, 1952). This circular ordering derives from multidimensional scaling analyses of judgements of facial expressions (Russell & Bullock, 1986b), self-report data from adults and children (Russell & Ridgeway, 1983) and semantic similarity ratings made by Chinese, Japanese, Gujarati and Croatian speakers (Russell, 1983). Russell & Bullock interpret this circular ordering as the product of fundamental similarity relations between the various emotion categories, and argue that it reflects the underlying dimensions of pleasantness and arousal.

The errors that children (and adults, for that matter) make in facial expression tasks are predicted by Russell & Bullock to be more likely to be selections of one or other of the 'neighbouring' emotion categories in their structural model than other category choices. In the Bullock & Russell (1984) study, the proportion of errors that fell into these predicted categories was 40.1% for 3-year-olds, 43.3% for 4-year-olds, and 54.7% for 5-year-olds, compared with a chance figure of 22.2%. In the Bullock & Russell (1985) study, subjects were asked to choose the target expression

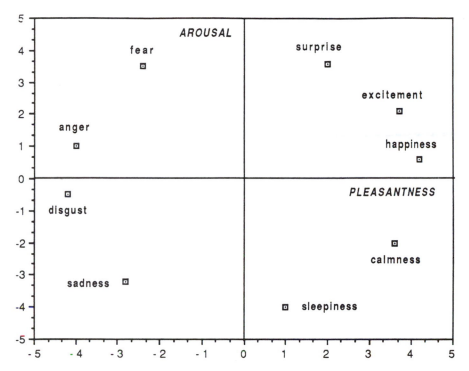

Figure 10.1 Circular structure of emotions in two-dimensional space (after Bullock & Russell, 1986)

from a pair of expressions, and as expected, the number of errors was found to be a direct function of the number of 'steps' in the structural model between the target expression and its foil in the stimulus pairing.

Bullock & Russell interpret the findings described thus far as resulting from the *breadth* of young children's categories of emotion. Because young children have broader categories of emotion than older children or adults, they make more errors when labelling or recognising facial expressions. More direct evidence of the relationship between category breadth and age comes from another study reported by Bullock & Russell (1986). Children were asked, 'Is this person x?', where x was one of the nine terms used in the earlier studies. On average, a facial expression was put into 4.0 categories by 3-year-olds, 2.5 categories by 4-year-olds, and 2.2 categories by 5-year-olds, out of the total of nine possible categories.

Russell & Bullock's research helps us to understand why young children make errors on facial expression tasks: they seem to have broader conceptions of emotion categories than their older counterparts, which result in a tendency to be overinclusive (by adult standards) when they are asked to match expressions to other expressions, to provide labels for expressions, or to pick expressions to match labels. As they grow older, their conceptions of what defines an emotion narrow, and so they approach more closely adult standards of performance on such tasks. This does not explain why certain expressions, such as happy and sad, seem to be more easily recognised or labelled by young children; this is an issue that will be addressed below, after reviewing the research literature on children's ability to make correct judgements about verbal descriptions of emotionally arousing situations.

Responses to verbal descriptions of emotionally arousing situations

Examining the accuracy with which children infer emotional states from descriptions of emotionally arousing situations begins to shed light on their understanding of the causes of emotion. In studies of this type, children are typically read short stories describing events that are likely to elicit particular emotional states, and are asked to provide a verbal label, select a verbal label, or choose a photograph of a facial expression to represent the emotion that would be experienced by the protagonist in the story. Sometimes the protagonist is someone else; in other studies the children are asked to imagine the described events as happening to them, and to say how they would feel in such circumstances.

Borke (1971) presented children aged between 3 and 8 years with a series of stories depicting a protagonist in situations that would normally elicit happiness, sadness, anger or fear, and asked the children to select one of four drawings of faces expressing these four emotions to 'complete' the stories. The responses of children aged between 3 and $3\frac{1}{2}$ years to the happy, sad and angry situations showed above-chance accuracy in selecting the appropriate expressions, although the happy situations were much more likely than the other two to elicit the correct response. The fear situations did not result in more selections of the afraid expression than would have been expected by chance, although children older than $3\frac{1}{2}$ years did perform better than chance. Children showed some tendency to confuse the sad and angry situations.

The ability of young children to distinguish between anger and sadness was a particular focus of the study reported by Thompson & Kieley (1987). They gave 5-year-olds and 8-year-olds sets of stories, 16 of which were expected to result in attributions of anger, and eight of which were expected to give rise to attributions of happiness or sadness. Responses were made by pointing to a face which expressed the feeling that the child thought would be experienced by the protagonist. Younger children made significantly fewer 'angry' responses to the anger stories. Although the younger children gave fewer 'angry' responses to all story types, by comparison with the older children, they were particularly likely to offer 'sad' as a response to stories depicting 'unjust punishment'. Deliberately drawing children's attention to the agency or intentionality of the actions depicted in the stories did increase the number of 'angry' responses, but not to a differential degree in the two age groups.

Evidence from other studies is generally consistent with this conclusion. For example, Barden *et al*. (1980) presented children ranging in age from 5 to 13 years with eight types of stories. Children responded by choosing from five emotion labels. For the story types that were expected to elicit negative affect, the majority response of 5-year-olds was 'sad' in five out of six cases, the exception being undetected dishonesty (where happiness was the majority response!). Another finding from this study was that when the investigators analysed children's responses to the stories without regard to accuracy, they found that the 5-year-olds used the term 'happy' significantly more often and the term 'scared' significantly less often than 9- to 10-year-olds or 12- to 13-year-olds.

Stein & Levine (1989) studied emotion knowledge in 4-year-olds, 7-year-olds and adults, by presenting them with narratives that varied along certain dimensions. The probability of 7-year-olds and adults choosing anger to describe the protagonist's response to the situation was significantly related to the degree to which the subjects inferred that there was intent to cause harm; the 4-year-olds, however, were just as likely to attribute sadness as anger, given that intent to cause harm was inferred.

Taken together, these findings suggest that while young children are able to make accurate attributions of happiness to protagonists who experience positive outcomes, and are very unlikely to attribute positive emotion in negative situations or negative emotion in positive situations, they do have greater difficulty than older children in distinguishing between different types of negative emotion. Few of the studies in which children are asked to match labels or photographs to verbal descriptions of situations have involved more than one positive emotion. This raises the question of whether young children might experience greater difficulty than older children in distinguishing between different types of positive emotion.

This possibility was examined in two studies conducted by the author and his students (Manstead, Anderson & Bromley, in preparation). In the first study, children in three age groups (4- to 5-year-olds, 7-year-olds and 10-year-olds) were presented with vignettes depicting episodes that were intended to elicit one of six emotions: happiness, excitement, surprise, sadness, anger or fear. These vignettes were written in the second-person, and the child was asked to say how he or she would feel in each situation. If the child was unwilling or unable to provide a label, a list of the six emotion terms was read aloud and the child was invited to choose one. The children's responses are summarised in Table 10.1.

It is evident that these responses vary significantly as a function of age group for four of the six emotions, the exceptions being happiness and

Table 10.1 Study 1: mean proportion of correct responses

	Age group (years)		
Emotion	4–5	7	10
Happy	1.000_a	0.984_a	0.992_a
Excited	0.125_a	0.383_b	0.859_c
Surprised	0.016_a	0.398_b	0.672_c
Sad	0.953_a	0.977_a	0.992_a
Cross	0.266_a	0.547_b	0.922_c
Scared	0.281_a	0.492_b	0.852_c

Means not sharing a common subscript differ significantly ($p < 0.05$)

sadness. For these two emotions the scores of the youngest groups are close to ceiling. Further analyses examined the frequency with which children used the different emotion terms in their responses, regardless of accuracy. The relevant means are shown in Table 10.2. There it can be seen that 'happy' and 'sad' were used spontaneously by children in the youngest group significantly more often than by their older counterparts, although the mean frequency of 'happy' responses by the youngest children differed only from the corresponding mean for the oldest group. By contrast, the frequency with which every other emotion term was used in responding to the vignettes increased steadily and significantly from one age group to the next. Thus the 'accuracy' of the youngest group's responses to the happy and sad vignettes has to be evaluated in the light of their high base-rate responding in these two categories.

Table 10.2 Study 1: mean number of spontaneous responses

	Age group (years)		
Emotion	4–5	7	10
Happy	7.94_a	7.44_a	5.03_b
Excited	0.31_a	1.59_b	3.44_c
Surprised	0.25_a	0.91_b	2.34_c
Sad	12.50_a	8.96_b	4.84_c
Cross	1.25_a	2.16_b	3.72_c
Scared	0.25_a	2.00_b	3.72_c

Means not sharing a common subscript differ significantly ($p < 0.05$)

Further insight into this issue is provided by analyses of the patterns of errors made by children. Of course, there were few errors for any age group in response to the happy and sad vignettes, but for the other four types of vignette there were some interesting patterns, as can be seen in Figure 10.2 (a–d). For the excited vignettes (Figure 2a), there was a marked tendency for children in the youngest group to respond with 'happy'; just as this tendency declined as a function of age, so the tendency to say 'excited' increased. For the surprised vignettes (Figure 2b), there was a more complex picture: here the youngest group tended either to say 'sad' or 'happy', which reflects the ambivalent valence of surprise (i.e. surprises can be pleasant or unpleasant). The number of 'sad' responses declined sharply with age, and there is a corresponding increase in the number of 'surprise' responses. For 'cross' (Figure 10.2c) and 'scared' (Figure 10.2d) the distributions are similar: in both cases, there was a noticeable tendency for the youngest group to respond with 'sad'; this tendency declined sharply with age, and the tendency to offer the correct response increased equally markedly.

A possible weakness of this study is its dependence on linguistic ability. Children not only had to comprehend the meaning of the vignettes; they also had to produce a verbal label to describe how they would feel in the situation in question, or at least recognise the likely response from a set of six labels read out by the interviewer. This places an appreciable load on the child's cognitive and linguistic skills, and may underestimate the complexity of children's understanding of emotion. We therefore conducted a second study that was essentially a replication of the first, modified in such a way as to reduce as far as possible the dependence on the child's linguistic ability. This was achieved by turning the response task into a non-verbal one. Instead of indicating how they would feel by means of a *verbal* label, children in this follow-up study were asked to point to one of a number of photographs of facial expressions of emotion. The photographs were taken especially for this study, and depicted a child posing one of six facial expressions: happy, surprised, sad, cross, disgusted and scared.

The children who participated in this second study were 4- to 5-year-olds, 6- to 7-year-olds, or 8- to 9-year-olds. Having established that each child was able to recognise and label all photographs accurately and reliably, vignettes similar in style to those used in the previous study were presented. Children were asked to indicate their response to each vignette by pointing to one of the photographs. The mean proportions of accurate responses made by children in each of the three age groups are shown in Table 10.3. As in the earlier study, there were no significant age differences for responses to the happy and sad vignettes, but strong and significant differences for the surprise and scared vignettes. Responses to the disgust vignettes also showed a marked effect due to age. One difference from the

(a)

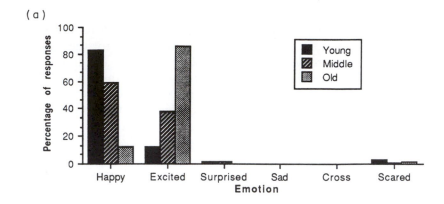

(b)

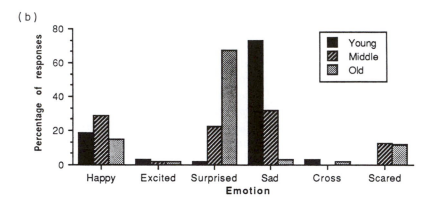

Figure 10.2
(a) Study 1: responses to 'excitement' vignettes.
(b) Study 1: responses to 'surprise' vignettes.

Table 10.3   Study 2: mean percentage of correct responses

	Age group (years)		
Emotion	4−5	6−7	8−9
Happy	0.950_a	0.903_a	0.828_a
Surprised	0.250_a	0.500_b	0.862_c
Sad	0.817_a	0.919_a	0.914_a
Cross	0.533_a	0.532_a	0.603_a
Disgusted	0.267_a	0.452_{ab}	0.621_b
Scared	0.333_a	0.565_b	0.759_b

Means not sharing a common subscript differ significantly
($p < 0.05$)

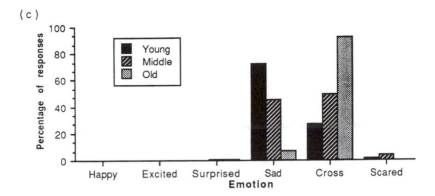

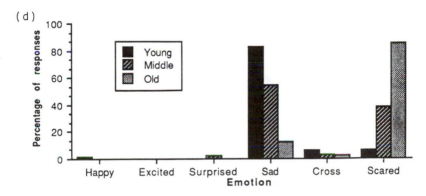

Figure 10.2 (continued)
(c) Study 1: responses to 'anger' vignettes.
(d) Study 1: responses to 'fear' vignettes.

earlier study is that there was no significant age difference in responses to the anger vignettes.

Analysis of the distribution of errors in responding to vignettes also echoed the earlier study. For the surprise vignettes (Figure 10.3a), there was a strong tendency for errors to arise from choosing the 'happy' photograph, and this tendency weakened as a function of age. For the scared vignettes (Figure 10.3b), younger subjects tended to choose the 'sad' photograph. Errors in responding to the disgust vignettes (Figure 3c) were somewhat more complex. The youngest children's modal error was to choose the 'sad' photograph, and this tendency declined with age;

however, there was also a tendency for children in the youngest group to choose the 'cross' photograph, and this tendency did not decline with age. Finally, the pattern of errors in response to the angry vignettes (Figure 10.3d) shows that the majority response for each age group was 'cross', but also that children in the youngest and middle groups were more inclined

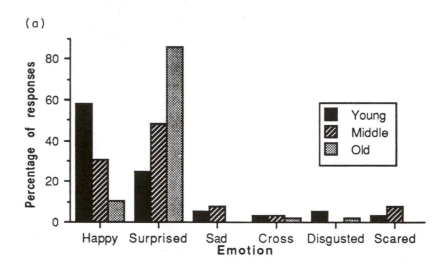

Figure 10.3
(a) Study 2: responses to 'surprise' vignettes.
(b) Study 2: responses to 'fear' vignettes.

(c)

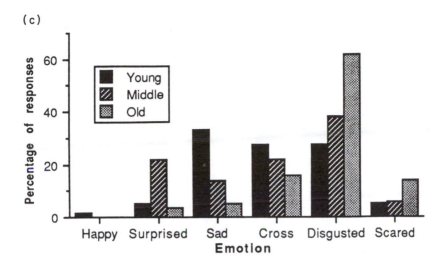

(d)

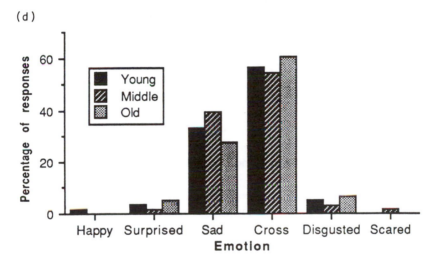

Figure 10.3 (continued)
(c) Study 2: responses to 'disgust' vignettes.
(d) Study 2: responses to 'anger' vignettes.

than the older group to choose the 'sad' photograph in response to the angry vignettes.

Overall, the results of this study are consistent with those of the first study. In both studies, children's ability to respond correctly to vignettes depicting prototypical emotion-eliciting situations other than happy and sad ones was found to vary as a function of age, with the older children performing better than the younger ones (the one exception being anger in Study 2). In both studies the distribution of errors shows that when children make by what adult standards would be considered 'errors', they do so in ways that are quite systematic. There was a marked tendency for the youngest children to choose 'happy' in response to positive vignettes, and to choose 'sad' in response to negative vignettes.

What might account for this pattern of findings? In several respects these results are reminiscent of the findings obtained by Russell & Bullock in their research on children's responses to facial expressions of emotion (Bullock & Russell, 1986). In addition to showing that the errors that children make on such tasks are not random, Bullock & Russell have demonstrated that multidimensional scaling of the perceived similarity relations between different facial expressions (which were assessed by asking subjects to sort photographs of facial expressions into piles) results in structural solutions that are very similar for 2-year-olds, 3-year-olds, 4-year-olds and adults. This similarity across age groups is used by Bullock & Russell as a basis for arguing that children as young as 2 years distinguish between facial expressions along the two 'fundamental' dimensions of pleasantness and arousal, just like adults. The fact that the circular ordering of emotions in two-dimensional space is as evident in the responses of 2-year-olds as it is in adults leads Bullock & Russell to argue that distinguishing expressions in terms of pleasantness and arousal reflects a basic or primitive way of structuring emotions. From this it follows that young children responding to vignettes would be likely to be accurate in inferring essentially positive affective reactions to pleasant situations and essentially negative affective reactions to unpleasant situations; however, their accuracy in making finer discriminations within positive and negative affective reactions might be more limited.

The results of our two studies are consistent with Bullock & Russell's argument. Moreover, these findings extend the empirical support for that argument into the domain of children's estimates of how they themselves would feel in specified situations, whereas Bullock & Russell's own research was concerned purely with children's judgements of other people's facial expressions. Young children's understanding of the emotion domain appears to be organised by a distinction between *positive* and *negative* emotions. Their inability to make finer discriminations reliably within these two general categories leads them to make 'errors' on tasks requiring them to infer emotion from another person's facial expression, or to predict their own emotion in a specified situation. The relatively high levels of accuracy often observed in children with respect to 'happy' and 'sad' expressions or situations need to be interpreted cautiously in the light of evidence that these terms seem to be used in a more inclusive way by young children.

Children's knowledge of the causes and consequences of emotion

The research reviewed in the previous section is, of course, relevant to the issue of children's understanding of the causes of émotion, in that being able to identify the 'correct' emotion that a protagonist would feel in a specified set of circumstances requires an understanding of what kinds of events give rise to certain emotions. Other researchers have examined this issue more directly, for example by presenting children with a set of emotions and asking them to say what would lead them to experience these emotions. Another issue addressed by research reviewed here is children's understanding of the consequences of emotion.

Trabasso, Stein & Johnson (1981) told children aged between 36 and 54 months stories in which the protagonist experienced one of six emotions, three positive and three negative, and asked the children to think of a possible cause for the emotion or of a possible consequence. The results showed: (a) that most of the children's replies (72% for causes; 73% for consequences) were judged appropriate by adults; (b) that the replies relating to causes differed from those relating to consequences; (c) that the sorts of causes and consequences offered by children in connection with positive emotions differed from those they offered in connection with negative emotions; and (d) that there was much less differentiation of causes and consequences within the positive emotions (happy, excited, surprised) or the negative emotions (sad, angry, scared). Thus although children seemed to know that different kinds of events were associated with positive and negative emotions, there was quite a high degree of similarity of story content within the positive or negative emotions.

A similar type of study was conducted by Harris et al. (1987). These investigators presented children in England, the Netherlands and Nepal with several emotions and asked them to think of situations that would be likely to elicit each emotion. Just as in the Trabasso et al. (1981) findings, there was a clear differentiation between the perceived causes of positive (happy, excited, proud) and negative (sad, angry, afraid, shy) emotions, but less clear discrimination within these two categories. Only in older children was there evidence of subclusters of causes (e.g. for ashamed and guilty) within the larger clusters of positive or negative emotions.

Russell (1990) conducted a study in the same vein, in which children aged between 4 and 5 years were asked to tell stories about the causes or consequences of various emotions. In one version of the task, the emotions were presented to the children in verbal form only (as in the Trabasso et al. and Harris et al. studies); in another, the emotions were presented only in the form of facial expressions; in a third version, both verbal labels and facial expressions were used to convey the emotions. Children's responses were scored in each of two ways: they were judged by four adults for plausibility with respect to the target emotion, and they were also judged blind by one adult who rated their plausibility for each of the 12 possible conditions (six emotions by cause vs consequence) and also guessed which of the 12 possibilities had given rise to each story. Overall, 73.6% of the responses given by children were judged by adults to be correct. Greatest accuracy was achieved when the children had access to both verbal and facial cues (88%), followed by verbal cues alone (74%), and then facial cues alone (61%). The 5-year-olds' responses were more likely to be judged correct than those of the 4-year-olds (77% vs 71%). The children's causal stories were judged correct more often than their stories about consequences (81% vs 67%). One interesting point that emerged from the 'blind' plausibility ratings is that 40% of the children's responses were judged to be plausible responses to more than one of the 12 conditions. When these plausibility ratings were subjected to multi-dimensional scaling, two clear dimensions emerged: cause vs consequence and positive vs negative. Thus the overlaps in plausibility were almost entirely due to stories for causes or consequences being judged to be plausible responses to more than one positive or negative emotion.

These results are highly consistent with those of Trabasso *et al.* and Harris *et al.* (1987). Children make clear distinctions between the causes and consequences of emotions, and between the causes and consequences of positive vs negative emotions, but their stories about causes or consequences do not vary greatly within positive or negative emotions. However, one further aspect of Russell's findings suggests that this charac-terisation of children's understanding may underestimate their abilities. When the blind judge's 'best guesses' were compared with the eliciting emotion, a significant association was observed. The results are sum-marised in Table 10.4. Although there was a marked tendency for best guesses to correspond to the eliciting emotion, it is interesting to note that 52% of the 'excitement' stories and 49% of the 'surprise' stories were guessed to be responses to 'happy'; by contrast, only 18% of the 'anger'

Table 10.4 Differentiation among positive and negative emotions (adapted from Russell, 1990)

Stimulus emotion	Response judged					
	Happy	Excited	Surprised	Sad	Angry	Afraid
Happy	85	9	5	5	0	2
Excited	17	16	0	0	1	0
Surprised	38	14	26	8	3	9
Sad	10	0	0	75	14	8
Angry	4	1	0	19	80	4
Afraid	12	5	0	6	7	78

stories and 7% of the 'afraid' stories were guessed to be responses to 'sad'. These results suggest that children may be better able to discriminate between the causes or consequences of different negative emotions than other studies lead us to believe, for although the pattern of errors shows some confusion between 'sad', on the one hand, and 'angry' and 'afraid', on the other, the degree of confusion is less than one might anticipate on the basis of other research on this topic. It would be interesting to know whether there is a clear developmental trend for children's perceptions of the causes and consequences of emotions to become more differentiated within the general categories of positive and negative emotion.

THEORETICAL MODELS OF CHILDREN'S UNDERSTANDING OF EMOTION

Bullock & Russell (1986) have proposed a model of the development of children's conceptualisation of emotion that is consistent with much of the evidence reviewed in this chapter. They argue that young children begin by perceiving the emotions of others in terms of the dimensions of pleasantness and arousal:

> A variety of events in the child's world can be given meaning in terms of emotion: subjective experiences that the child undergoes, certain words spoken by caregivers, and facial and vocal expressions of the caregivers. Our proposal is that the child initially gives meaning to each such event in terms of pleasure and arousal. A subjective experience might be felt as pleasant and aroused; the caregiver's sad demeanor appears unpleasant and unaroused. This hypothesis does not deny that very young children discriminate and even categorize different emotions. What it does is specify the basis of discrimination and categorization as pleasure and arousal dimensions, rather than adultlike categories appropriately labeled anger, fear, and the like.
>
> (Bullock & Russell, 1986, p. 226)

According to this account, the 2- to 3-year-old's representation of emotion is relatively undifferentiated; as children grow older, their representations become increasingly differentiated, until they reach an adult-like taxonomy of emotional categories. The means by which the child proceeds from an undifferentiated to a differentiated representation of the emotion domain is, according to Bullock & Russell, through the learning of emotion 'scripts'. This is achieved by learning associations between context, facial expression, verbal utterances, subjective feelings and behavioural consequences:

> Children begin to associate expressions with the immediate contexts in which they occur. For example, the child notes the context in which a smile or frown occurs, notes that smiles or frowns go with certain tones of voice, notes that an unpleasant and aroused expression in the context of spilled milk is

different from the unpleasant and aroused expression in the context of soiled diapers or a cut finger. The child learns to associate pairs of elements. These two-element combinations are the basis of emotion scripts...

(Bullock & Russell, 1986 p. 228)

This learning process is facilitated by two factors. First, parents, teachers, older siblings and others tend to label certain events in terms of emotions. These events include the child's own experiences, as well as the experiences of others whom the child might observe. This classification process is likely to encourage the child to think of the elements of such events as being correlated. Second, the components of emotion scripts do, of course, tend to be correlated. Although emotion scripts do not always include the same features in the same sequence, there is sufficient invariance across episodes of, say, anger for it to be reasonable to assert that there is a core script for anger. This invariance will naturally assist the child's acquisition of the script.

Although Bullock & Russell's theoretical model provides a useful starting-point, it leaves many questions unanswered. First, exactly why and how is the young child's concept of emotion constrained by the two dimensions of pleasantness and arousal? Is the ability to make such discriminations innate or acquired? The literature on infants' responses to facial expressions of emotion suggests that the ability to extract meaning from facial expressions does not emerge until the age of 12 months or so, which certainly leaves open the possibility that discriminations in terms of pleasantness and arousal are learned. It needs to be remembered in this connection that the infant is exposed to a huge number of examples of facial expressions during the first year of life. In their observational research on mother–infant interaction, Malatesta & Haviland (1982) found that, on average, mothers of 3- to 6-month-old infants exhibit more than eight emotion-signal changes per minute. On this basis these investigators calculated that simply between the ages of 3 and 6 months the average infant is exposed to no fewer than 32 500 facial expressions of emotion.

A second issue that arises from Bullock & Russell's theoretical analysis concerns the elements of emotion scripts. It is one thing to argue that emotion knowledge takes the form of scripts, but quite another to be able to specify what these scripts need to contain in order for the child to be able to make adult-like discriminations.

The model advanced by Stein & Levine (1987, 1989) shows one way in which Bullock & Russell's analysis could be developed. These investigators propose a set of criteria in terms of which discriminations between emotional states are made. In common with other emotion theorists, they argue that emotions are closely related to goals and values. That is, emotions will be experienced when people detect some change in their ability to achieve a goal or maintain a valued state. What type of emotion is experienced will depend on the way in which the person evaluates the significance of the change.

According to Stein & Levine, the important difference between happiness, on the one hand, and sadness and anger, on the other, is in terms of the combination of goals and outcomes that result when the individual notices some change in ability to attain or maintain a valued state. Thus, 'happiness occurs when people are able to attain what they want or to avoid what they do not want' (Stein & Levine, 1989, p. 346). Anger and sadness, by contrast, are experienced when the person fails to attain or maintain a desired state or fails to avoid or leave an undesired state. Thus happiness can be distinguished from sadness and anger simply in terms of goal achievement, and the comparative simplicity of this distinction might be the basis for the early emergence of the child's ability to make accurate discriminations between positive and negative emotions. Two dimensions are necessary for making the distinction between sadness and anger, according to Stein & Levine: focus of attention once the goal failure has occurred, and inferences about the possibility of goal reinstatement. For anger to be experienced, the individual has to focus on the conditions that caused the goal failure, whereas sadness is experienced when the individual focuses on the implications or consequences of goal failure. Whether or not the individual needs to infer the intention to cause harm or simply to believe that an obstructed goal can be reinstated is a matter of dispute in the theoretical literature on the cognitive antecedents of emotion (Ortony, Clore & Collins, 1988; Oatley & Johnson-Laird, 1987). Either way, the greater complexity of the anger–sadness distinction helps to account for the greater difficulty that young children have in making a distinction between these states. The fact that 4-year-olds' attributions of anger to a protagonist in Stein & Levine's (1989) study were unrelated to their inferences of intent to harm, unlike those of 7-year-olds and college students, suggests that at this age children have not fully acquired the key components of the 'adult' anger script.

Although the above account has emphasised the potential for integrating Bullock & Russell's (1986) analysis with theoretical models, such as that of Stein & Levine (1987, 1989), that are rooted in the cognitive antecedents of emotional states, there is one point of difference between the two accounts that should not pass without comment. Whereas Bullock & Russell's analysis focuses principally on the links between a situation and an individual's emotional response, Stein & Levine's analysis focuses more on the relationship between an individual's values and goals and what happens in the situation. As Harris (1989) has observed, much of the evidence concerning children's understanding of emotion could be accounted for by assuming that children simply learn the associations between emotions and situational events, in a script-like sequence. However, if children's representations of emotion really do take the form of emotion scripts that are built up through learning the associations between experienced or observed emotions, situational antecedents and behavioural consequences, children's understanding of emotion would be limited by what they themselves had experienced either directly or vicariously. Harris argues that this would preclude children from understanding that two people could react to the same situation with different emotions because of their differing desires or beliefs, or that one person's emotional reactions could vary simply as a function of the correspondence between belief and reality. Yet there is evidence that children can do just this.

Harris *et al*. (1989) report three experiments in which children aged between 3 and 7 years were tested for their understanding of the impact of beliefs and desires on emotion. For example, in one experiment children were introduced to various toy animals and were told a story about each type of animal. The children were told that the animal wanted a snack or drink but liked only one type of food/drink, and not another (e.g. 'Ellie the Elephant wants a drink, but she only likes one type of drink and that is Coke. She doesn't like milk, she only likes Coke'). Then, unknown to this animal, a second animal, Mickey the Monkey, who was 'always playing tricks on the other animals', replaced the contents of a familiar container with the alternative drink or food (e.g. he emptied the can of Coke and refilled it with milk). For some children, the food or drink that was removed from the container was the animal's favourite food; for other children, the food or drink that was removed was the animal's disliked food or drink. The children were asked to predict and explain the animal's emotion both before opening the container and after discovering its contents. If children took account of the animal's beliefs and desires, they should predict different emotional reactions before and after opening the container. In other words, they should be able to discount their own knowledge of the contents and take account of the animal's mistaken belief before the container is opened. Perhaps unsurprisingly, children were accurate in predicting the animal's emotion on opening the container: 13 out of 16 4-year-olds, 13 out of 16 5-year-olds, and all 16 6-year-olds made the correct prediction in all four stories. This shows that even the youngest children are generally able to take account of another's desires in predicting how that person will respond emotionally. However, children did less well in predicting how the animal would feel *before* opening the container: 2 out of 16 4-year-olds, 7 out of 16 5-year-olds, and 9 out of 16 6-year-olds consistently took account of the animal's mistaken belief. When the justifications for their predictions were analysed, it was found that those children who predominantly made correct predictions were likely to refer to the *apparent*, rather than the real, contents of the container.

On the basis of these findings and those from their other experiments, Harris *et al*. (1989) concluded that children as young as 4 years old are able to deploy a theory-like conception of mind in predicting another's emotional reactions to events, in that they take account of that person's desires. Although children at this age are less good at taking account of another's false beliefs, at least some are able to do so, and the number who can steadily increases as a function of age. In accounting for these findings, Harris (1989) argues that predictions of someone else's emotions involve a two-step thought experiment: first, the goals or beliefs of that person are imagined, and second, one estimates one's own emotional reactions, given these goals and beliefs. The results of this thought experiment serve as the basis for predicting the other person's emotions. In the case of 3- or 4-year-olds, they are able to imagine someone keenly wanting a particular food or drink, and how they themselves would feel on obtaining a desired item. This helps them to predict how the other person would feel on getting a favourite food or drink. However, they apparently find it more difficult to imagine someone else having a mistaken belief about what food is in the container, and are therefore inclined to make predictions based on what is actually in the container. Older children are better able to imagine another's mistaken beliefs, and therefore make predictions based on how they themselves would feel if they entertained these mistaken beliefs. The predicted emotion therefore takes account of what the person expects to find, as opposed to what is actually in the container.

The research reported by Harris *et al.* (1989) suggests that children's representations of emotion include some awareness of the role played by beliefs and desires. This points to ways in which the emotion script proposed by Bullock & Russell (1986) needs to embrace more than the associations between elements such as situational antecedents, expressions, experiences and consequences. It would appear that children as young as 3 or 4 years are capable of taking into account their own and others' desires when thinking about emotional reactions. Of course, this is quite consistent with the apparent ease with which young children make distinctions between positive and negative emotions: positive emotions are those that result from desires being satisfied, while negative ones are those that result from desires remaining dissatisfied or being blocked. As they grow older, children are able to incorporate more sophisticated elements into their emotional scripts. One such element might be beliefs, especially mistaken beliefs. Other elements might be inferences about intent, or other attributions. Still others might be knowledge of how the event in question would relate to the goals and values of specific others, or to social norms. There is a clear and pressing need for further research that systematically maps the relationship between what children know about themselves, others and society, and the degree to which they are able to make discriminations between emotions in terms of facial (or other non-verbal) expressions, situational antecedents and consequences, and how they and others would react under hypothetical circumstances.

ACKNOWLEDGMENTS

I would like to thank Paul Harris, Jim Russell, Hugh Wagner, and the editors for their helpful comments on an earlier version of this chapter.

REFERENCES

Barden, R.C., Zelko, F.A., Duncan, S.W. and Masters, J.C. (1980). Children's consensual knowledge about the experiential determinants of emotion, *Journal of Personality and Social Psychology*, **39**, 968–976.

Barrera, M.E. and Maurer, D. (1981). The perception of facial expressions by the three-month-old, *Child Development*, **52**, 203–206.

Borke, H. (1971). Interpersonal perception of young children: egocentrism or empathy? *Developmental Psychology*, **5**, 263–269.

Bretherton, I. and Beeghly, M. (1982). Talking about internal states: the acquisition of an explicit theory of mind, *Developmental Psychology*, **18**, 906–921.

Bullock, M. and Russell, J.A. (1984). Preschool children's interpretation of facial expressions of emotion, *International Journal of Behavioral Development*, **7**, 193–214.

Bullock, M. and Russell, J.A. (1985). Further evidence on preschoolers' interpretations of facial expressions of emotion, *International Journal of Behavioral Development*, **8**, 15–38.

Bullock, M. and Russell, J.A. (1986). Concepts of emotion in developmental psychology. In C.E. Izard and P.B. Read (eds), *Measuring Emotions in Infants and Children, Vol. 2* (pp. 203–237). New York: Cambridge University Press.

Dunn, J., Kendrick, C. and MacNamee, R. (1981). The reaction of first-born children to the birth of a sibling: mother's reports, *Journal of Child Psychology and Psychiatry*, **22**, 1–18.

Felleman, E.S., Barden, R.C., Carlson, C.R., Rosenberg, L. and Masters, J.C. (1983). Children's and adults' recognition of spontaneous and posed emotional expressions in young children, *Developmental Psychology*, **19**, 405–413.

Field, T.M., Woodson, R., Greenberg, R. and Cohen, D. (1982). Discrimination and imitation of facial expression by neonates, *Science*, **218**, 179–181.

Field, T.M., Woodson, R., Cohen, D., Greenberg, R., Garcia, R. and Collins, K. (1983). Discrimination and imitation of facial expressions by term and preterm neonates, *Infant Behavior and Development*, **6**, 485–489.

Gates, G. (1923). An experimental study of the growth of social perception, *Journal of Educational Psychology*, **14**, 449–461.

Harrigan, J.A. (1984). The effects of task order on children's identification of facial expressions, *Motivation and Emotion*, **8**, 157–169.

Harris, P.L. (1989). *Children and Emotion: The Development of Psychological Understanding*. Oxford: Blackwell.

Harris, P.L., Olthof, T., Meerum Terwogt, M. and Hardman, C.E. (1987). Children's knowledge of the situations that provoke emotion, *International Journal of Behavioral Development*, **10**, 319–343.

Harris, P.L., Johnson, C.N., Hutton, D., Andrews, G. and Cooke, T. (1989). Young children's theory of mind and emotion, *Cognition and Emotion*, **3**, 379–400.

Izard, C.E. (1971). *The Face of Emotion*. New York: Appleton-Century-Crofts.

Kaitz, M., Mechulach-Sarfaty, O., Auerbach, J. and Eidelman, A. (1988). A reexamination of newborns' ability to imitate facial expressions, *Developmental Psychology*, **24**, 3–7.

LaBarbera, V.D., Izard, C.E., Vietze, P. and Parisi, S.A. (1976). Four- and six-month old infants' visual responses to joy, anger, and neutral expressions, *Child Development*, **47**, 535–538.

Malatesta, C.Z. and Haviland, J.M. (1982). Learning display rules: the socialization of emotion expression in infancy, *Child Development*, **53**, 991–1003.

Manstead, A.S.R., Anderson, K. and Bromley, J. (in preparation). Children's recognition of situations that evoke emotion. University of Manchester.

Nelson, C.A. (1985). The perception and recognition of facial expressions in infancy. In T.M. Field and N.A. Fox (eds), *Social Perception in Infants* (pp. 101–125). Norwood, New Jersey: Ablex.

Nelson, C.A. (1987). The recognition of facial expressions in the first two years of life: mechanisms of development, *Child Development*, **58**, 889–909.

Nelson, C.A. and Horowitz, F.D. (1983). The perception of facial expressions and stimulus motion by 2- and 5-month-old infants using holographic stimuli, *Child Development*, **54**, 868–877.

Oatley, K. and Johnson-Laird, P. (1987). Toward a cognitive theory of emotion, *Cognition and Emotion*, **1**, 29–50.

Odom, R.D. and Lemond, C.M. (1972). Developmental differences in the perception and production of facial expressions, *Child Development*, **43**, 359–369.

Ortony, A., Clore, G. and Collins, A. (1988). *The Cognitive Structure of Emotion*. New York: Cambridge University Press.

Russell, J.A. (1983). Pancultural aspects of human conceptual organization of emotions, *Journal of Personality and Social Psychology*, **45**, 1281–1288.

Russell, J.A. (1990). The preschooler's understanding of the causes and consequences of emotion, *Child Development*, **61**, 1872–1881.

Russell, J.A. and Bullock, M. (1985). Multidimensional scaling of emotional facial expressions: similarities from preschoolers to adults, *Journal of Personality and Social Psychology*, **48**, 1290–1298.

Russell, J.A. and Bullock, M. (1986a). On the meaning preschoolers attribute to facial expressions of emotion, *Developmental Psychology*, **22**, 97–102.

Russell, J.A. and Bullock, M. (1986b). Fuzzy concepts and the perception of emotion in facial expressions, *Social Cognition*, **4**, 309–341.

Russell, J.A. and Ridgeway, D. (1983). Dimensions underlying children's emotion concepts. *Developmental Psychology*, **19**, 795–804.

Schlosberg, H. (1952). The description of facial expressions in terms of two dimensions, *Journal of Experimental Psychology*, **44**, 229–237.

Sorce, J.F., Emde, R.N., Campos, J.J. and Klinnert, M.D. (1985). Maternal emotional signaling: its effects on the visual cliff behavior of 1-year-olds, *Developmental Psychology*, **21**, 195–200.

Stein, N.L. and Levine, L.J. (1987). Thinking about feelings: the development and organization of emotional knowledge. In R.E. Snow and M. Farr (eds), *Aptitude, Learning and Instruction: Cognition, Conation and Affect, Vol. 3* (pp. 165–198). Hillsdale, New Jersey: Lawrence Erlbaum.

Stein, N.L. and Levine, L.J. (1989). The causal organisation of emotional knowledge: a developmental study, *Cognition and Emotion*, **3**, 343–378.

Stifter, C.A. and Fox, N.A. (1987). Preschool children's ability to identify and label emotions, *Journal of Nonverbal Behavior*, **11**, 43–54.

Thompson, A.E. and Kieley, M. (1987). Children's differentiation of anger and sadness concepts. Unpublished manuscript, Harvard University.

Trabasso, T., Stein, N.L. and Johnson, L.R. (1981). Children's knowledge of events: a causal analysis of story structure. In G. Bower (ed.), *Learning and Motivation, Vol. 15* (pp. 237–282). New York: Academic Press.

Walker-Andrews, A.S. (1986). Intermodal perception of expressive behaviors: relation of eye and voice? *Developmental Psychology*, **22**, 373–377.

Young-Browne, G., Rosenfeld, H.M. and Horowitz, F.D. (1977). Infant discrimination of facial expression, *Child Development*, **48**, 555–562.

Zahn-Waxler, C. and Radke-Yarrow, M. (1982). The development of altruism: alternative research strategies. In N. Eisenberg-Berg (ed.), *The Development of Prosocial Behavior*. New York: Academic Press.

Zahn-Waxler, C., Radke-Yarrow, M. and King, R.A. (1979). Child rearing and children's prosocial dispositions towards victims of distress, *Child Development*, **50**, 319–330.

11 Metalinguistic Awareness: The Development of Children's Representations of Language

ELLEN BIALYSTOK
York University

The identification of a distinct aspect of development in which children become able to examine their knowledge about a domain, apart from their ability to use that knowledge in performance, can be traced to about the mid-1970s. The term 'meta' came to be applied to this aspect of knowledge development both in its general sense for cognitive operations, *meta-cognition*, and its specific application to domains of knowledge, in particular *metamemory* and *metalinguistic* awareness. In an important early reference, Flavell (1977) used the term 'meta' to describe the cognitive abilities of adolescents:

> Another way to conceptualize it is to say that formal operations constitute a kind of 'metathinking,' i.e., thinking about thinking itself rather than about objects of thinking. Children certainly are not wholly incapable of this and other forms of 'metacognition,' e.g., thinking about other psychological processes such as language, perception, and memory.
>
> (Flavell, 1977, p. 107)

Interestingly, Flavell was using the term in order to describe one of the important changes that occur with Piaget's formal operational thought. That is, the term was invoked as a means of explicating a notion that Piaget had already conceptualized but had expressed with a different terminology. Throughout the literature, there is a recurring, although sporadic, theme in which the emergence of metacognitive abilities is related in some manner to the development of Piagetian operational thought (Hakes, 1980; Van Kleeck, 1982). The similarities are compelling, but no direct evidence has yet linked the specific accomplishments that are called 'meta' to precise aspects of development from a Piagetian interpretation in a way that could serve as an explanation for either one.

The delineation of the proper domain for metacognition has always been somewhat contentious. The term itself has suffered from the vagaries of multiple definitions and the idiosyncrasies of interpretation by different

Systems of Representation in Children: Development and Use. Edited by C. Pratt and A.F. Garton
© 1993 John Wiley & Sons Ltd

researchers. Brown *et al.* (1983, p. 107) point to one important confusion in definition. They note that the term 'metacognition' has been used in the psychological literature to refer to both 'knowledge about cognition and regulation of cognition'. These two uses are virtually contradictory. The first use, knowledge about cognition, includes such properties as 'stable', 'stateable', 'fallible' and 'late' developing. None of these features is shared by the second use, regulation of cognition, even though the same term, metacognition, is applied to both.

Rather than signalling a contradiction, it may be that these two functions may reflect two different but equally essential components of the processing that determine the difference between cognition and metacognition. The first of these is the requirement for specific types of knowledge structures and the properties entailed by them. The second is the requirement for a degree of intentionality in cognitive processing. The possibility that these are two functionally distinct but equally important aspects of metacognitive processing is the basis for the discussion of metalinguistic awareness presented in this chapter.

The first aspect of metacognitive processing is emphasized by Brown *et al.* (1983) in their description of the knowledge basis upon which metacognition proceeds. This attention to knowledge structures has been a particular focus of study in the work on metamemory, such as that reported by Flavell & Wellman (1977). The tradition in this research is to ask children to describe their strategies for remembering and to encourage them to examine these strategies. In this way, children's knowledge of memory strategies is put forth as an object of study and discussed in much the same way as other factual knowledge is treated. This approach has obvious implications for strategy training.

Flavell (1977) finds theoretical origins for the second aspect of metacognition in Luria's (1959, 1961) description of the growth of self-regulation. Flavell (1977) asserts that 'the emergence of some capacity for voluntary self control is clearly one of the really central and significant cognitive-developmental hallmarks of the early childhood period' (p. 64). Although he traces the inception of this ability to early childhood, he is careful to point out that considerable development is necessary before the child has truly gained control over cognitive processes. Hence there is no contradiction with his claims, cited above, that metacognition is essentially an achievement of formal operational thought.

CONCEPTUALIZING METALINGUISTIC ABILITY

Investigations of children's metaknowledge of language formally pre-date the general study of metacognition. Nonetheless, the same definitional disputes that were apparent for metacognition echo throughout the investigations of this sub-area. One of the first references to metalinguistic awareness was made by Cazden (1974): 'The ability to make language forms opaque, and attend to them in and for themselves, is a special kind of language performance, one which makes special cognitive demands, and seems to be less easily and less universally acquired than the language performances of speaking and listening' (p. 29). Although Cazden signalled the ways in which metalinguistic uses of languages were to be differentiated from speaking and listening, she did not identify what was 'special' about the cognitive demands made by these language functions. A more detailed definition was offered by Tunmer & Herriman (1984): 'the ability to reflect upon and manipulate the structural features of spoken language, treating language itself as an object of thought, as opposed to simply using the language system to comprehend and produce sentences' (p. 12). Later in the same paper they define metalinguistic in the following way: 'the use of "control" processing to perform mental operations on the *products* of the mental mechanisms involved in sentence comprehension and production' (Tunmer & Herriman, 1984, p. 16). These are only three of a large number of definitions that have been proposed for metalinguistic awareness. Although they differ in many ways, these definitions consistently point to two features of metalinguistic awareness: the attention to language forms and the manipulation of linguistic units. These again correspond to the two aspects of metacognition identified by Brown *et al.* (1983).

One of the primary conflicts surrounding conceptualizations of metalinguistic ability is whether these skills are continuous with the linguistic skills involved in language comprehension and production (Clark, 1978) or mark a distinct departure from those skills (Hakes, 1980). Evidence for either side of this debate depends largely on what one agrees to consider as metalinguistic, but the controversy nonetheless signals a real theoretical opposition about the construct. The definitions largely leave unspecified the critical elements that could decide this issue. At what point is attention to language forms meta? What is the nature of manipulation of language that catapults performance into the meta domain? Definitions have generally not set explicit limits on these critical issues.

Ultimately, the issue of definition has probably been best handled operationally. A number of methodologies for assessing children's level of metalinguistic competence have been developed, refined and proven useful for exploring children's development. Most assessments of children's metalinguistic awareness have been confined to exploring only one aspect of linguistic structure. The primary divisions in this regard are phonological awareness, word awareness, syntactic awareness and pragmatic awareness.

Phonological awareness

Phonological awareness is defined by Nesdale, Herriman & Tunmer (1984, p. 56) as, 'the extent to which the young child can both segment the spoken word into its component phonological units and synthesize these units to produce a word'. Put this way, the skill appears not only fundamental to high-level linguistic processing but also to a variety of skills involved with oral uses of language. The assessment of children's ability to carry out phonological segmentation and integration tasks has included such activities as isolating phonemes in words and indicating their recognition of phonemic units in various ways. In some tasks, children have been asked to clap or tap to indicate the number of phonological units in a word (Liberman *et al.*, 1974). In other tasks, children are recursively instructed to 'say a little bit' of a word and then each successive unit that is produced until the child reaches some unsegmentable level (Fox & Routh, 1975). Calfee (1977) simplified this procedure of saying just a little bit of the word by modelling the answers for the child, telling them for example, 'If I say greet, you should say eat'. Kindergarten children did extremely well on these simple tasks, but it is not clear that they needed to understand anything about phonological units being investigated in order to succeed.

An interesting phonological awareness task is the phonemic oddity test, developed by Bryant & Bradley (Bradley & Bryant, 1983, Bryant & Bradley 1985). Children are presented with a series of three words. Two of the words are consistent with a phonological pattern while the third deviates from that pattern. The child's task is to identify the word that does not fit with the other two. The task is very difficult when the pattern is indicated by the medial sound (such as, pin, bin, *den*) or final sound (such as, bun, gun, *hut*) rather than by the initial one (such as bun, bud, *rug*). According to Bryant and his colleagues (Bradley & Bryant, 1983; Bryant & Goswami, 1987), phonological awareness, especially as measured by the oddity task, is causally related to children's progress in learning to read. By 4 years of age, children are quite successful in solving the oddity test, even though they are unable to tap correctly the number of sounds in a word until about 6 years of age.

Word awareness

Word awareness is the extent to which children can demonstrate that they understand that words are the primary meaning constituents of language and that they know about the properties of words. Bowey & Tunmer (1984) claim that 'fully developed word awareness would involve the following three components: awareness of the word as a unit of language, awareness of the word as an arbitrary phonological label (the word–referent distinction), and comprehension of the metalinguistic term word' (p. 73). These three conditions for word awareness do not emerge simultaneously but develop gradually as children become more sensitive to the structural properties of language.

Some of the earliest systematic studies of metalinguistic awareness were carried out on children's awareness of word. Children's performance on these word awareness problems is surprisingly weak. Although it is not surprising that children fail to provide adequate definitions for *word* (Berthoud-Papandropoulou, 1978), they fail as well to indicate that they understand that words are the primary unit of oral speech.

The basis of word awareness is the distinction between a word and its referent, and it is this understanding that has most eluded children. Papandropoulou & Sinclair (1974) report that when children were asked to produce a long word, they would provide 'train', a short word that names a long object. This separation between words and their referents is also the insight that allows children to solve Piaget's (1929) sun–moon problem in which children are asked about the names for celestial objects if the sun and the moon were to switch labels. These problems are not solved until children are about 6 or 7 years old.

A common method for measuring children's awareness of word and their ability to distinguish between words and their referents is to ask them to count the number of words in a sentence (Holden & McGinitie, 1972). Again, performance on these problems is typically poor until about 6 years, but task modifications can elicit reliable performance in children as early as 4 years of age (Bowey, 1988).

Syntactic awareness

Early studies used children's notions of sentence well-formedness, based primarily on word order constraints, to demonstrate that children were able to make decisions about the form of utterances as distinct from their meanings. In these early studies, children as young as $2\frac{1}{2}$ years old were able to make simple judgements of sentence acceptability with consistent accuracy (Gleitman, Gleitman & Shipley, 1972; de Villiers & de Villiers, 1972). The research by de Villiers & de Villiers, and subsequent research by Gleitman & Gleitman (1979), however, showed that children may have been responding to the semantic intentions in these sentences, accepting anything that they could interpret as a good sentence, rather than making judgements on the basis of grammatical well-formedness. In a larger study, Hakes (1980) showed the continuing improvement in children's judgements between the ages of 4 and 8 years. This improvement is attributable to the increasing degree to which children were able to base their judgements of acceptability on the form rather than semantic content. More stringent tests of notions of grammatical acceptability are obtained on correction tasks in which errors must not only be noted but also corrected. Bowey (1988) reports results from a series of studies of this type and sets higher limits on the criteria for determining that children have syntactic awareness.

Pragmatic awareness

This somewhat nebulous aspect of metalinguistic awareness captures a variety of abilities involved in children's awareness of the use of language in contexts. Pratt & Nesdale (1984) describe it as follows: 'pragmatic awareness is concerned with the awareness or knowledge one has about the relationships that obtain within the linguistic system itself ... and with the relationships that obtain between the linguistic system and the context in which the language is embedded' (p. 105).

One productive method for assessing children's pragmatic awareness has been through tasks in which children are expected to make judgements about the adequacy of specific messages for their interpretation by another child (Flavell *et al.*, 1981; Beal & Flavell, 1982; Markman, 1981). Another method is to elicit judgements from children concerning the degree of politeness of various utterances (Bates, 1976). Children's ability to solve these kinds of tasks generally emerges later than other aspects of linguistic awareness.

Obstacles of the integration of metalinguistic abilities

As most of the empirical studies of metalinguistic development in children have been confined to one of these varieties of language awareness, direct comparisons of their respective courses of development have been difficult. Differences in the timing of the appearance or the pattern of development for any one of these sub-areas of metalinguistic skill could be traced to a variety of methodological factors rather than to systematic differences among these abilities themselves. Nonetheless, attempts have been made to integrate the different accomplishments. Rozin & Gleitman (1977), for example, claim that there is a constant order of emergence for various metalinguistic abilities and that this order is determined by the level of representation needed for each. Phonological representation is the lowest and semantic-pragmatic representation is the highest on this scale. Further, deep representations are easier to access than surface representations because surface representations are less well processed. Hence, phonological aspects of language should be available for metalinguistic processing earlier than semantic or pragmatic ones. But with no way of equating the task difficulty of the instruments used to assess these aspects of linguistic awareness, the argument seems not only arbitrary, but counterintuitive. Nesdale & Tunmer (1984), in fact, suggest that pragmatic awareness might appear earlier than other types since the aspects of language with which it deals are more public and more commented upon. These pragmatic features include such formal manipulations as the speech adjustments made for the benefit of specific listeners or the deference made to specific social contexts.

In spite of these difficulties, the separation of metalinguistic awareness into these specific types of competencies has allowed descriptive attempts to advance. Within each type of language competence, there is a course of development through which the child is ultimately led to awareness of the system. The integration of these individual descriptions into a coherent model of metalinguistic competence has been considerably less successful than the advances made in understanding the discrete developments for each area. In fact, the need to account for the great diversity in the development of each area may have precluded the formation of more general descriptions. Yet, it would seem that a more general description is necessary to evaluate the construct of metalinguistic awareness and to decide if it adds theoretically to our understanding of children's language development.

Two confusions permeate the metalinguistic literature and prevent the emergence of such general descriptions. The first is a terminological confusion (that undoubtedly betrays a conceptual confusion) between metalinguistic task, metalinguistic awareness and metalinguistic skill. The second is a conceptual confusion (that is likely a territorial debate) between linguistic proficiency and metalinguistic proficiency. These confusions need to be clarified before a model of metalinguistic proficiency can be developed.

The term metalinguistic appears to be used interchangeably to describe tasks, skills and levels of awareness. When applied to tasks, certain uses of language, such as making repairs or judgements about well-formedness, are classified as being metalinguistic or not. A learner performing a task classified as metalinguistic is demonstrating metalinguistic ability (Clark, 1978). When the term is applied to skills, learners are considered to have demonstrated metalinguistic ability when they can focus on language forms irrespective of any particular task for assessing this skill. The term metalinguistic in this case is describing a singular processing ability determined by what information can be brought into attention irrespective of the task or of the learner's mental state (Lundberg, 1978). Applied to levels of awareness, virtually any performance can have metalinguistic properties if it is carried out with the deliberate control and awareness of the language learner. On this view, it is not sufficient merely to perform a metalinguistic task (such as repair), nor to have demonstrated an independent ability to focus on language forms, but performance must indicate as well that the learner is in a particular mental state, namely that the learner is aware of the forms and functions of the language being manipulated (Bowey, 1988).

These three applications are sometimes signalled by the different terms 'metalinguistic task', 'metalinguistic ability' and 'metalinguistic awareness'. The problem is that these terms are not used systematically to distinguish among the three applications, nor do they indicate which of the definitional features is being assumed. For this reason, little effort has been made to consider the possible relations among the uses of these terms. Rather, the terms have been applied loosely to the variety of behaviours and abilities described above but without systematic constraint on which one more closely described the intended meaning.

The second confusion is the identification of some valid, or at least reliable, criterion for deciding that language performance has transcended the realm of ordinary linguistic processing and become metalinguistic. This problem of setting some objective threshold applies to all three uses of the term, that is as a task, an ability, or a level of awareness. Although conversation is not normally considered to be a metalinguistic task, pausing to repair an utterance may make it so, but what about false starts and hesitations? The threshold of learner ability that signals passage into the sphere of the metalinguistic is equally slippery. This 'threshold' is particularly elusive because of differences in children's control over the different aspects of language: sound, word, etc. Has a child who has demonstrated phonemic awareness but not syntactic awareness provided sufficient evidence for metalinguistic ability? Finally, level of awareness as a criterion for determining the presence of metalinguistic awareness is a difficult construct. Awareness itself is practically impossible to define, let alone measure (see Allport, 1988). The relationship between awareness and metalinguistic functioning may well work in the direction opposite to the expected one: the act of bringing some aspect of structure into conscious awareness is in itself responsible for the development of metalinguistics awareness. In this way, it could not be used as a criterion for evidence of metalinguistic awareness.

The use of the term metalinguistic to describe developmental changes in children's language proficiency has, to say the least, been less than satisfactory. The description of children's emerging awareness of the phonological, segmentational, syntactic and pragmatic aspects of language is rich and interesting but difficult to interpret. This difficulty applies both to the attempt to relate the achievements to each other (e.g. Bowey, 1988; Hakes, 1980; Smith & Tager-Flusberg, 1982) and to relate metalinguistic awareness to such accomplishments as learning to read (for opposing views, see Ehri, 1979, and Bryant & Goswami, 1987). Children undoubtedly undergo significant changes in their conceptualization of language, and these changes undeniably include the emergence of explicit linguistic concepts. Yet theoretical descriptions of this transformation have left certain problems unanswered.

Dispersed throughout the various accounts in the literature are two parts of an explanation for children's growing ability to use language in these specialized ways. These two parts converge upon the two meanings for metacognition described above: the need for explicit formal knowledge and the need for intentionality and control. Some accounts are more committed to detailing the requirements for structural knowledge needed to solve metalinguistic problems. Gleitman & Gleitman (1979), for example, set out that portion of explicit knowledge of the principles of language that develops in childhood. On these views, important contributions to children's ability to solve metalinguistic problems are determined by children's knowledge of the forms and functions of language.

The second part of the explanation is the need for children to gain control over their solutions to problems. Hakes makes the point most explicitly:

> Both metalinguistic and concrete operational development involve an increasing ability to control the course of one's own thought. The change is from a relatively automatic, relatively spontaneous application of the sorts of heuristic strategies available early to a more controlled, more deliberate choice between those processes and others that are available *only* by choice
>
> (Hakes, 1980, p. 39)

Bowey (1988) and Clark (1978) also stress that constructs similar to intentional control are the determining feature of metalinguistic performance. Both of these aspects of children's performance in solving metalinguistic problems, namely availability of language forms and structures, and ability to choose among processing options, must enter into an explanation of how children become able to solve metalinguistic problems.

LANGUAGE PROCESSING AND METALINGUISTIC SKILLS

This section outlines a framework for explaining the emergence of children's ability to solve metalinguistic problems. The premise is that metalinguistic awareness is continuous with children's developing language proficiency. The central concept in explaining this development of children's language abilities from conversational up to metalinguistic uses is representational change. Changes in children's representation of language throughout childhood allow children to use language in more complex and more specialized ways. The notion of representational change as a mechanism for development has been explicated by Karmiloff-Smith (1986) to explain the way in which representations evolve to support increasingly complex performance in language and thought. Following this view, metalinguistic awareness must be explained within a dynamic model that includes the representational and organizational processes that are responsible for language acquisition from the point of ordinary comprehension and production.

The contribution of the term 'meta' to descriptions of language proficiency is that it promotes the notion of differentiated representation. This differentiation of general language proficiency should be: (a) process-dependent, that is, explained in terms of ongoing cognitive processes, and (b) functionally motivated, that is, allows children to solve specific problems or to use language in unique ways.

Language proficiency is conceptualized as emerging from the development of two related but functionally independent processing components. These are called *analysis of representational structures* and *control of attentional processing*. Each component is specialized for a different aspect of processing and each develops in response to different experiences. Metalinguistic functioning requires high levels for one or both of these components. Meta, on this view, describes a level of processing (metalinguistics ability) that presupposes certain qualities of the representation (metalinguistic awareness) and allows the learner to solve certain types of problems (metalinguistic task). A description of any one of these features in the absence of the others gives the limited and false impression that 'meta' is the sole property of one aspect of this complex interaction.

These two processing components reflect the two aspects of meta-cognition mentioned earlier. They find expression as well in a variety of conceptions of metalinguistic awareness. In different interpretations, one or the other, and sometimes both, are stressed, but rarely are these two aspects of metalinguistic functioning made explicit. The central point in conceptualizing metalinguistic awareness as a distinct achievement is to create the possibility for the joint examination of these two processing components. Nonetheless, these same components are involved in a range of language uses and are not specific to metalinguistic ones. In fact, the only factor which differentiates their involvement in metalinguistic uses from their involvement in ordinary language comprehension and production is that somewhat higher values or more sophisticated levels are required to function in metalinguistic situations. But these are higher values of the *same* processing components. Processing is no different for metalinguistic tasks than for ordinary language uses.

Language proficiency involves other processes as well, such as the 'fast processes' described by Jackendoff (1987). These are not considered here because they are essentially inaccessible to study and impervious to development. The distinction between fast processes and slower processes (there seems not to be a good name for these) is most useful as a means of distinguishing between encapsulated modular processes (fast) and general central processes (slow) (Fodor, 1983; Jackendoff, 1987). Following from this distinction, metalinguistic functioning would be under the jurisdiction of the central processor. It is, by its nature, a deliberate and intentional operation applied to language.

It may even be possible in principle to reject the distinction between modular and central processes and include an explanation for the fast processes in the same model as the slow (central) ones. This would be the strong assertion of the hypothesized continuity between metalinguistic processes and ordinary linguistic ones. On this strong view, the general central processes that are at issue in the current description are the same ones that characterize functioning in the fast processes as well, perhaps in modular systems. Jackendoff (1987) sets up the logic for this view but rejects the conclusion. He argues that in his highly differentiated system (much more finely segmented than that of Fodor) the *same* operations exist across modules but are instantiated differently. The same argument could apply to the distinction between modular and central processes: the same operations would define processing of both types but their instantiation as either a central or fast process would produce superficial differences in their functioning. Such an interpretation would challenge the need for a distinction between central and modular processes.

Analysis of representational structures

The need for a processing component for analysis is based on the view that children's representations of knowledge undergo significant and systematic change. Some theorists, such as Keil (1983) and Chi (1981), attribute the bulk of cognitive growth to quantitative increases in the knowledge base. Others, such as Carey (1985), consider that changes in the organization of that knowledge are a more profound factor in cognitive growth than are the incremental changes in how much is known. It seems that both positions are correct in that each of these aspects of growth contributes substantially to cognitive development.

On the present view, qualitative changes in representation are considered to be fundamental to the development of proficiency. The same knowledge at different points in development can support different kinds of performance because that knowledge is represented differently in the mind of the child. Differences in level of proficiency are attributable in part to qualitative differences in the form in which the relevant knowledge is represented. Specifically, different levels of analysis, or explicitness, of the representations allow that knowledge to be used for different purposes, and these organizational changes are revealed in different kinds of performance the child is capable of achieving.

Analysis is defined as the process of restructuring and recoding conceptual representations organized at the level of meanings (knowledge of the world) into explicit representations of structure organized at the level of symbols. The higher-order symbolic representations differ from conceptual representations in that they: (1) are organized around a different set of categories, i.e. formal symbolic categories, (2) contain explicit information about the structure of those categories, and (3) are less dependent upon contexts and therefore more general and transferable concepts. The effect of these characteristics is that analysed representations are abstract general structures that can be translated into other symbol systems.

Consider these three characteristics in turn. The assumption in the first point is that the process of analysis involves reorganizing the child's knowledge to conform with the categories designated by specific symbol systems. In language, these categories are primarily based on the units of the linguistic system, such as words, sounds and letters. Classes of words can also serve as organizing units. Karmiloff-Smith (1986) describes the process by which children learning French as a first language originally have separate representations for each instantiation of the determiners, *un* and *une*. Their knowledge of these words is known only in the context of a procedure for producing utterances that links each to certain nouns: *un couteau, une chaise*. In these contexts the meaning of the determiner is ambiguous as it means both *a* and *one*. Through the process of redescription, these discrete terms are collected from their individual contexts of use and are organized into a single category, in this case the linguistic category of determiners. Before that reorganization, commonalities between these terms were not part of the child's knowledge of *un* and *une*.

The second characteristic of analysed representations is that the structure of the knowledge is explicit with the meaning. This explicitness of structure allows the child to attend to either one of these features—they are both available. Most metalinguistic tasks are assessments of the child's ability to indicate control over precisely this feature of representation. In many grammaticality judgement tasks, sentences must be judged for their well-formedness even though the sentence itself conveys some coherent meaning. Children's ability to make these judgements depends upon their having representations for the sentence forms along with the representations they can construct for those meanings. Similarly, such metalinguistic tasks as counting the number of words in sentences requires that the formal structure of the sentence be accessible to child along with its meaning.

Third, analysed representations can represent the contextually bound information of a conceptual representation in different symbol systems. Spatial knowledge about location, for example, can be represented in language by means of the spatial lexicon, in maps by means of the conventions of scale and perspective for signifying location, and in number by means of quantifying expressions for relative distances and sizes. Each symbol system has its own structure, its own constraints and, to some extent, its own meanings that it can encode. Through the process of analysis, symbolic representations can be built up in each of these systems as a formal means of representing a domain of knowledge. Because formal representations are abstract, they can be compared across domains. Research addressing the way in which children develop the ability to represent symbolic information in other domains using different symbol systems such as maps (Liben & Downs, 1989) and number (Durkin, Chapter 8; Fuson, 1988) has produced results that are compatible with the notion of analysis and the observations regarding the course of analysis for linguistic representations.

Children's analysis of linguistic representations evolve through a series of three stages that are more or less distinct. I call these stages 'conceptual representation', 'formal representation' and 'symbolic representation'. These levels differ by incrementally changing their value on a dimension of contextual-dependency, with conceptual representation being contextually dependent and symbolic representation being contextually independent.

Conceptual representation is the encoding of the world of meanings in the absence of knowledge of language structure. Although young children can speak in grammatically well-formed utterances and make acceptability judgements about formal aspects of language, there is no evidence that children have explicit concepts for these structures. Children's use of language in early conversations, rather, is largely based on routine chunks or patterns (Bowerman, 1982) that are used as procedures (Karmiloff-Smith, 1986). As Macnamara (1972) argued long ago, it is possible for children to understand the speech addressed to them on the basis of context without the need for employing formal linguistic knowledge to interpret utterances. Indeed, the rules of that formal system undoubtedly surpass their comprehension capacity. Within this view, there are different possibilities for the status of formal language rules. For Karmiloff-Smith, they are represented but are embedded as part of a procedure for production or comprehension. Children have access only to the procedure. For Macnamara, they are not represented at all but are worked out later.

Formal representations are the explicit codings of language structure. These representations include the identification of the units of language: word, sound, sentence. At about 4 or 5 years of age, children can identify sounds in words, segment sentences into words if concrete supporting materials are supplied, and decide that a sentence violates some structural rule. In real terms, this last decision may constitute little more than a matching judgement between a heard sentence and some known pattern. Children who can solve these tasks have explicit concepts of sound, word and sentence, although the boundaries on these concepts are fuzzy and errors are made. Children with only conceptual representations for language are unable to solve any of these tasks and in some cases the instructions do not even make sense. Younger children cannot even understand the separation between words and their references, so answering questions about the properties of words as opposed to the properties of their referents is impossible. The striking example of this is the result by Papandropoulou & Sinclair (1974) in which children provided 'train' as an example of a long word. The questions used in word awareness tests typically require that the child has represented language in terms of formal categories.

Symbolic representations are abstractions from that formal system based on the explicit symbolic coding of selected features, attributes and functions. At this level, what is represented is a set of symbols that *refer to* or *stand for* concepts represented at the level of meanings. The feature that distinguishes symbolic representation from formal representation is that it is relational. Once children have explicated the formal properties of language and represented these as meaningful structures, they must still learn about the relations that connect the language system to meanings. When letters, sounds and words are represented formally (the second level of representation), they are understood as objects. Letters can be written because they have particular visual and phonological properties: the letter *b* has a certain shape and makes the sound *buh*. This is comparable to knowledge of objects: dogs have four legs and make the sound *bow-wow*. When letters, sounds and words are represented symbolically (the third level of representation), they are understood as symbols with no meaning of their own whose function is to signify a meaning. Symbolic representation is organized around the relation *stands for*: the letter b *stands for* the sound *buh*. Children can learn to read only when written language has moved from formal representation to symbolic representation (Bialystok, 1991a).

This view of representation, in which changes in form reflect increases in abstractness, converges with a number of discussions in the literature on the development of children's representations of knowledge. Mandler (1983) distinguishes between two senses in which representation is used in the developmental literature. First is the meaning in which representation refers to the structure and organization of knowledge. Second is the sense in which representation involves the use of symbols. Words and artifacts are symbols that stand for concepts. Representation in this sense must address the problem of the relation between the mental symbol and its referent. These two senses refer to ordered levels of representation in the present framework. Although the symbolic form is developmentally more advanced, all three remain viable representational structures. Metalinguistic tests usually require representation minimally at the second level, that of formal structure.

Control of attentional processing

The second processing component is the selective attention directed to different representations or different aspects of a representation as language is used in real time. This processing component becomes most apparent when language contains conflict or ambiguity. In these cases, two or more representations may be constructed, each of which bears some relation to the task. The correct solution, however, requires attending to only one of these possible representations. Attending to the competing representation may either simply slow down the process of understanding or using the language, or sometimes mislead the child to an incorrect solution. Selective attention, then, is the process by which relevant representations are constructed and made available to the child.

The real time constraint on the operation of control of processing makes the functioning of this component the basis for the emergent phenomenon of fluency or automaticity. If less attention is needed in a language task, then the solution appears to emerge with greater fluency or automaticity. Tasks that can be executed fluently, then, should be those in which conflict and ambiguity are minimal. The claim here is that the process is exactly the same, but when language use is effectively carried out within real time constraints because the attention requires less effort, the phenomenal interpretation is that the process is carried out automatically or fluently.

Most language uses present some degree of ambiguity. Even the simple act of carrying on a conversation provides the speaker with at least two alternative signals to which attention can be paid: the use and structure of the formal symbol system and the set of meanings that symbol system has been invoked to represent. These alternatives are scarcely noticed in conversational uses of language since the meaning is so clearly the relevant level of representation for language comprehension and production. Other uses of language, however, demand different degrees of attention to these two aspects.

The competition for attention in language processing takes two forms. The simplest case is the need to pay differential attention to aspects of the linguistic representation that is being constructed during some language use. The more difficult case is a conflict between two different types of representations that are relevant, each of which bears some relevance to the situation. This conflict may involve linguistic and non-linguistic representations.

Choosing between aspects of a linguistic representation—the first type of competition—may involve the choice between attending more carefully to forms or to meanings, to phonology or to syntax, etc. Different uses of language place different values on the relative importance of these linguistic features. Reading demands considerably more attention to normal features of language than does conversation, and metalinguistic tasks are notorious for the formal detail they frequently require for their solution. But all of these features are linguistic. As children's level of analysis of linguistic representation increases towards more formal representation, these structural features become available for inspection.

Some tasks require that the child choose between two representations constructed at entirely different levels of analysis, such as a conceptual and a symbolic representation. This is the second type of competition. Both may be true descriptions but only one will lead to the correct solution. Syllogisms are an example of this type of problem. Scribner & Cole (1981) showed that non-literate adults in Liberia were unable to solve syllogisms of the following type: 'All the women in Monrovia are married. Kemu lives in Monrovia. Is Kemu married?'. A conceptual representation of the information in this syllogism encodes the meanings, and the solution to the question is an empirical one: 'I don't know Kemu so I don't know if she is married'. A symbolic representation of the syllogism includes the formal logical structure of the problem. The solution that follows from this representation is that 'Kemu is married'. Literate subjects in the study by Scribner & Cole were able to provide this formal answer. The solution requires selective attention. Both the conceptual and the symbolic representations are correct from a particular perspective, but the designated correct solution requires attending to only one of these.

The three-mountain task is another example of a problem that requires a great deal of selective attention. Contrary to the early claims made by Piaget & Inhelder (1956), children indeed realize that the doll sees something different from the child (see Newcombe, 1989, for review). The child must decide, however, which legitimate representation that can be constructed for the display will provide the correct solution to the problem: do I pay attention to the representation that is correct from my own point of view or to an alternative representation that is correct from the observer's point of view? Both are correct representations of the display, but the problem requires choosing the one that is correct for the question asked. Since it is considerably more difficult to construct the representation from the observers's point of view, children may settle for their own.

Jackendoff (1987) presents a model which assigns a central role to a processing construct similar to the control component of the present framework. The problem to be explained for cognition, Jackendoff argues, is consciousness: what is available to consciousness and what are the descriptive properties of conscious awareness? To this end, he distinguishes consciousness from attention. Attention is high-level processing, phenomenally, what we pay attention to in carrying out activities, cognitive or physical, and what we need less of when we become more skilled in an activity. Skilled performers in all these activities need to pay less attention to the representations as their implementation requires less high-level processing.

Jackendoff (1987) identifies two separate functions for attention—the selection function and the directing function. The selection function selects relevant structures from long-term memory and calls them up for active processing in the solution to a problem. The directing function 'is responsible for choosing which portions of the designated set of representations are to be subjected to high-intensity processing. Thus one may conceive of the selection function and the direction of attention as successively narrowing the domain to which attention can apply' (p. 282). These two functions for attention correspond to the two levels of choice described above for control: selecting the relevant representation and selecting aspects of a particular representation that are relevant to the solution. Defined this way, metalinguistic tasks generally require high levels of selective attention.

META IS A FOUR-LETTER WORD: IS THE CONCEPT NECESSARY?

The mechanism for language processing given by this framework is a system in which two complementary components are invoked. These components are responsible for the analysis of the representation and for the control of attention to relevant aspects of a representation or to competing representations. Different types of language use, e.g. having a conversation, reading, writing, are solved by different levels of involvement for these components. Some activities, such as conversation, require relatively low levels of mastery for both components, while others, such as writing or solving metalinguistic problems, make considerably higher demands on one or both processing components. Language proficiency is demonstrated when the task demands for levels of analysis and levels of control do not exceed the language user's level of mastery of those processing components.

The main point is that the processing components that are responsible for solving metalinguistic tasks are *the same* ones that bear responsibility for other types of language processing as well. In this case, is a separate concept of metalinguistic ability necessary? Metalinguistic tasks typically require high levels of the components for their solution, but these levels are attained gradually: children increasingly develop competence with both component processes, although the specific experiences that nurture the growth of each are undoubtedly different. In this sense, the ability to solve metalinguistic tasks emerges gradually out of children's established proficiency for speaking and understanding language. Therefore it may be asked if the construct 'metalinguistic' serves any useful function.

One possible benefit of this view that indirectly justifies the use of metalinguistics as a distinct construct is in the precision that can be added to both descriptions of language tasks and descriptions of children's abilities. First, for language tasks, the implication is that metalinguistic tasks should be scalable according to their individual demands for analysis and control. If metalinguistic tasks differ in these ways, it should be possible to determine a matrix of difficulty for a variety of tasks. Such an analysis should override classification based on content, such as phonemic awareness, word awareness, syntactic awareness and the like. If content-based distinctions turn out to be differentially difficult, the explanation for that difference should be in the level of processes needed to solve the task used to assess that ability and not inherent in the content itself.

Evidence in support of the claim that the relation among metalinguistic tasks is based on their reliance upon levels of processing for analysis and control rather than their reliance upon specific content is provided through correlational and regression analyses of children solving batteries of metalinguistics tasks. By analysing the demands of each task for its dependence upon high levels of analysis or control, correlational matrices show patterns of correspondence among different tasks that make the same processing demands, irrespective of content, but not among tasks that differ in their processing demands, even if the content and task method are essentially the same (Bialystok, 1988b).

An example of a distribution of metalinguistic tasks according to the demands for analysis and control is presented in Figure 11.1. The placement of metalinguistic tasks in this matrix takes increasing levels of analysis and control required for the solution to specific tasks to be indicated by higher values along the x and y axes respectively. There is no scale to quantify the changes as the intention is only to express relative values of the two components in order to compare the processing demands of pairs of metalinguistic tasks.

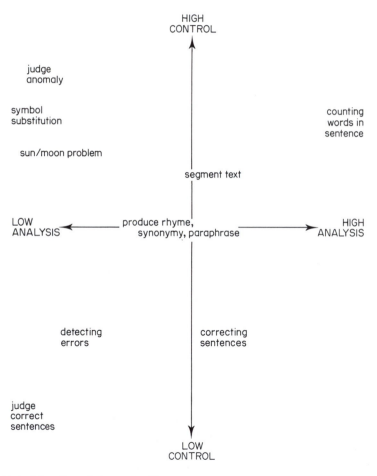

Figure 11.1 Metalinguistic uses of language

The tasks positioned in the matrix cross the boundaries that distinguish them by content. Judging sentence acceptability is traditionally a test of syntactic awareness. Producing rhyme is a test of phonological awareness. Counting the number of words in a sentence is typically classified among tests of word awareness. These tasks have all been used in different contexts to assess aspects of metalinguistic skill, but when compared directly, the correspondences are construed as processing similarities rather than content-determined classifications. A more detailed description of these relative placements and the empirical evidence that supports those positions is provided elsewhere (Bialystok, 1991b). Findings such as these challenge the utility of descriptions that classify metalinguistic skills according to content-determined sub-areas.

The second implication of the present view is that children's ability to solve specific language tasks may be predicted and described more precisely. Children may be expected to solve those problems for which they have mastered requisite levels of skill in the necessary processing components. This approach resolves the conflict between considering metalinguistic as a problem type (metalinguistic task), as an ability (metalinguistic skill), or as a description of consciousness (metalinguistic awareness). The conception is interactive: metalinguistic refers to the level of functioning at which children's mastery of analysis of linguistic representations and selective control of linguistic processing permits them to solve tasks containing certain characteristic features. Typically, the problems are *about* language (metalinguistic task criterion), and the solution frequently demands attention to the formal structure of the system (metalinguistic ability criterion). This approach provides a more precise means of describing an aspect of language proficiency.

Evidence for this claim depends on demonstrating that children with specific levels of skill in the component processes of analysis and control can solve linguistic problems that have been gauged to require that level of skill. Thus, children whose linguistic representations have achieved high levels of analysis should be more able to solve problems requiring explicit knowledge of structure than children whose linguistic representations are less well analysed. Similarly, children for whom attentional control strategies are well developed should perform better than children who are less able to control attention on tasks that are especially demanding on this processing component.

One way of testing these predictions has been to use between-group methods (Bialystok, 1986, 1988a). Analysis of linguistic representations is promoted, among other things, by the child's experience with literacy. Comparing children at different literacy levels provides a rough indication of how changes in analysis affect the ability to solve problems, especially if these metalinguistic problems are presented orally. Control of processing is promoted, among other things, by bilingualism. Comparing monolingual and bilingual children provides a rough indication of how changes in control affect the child's ability to solve metalinguistic problems. These comparisons showed advantages for children at higher levels of literacy in solving metalinguistic tasks based on high demands for analysis of linguistic knowledge, and advantages for bilingual children in solving metalinguistic tasks based on high demands for control of processing.

In spite of modest advances in descriptive precision, it still might be argued that this attempt to describe metalinguistic functioning as being continuous with other forms of language processing obviates the need for the construct. It may be that metalinguistic functioning is an optional extension of children's language proficiency that serves no particular purpose. Certainly if the achievement is to be explained within the same terms as other facets of language proficiency there is no theoretical advantage to distinguishing this as an important or separate accomplishment. No special processes are involved or developed, and no distinctive operations are established. The construct, then, adds more confusion than clarification to our understanding of children's language abilities.

But that view would be a misinterpretation of the significance of these processing components and the achievement that children have attained when they can solve metalinguistic tasks. The fact that children become able to represent information in forms that are formal and relational abstractions of information that they knew in another context and that they become able to control attentional resources in response to changes in task demands are significant accomplishments. These achievements are manifested in language proficiency when children become able to solve metalinguistic problems, but the implications of these abilities are far greater. The kinds of processing that underlie children's metalinguistic functioning are precisely the skills that are central to intelligent thought. When children can function metalinguistically, they not only understand that *meta* is a four-letter word, they also understand something about the way in which information is conveyed in a literate world.

REFERENCES

Allport, A. (1988). What concept of consciousness? In A.J. Marcel & E. Bisiach (eds), *Consciousness in Contemporary Science*. Oxford: Oxford University Press.

Bates, E. (1976). *Language and Context: The Acquisition of Pragmatics*. New York: Academic Press.

Beal, C.R. and Flavell, J.H. (1982). The effect of increasing the salience of message ambiguities on kindergarteners' evaluations of communicative success and message adequacy, *Developmental Psychology*, **18**, 43–48.

Berthoud-Papandropoulou, I. (1978). An experimental study of children's ideas about language. In A. Sinclair, R.J. Javella and W.J.M. Levelt (eds), *The Child's Conception of Language*. Berlin: Springer-Verlag.

Bialystok, E. (1986). Factors in the growth of linguistic awareness, *Child Development*, **57**, 498–510.

Bialystok, E. (1988a). Levels of bilingualism and levels of linguistic awareness, *Developmental Psychology*, **24**, 560–567.

Bialystok, E. (1988b). Aspects of linguistic awareness in reading comprehension, *Applied Psycholinguistics*, **9**, 123–139.

Bialystok, E. (1991a). Letters, sounds, and symbols: changes in children's understanding of written language, *Applied Psycholinguistics*, **12**, 75–89.

Bialystok, E. (1991b). Metalinguistic dimensions of bilingual proficiency. In E. Bialystok (ed.), *Language Processing in Bilingual Children*. London: Cambridge University Press.

Bowerman, M. (1982). Starting to talk worse: clues to language acquisition from children's late speech errors. In S. Strauss (ed.), *U-shaped Behaviour Growth*. New York: Academic Press.

Bowey, J.A. (1988). *Metalinguistic Functioning in Children*. Geelong, Australia: Deakin University Press.

Bowey, J.A. and Tunmer, W.E. (1984). Word awareness in children. In W.E. Tunmer, C. Pratt and M.L. Herriman (eds), *Metalinguistic Awareness in Children: Theory, Research, and Implications*. Berlin: Springer-Verlag.

Bradley, L. and Bryant, P.E. (1983). Categorising sounds and learning to read—a causal connection, *Nature*, **39**, 419–421.

Brown, A., Bransford, J., Ferrara, R. and Campione, J. (1983). Learning, remembering, and understanding. In P. Mussen (series ed.), J.H. Flavell and E. Markman (vol. eds), *Handbook of Child Psychology, Vol. 3: Cognitive Development* (pp. 77–166). New York: Wiley.

Bryant, P.E. and Bradley, L. (1985). *Children's Reading Problems*. Oxford: Basil Blackwell.

Bryant, P.E. and Goswami, U. (1987). Phonological awareness and learning to read. In J.R. Beech and A.M. Colley (eds), *Cognitive Approaches to Reading*. New York: Wiley.

Calfee, R.C. (1977). Assessment of independent reading skills: basic research and practical applications. In A.S. Reber and D.L. Scarborough (eds), *Toward a Psychology of Reading*. Hillsdale, New Jersey: Lawrence Erlbaum.

Carey, S. (1985). *Conceptual Change in Childhood*. Cambridge, Massachusetts: MIT Press.

Cazden, C.R. (1974). Play with language and metalinguistic awareness: one dimension of language experience, *The Urban Review*, **7**, 28–39.

Chi, M.T.H. (1981). Knowledge development and memory performance. In M. Friedman, J.P. Das and N. O'Connor (eds), *Intelligence and Learning*. New York: Plenum Press.

Clark, E.V. (1978). Awareness of language: some evidence from what children say and do. In A. Sinclair, R.J. Jarvella and W.J.M. Levelt (eds), *The Child's Conception of Language*. Berlin: Springer-Verlag.

De Villiers, P.A. and de Villiers, J.G. (1972). Early judgements of semantic acceptability by children, *Journal of Psycholinguistic Research*, **1**, 290–310.

Ehri, L. (1979). Linguistic insight: threshold of reading acquisition. In T.G. Waller and G.E. MacKinnon (eds), *Reading Research: Advances in Theory and Practice*. New York: Academic Press.

Flavell, J.H. (1977). *Cognitive Development*. Englewood Cliffs, New Jersey: Prentice-Hall.

Flavell, J.H. and Wellman, H.M. (1977). Metamemory. In R.V. Kail Jr, and J.W. Hagen (eds), *Perspectives on the Development of Memory and Cognition*. Hillsdale, New Jersey: Lawrence Erlbaum.

Flavell, J.H., Speer, J.R., Green, F.L. and August, D.L. (1981). The development of comprehension monitoring and knowledge about communication, *Monographs of the Society for Research in Child Development*, **46**.

Fodor, J. (1983). *Modularity of Mind*. Cambridge, Massachusetts: MIT Press.

Fox, F. and Routh, D.K. (1975). Analysing spoken language into words, syllables, and phonemes: a developmental study, *Journal of Psycholinguistic Research*, **9**, 115–119.

Fuson, K. (1988). *Children's Counting and Concepts of Number*. New York: Springer-Verlag.

Gleitman, L.R. and Gleitman, H. (1979). Language use and language judgment. In C.F. Fillmore, D. Kempler and W.S.-Y. Wang (eds), *Individual Differences in Language Ability and Language Behavior*. New York: Academic Press.

Gleitman, L.R., Gleitman, H. and Shipley, E.F. (1972). The emergence of the child as grammarian, *Cognition*, **1**, 137–164.

Hakes, D. (1980). *The Development of Metalinguistic Abilities in Children*. New York: Springer-Verlag.

Holden, M.H. and McGinitie, W.H. (1972). Children's conceptions of word boundaries in speech and in print, *Journal of Educational Psychology*, **63**, 551–557.

Jackendoff, R. (1987). *Consciousness and the Computational Mind*. New York: Academic Press.

Karmiloff-Smith, A. (1986). From metaprocess to conscious access: evidence from children's metalinguistic and repair data, *Cognition*, **28**, 95–147.

Keil, F. (1983). On the emergence of semantic and conceptual distinctions, *Journal of Experimental Psychology: General*, **112**, 357–385.

Liben, L.S. and Downs, R.M. (1989). Understanding maps as symbols: the development of map concepts in children. In H. Reese (ed.), *Advances in Child Development and Behavior*, **22**, 146–201.

Liberman, I.Y., Shankweiler, D., Fischer, F.W. and Carter, B. (1974). Explicit syllable and phoneme segmentation in the young child, *Journal of Experimental Child Psychology*, **18**, 201–212.

Lundberg, I. (1978). Aspects of linguistic awareness related to reading. In A. Sinclair, R.J. Jarvella and W.J.M. Levelt (eds), *The Child's Conception of Language*. New York: Springer-Verlag.

Luria, A.R. (1959). *Speech and the Development of Mental Processes in the Child: An Experimental Investigation*. (J. Simon, ed.), London: Staples Press.

Luria, A. (1961). *The Role of Speech in the Regulation of Normal and Abnormal Behavior* (J. Tizard ed.). New York: Liveright.

Macnamara, J. (1972). The cognitive basis of language learning in infants, *Psychological Review*, **79**, 1–13.

Mandler, J.M. (1983). Representation. In J.H. Flavell and E.M. Markman (eds), *Handbook of Child Psychology, Vol. III: Cognitive Development*. New York: Wiley.

Markman, E. (1981). Comprehension monitoring. In W.P. Dickson (ed.), *Children's Oral Communication Skills*. New York: Academic Press.

Nesdale, A.R. and Tunmer, W.E. (1984). The development of metalinguistic awareness: a methodological overview. In W.E. Tunmer, C. Pratt and M.L. Herriman (eds), *Metalinguistic Awareness of Children*. New York: Springer-Verlag.

Nesdale, A.R., Herriman, M.L. and Tunmer, W.E. (1984). Phonological awareness in children. In W.E. Tunmer, C. Pratt and M.L. Herriman (eds), *Metalinguistic Awareness in Children*. New York: Springer-Verlag.

Newcombe, N. (1989). The development of spatial perspective taking. In H.W. Reese (ed.), *Advances in Child Development and Behavior*, **22**, 203–247.

Papandropoulou, I. and Sinclair, H. (1974). What is a word? Experimental study of children's ideas on grammar, *Human Development*, **17**, 241–258.

Piaget, J. (1929). *The Child's Conception of the World*. London: Routledge and Kegan Paul.

Piaget, J. and Inhelder, B. (1956). *The Child's Conception of Language*. London: Routledge and Kegan Paul.

Pratt, C. and Nesdale, A.R. (1984). Pragmatic awareness in children. In W.E. Tunmer, C. Pratt and M.L. Herriman (eds), *Metalinguistic Awareness in Children*. New York: Springer-Verlag.

Rozin, P. and Gleitman, L.R. (1977). The structure and acquisition of reading (II): the reading process and the acquisition of the alphabetic principle. In A.S. Reber and D.L. Scarborough (eds), *Towards a Psychology of Reading*. Hillsdale, New Jersey: Lawrence Erlbaum.

Scribner, S. and Cole, M. (1981). *The Psychology of Literacy*. Cambridge, Massachusetts: Harvard University Press.

Smith, C.L. and Tager-Flusberg, H. (1982). Metalinguistic awareness and language development, *Journal of Experimental Child Psychology*, **34**, 449–468.

Tunmer, W.E. and Herriman, M.L. (1984). The development of metalinguistic awareness: a conceptual overview. In W.E. Tunmer, C. Pratt and M.L. Herriman (eds), *Metalinguistic Awareness in Children*. New York: Springer-Verlag.

Van Kleeck, A. (1982). The emergence of linguistic awareness: a cognitive framework, *Merrill-Palmer Quarterly*, **28**, 237–265.

12 Reading and Development

PETER BRYANT
University of Oxford

It goes without saying that to learn to read is to acquire a new system of representation, but it is worth making the point that at least two levels of representation are involved. Children must learn that written words and sentences mean something—that they represent meaningful speech. But they also have to learn that individual alphabetic letters represent sounds, as do sequences of letters. The two levels are connected, of course, for there is no point in knowing how letters represent sounds unless one also knows that these sounds usually add up to meaningful words: but the knowledge about language which children need in order to come to grips with these two forms of representation is rather different. To understand that written words and sentences represent spoken words and sentences one must have an idea of how spoken language consists of words and sentences: but to grasp the significance of alphabetic letters one has to realise that spoken words and syllables can be broken down into segments of sound which, on their own, mean nothing.

There are really two questions to be asked about children's learning of both these levels of representation in written language. The first is about the way in which initially they come to understand in a general way how the system works. When, and how, do children realise that each cluster of letters, separated from other clusters by a space on the page, represents a word, and that each of the letters in that cluster usually represents a phoneme? The second question is about their learning of the mechanics of the system, and it concerns the way in which they learn to use the alphabetic code and the semantic and syntactic constraints in the passages in front of them in order to read.

THE FIRST QUESTION—LEARNING WHAT FORM THE UNITS TAKE

There has been remarkably little work on the first of these two questions, but undoubtedly the best of it is done by Ferreiro and her colleagues (Ferreiro & Palacio, 1982; Ferreiro & Teberosky, 1982) with Argentine and Mexican children. Their starting point was Piaget's theory about cognitive development and it follows that their main point was that children are not just taught to read: they have to 'construct' reading for themselves, and

Systems of Representation in Children: Development and Use. Edited by C. Pratt and A.F. Garton
© 1993 John Wiley & Sons Ltd

a great deal of that construction involves working out what written language is.

Ferreiro & Teberosky argue, convincingly, that aspects of written language that we take for granted are not so obvious to young children. It takes them some time to learn that the separate clusters of letters represent separate words, that every spoken word in the speech which is represented in written language is written down, and that alphabetic letters represent phonemes.

At the beginning children have to work out for themselves the relation between written and spoken language. Initially (the 'pre-syllabic stage') they do not realise that letters and strings of letters symbolise sounds, or that clusters of letters represent words or even that the spoken words represented are presented in any particular order. Later they begin to understand that each written word represents a spoken word, but they still misunderstand the nature of the relationship between individual letters and sounds. Their first idea in this stage (the 'syllabic stage') is that alphabetic letters represent syllables and, to begin with, they often treat this relationship in a purely quantitative way, representing, for example, the word 'caballo' by 'XTS'. Later these syllabic spellings begin to bear a phonetic relationship to the word as well, for example, 'AAO' for 'caballo'. This is the point at which they begin to understand that different letters represent different sounds, but they are still concentrating on the wrong phonological unit. Finally (the 'alphabetic stage'), the children realise that letters denote phonemes.

This is a developmental hypothesis, and it makes some surprising and interesting suggestions, but it concentrates on the pre-reading period and abandons the child at the threshold of learning to read. So, it deals only with the first of our two questions. How children learn about specific letter–sound relationships, how they eventually understand orthographic rules, how they use their linguistic knowledge to help them decipher text—these are not questions which Ferreiro tries to answer. In general, her attempt to apply Piagetian theory to the pre-reading period is remarkably successful, but we still have to find an answer to our second question.

THE SECOND QUESTION—LEARNING HOW TO USE THE UNITS

Representing sounds with letters

In order to learn how to represent the sounds in spoken words with written letters, one must be able to break the spoken words up into the appropriate phonological segments in the first place. So, if learning about letter–sound relationships plays an important part in learning to read, the strength of a child's phonological skills must also be a significant factor. There are many psychologists who are convinced of the central importance of phonological skills in learning to read (for a review, see Goswami & Bryant, 1990). They argue that the main barrier to learning these connections is the difficulty that children often have in breaking words up into phonological segments or at any rate into phonological segments that are represented by letters or strings of letters. But among the people who hold this view there is nevertheless strong disagreement on one question. The question is where the necessary phonological skills come from. Some psychologists take the view that the phonological skills which children must acquire when learning to read are quite different from anything that they have achieved until then, and thus that there is little or no connection between children's early phonological experiences and reading: for them, reading is a phonologically 'unnatural' act (Gough & Hillinger, 1980). Others are convinced that children's early phonological skills and experience play a critical role in helping them surmount the considerable phonological barriers that face them when they begin to read and to spell.

First, we have to establish that there is a connection. This is quite easy to do. There are many studies which show a close relation between children's performance in phonological tasks of one sort or another and their reading level (e.g. Stanovich, Cunningham & Cramer, 1984; Liberman, Shankweiler & Liberman, 1989). In some of these studies the children's reading levels were assessed at the same time as they were given the phonological tasks. Other studies were predictive: the children's phonological skills were measured some time before the reading tests were given. Either way a consistent relationship between the two variables has always emerged, and it is one that remains significant even after quite stringent controls are taken for differences in IQ and in the children's social background.

The results of several intervention studies also support the idea of a strong relationship between children's phonological skills and the progress that they make in reading. One is a remarkable study by Lundberg, Frost & Petersen (1988) in Denmark of two groups of children, one of which was given concentrated training in phonological skills at nursery school while the other received the same amount of extra attention but in the form of experiences which were not in any way phonological. The first of these two groups made more progress than the second later on when they went to school and were taught to read. Another study comprises some work of our own (Bradley & Bryant, 1983) in which we showed that children of 6 and 7 years given extra experience in the form of rhyming games make more progress in reading than do comparable control groups.

These studies show that a child's ability to analyse the sounds in words plays a significant role in his or her reading, but this still leaves us with a causal question which, as it happens, is a version of the question that was posed earlier about continuity or discontinuity. There are again two possibilities. One is that the development here is a continuous one (Bryant &

Goswami, 1987; Goswami & Bryant, 1990). Children acquire certain phonological skills and presumably become more skilled phonologically throughout the preschool period, and these early phonological skills form the basis of their learning about letter–sound relationships when they begin to read. The other possibility (Content *et al.*, 1982) is that the phonological routines that they have to learn about in reading are at a different level and take a completely different form to any phonological analyses that they have carried out until then. According to this second argument, children acquire new phonological skills which otherwise would not be part of their cognitive repertoire as a direct result of learning to read.

Let us deal first with this latter argument, which is a clear example of the idea that reading is an unnatural act and that it depends on artificial skills which children only acquire as a direct result of being taught to read. The idea rests on an assumption of the central importance of the phoneme. Single alphabetic letters represent single phonemes, by and large, and so, it is claimed, children have to learn how to break words up into their constituent phonemes in order to learn how to use the alphabet. But judgements about phonemes are notoriously difficult for young children, and most of them are impossible for children who have not yet learned to read. Two examples will be enough to make this point. One is the well-known tapping task devised by Isabelle Liberman and her colleagues (Liberman *et al.*, 1974). They tried to teach children to tap out the number of sounds in words that they heard. In one version of the task the children had to tap out the number of syllables in each word (three taps for 'elephant'), and in another it was the number of phonemes (three taps for 'cat'). The first task was a great deal easier than the second, but the most important result from the point of view of this discussion is that the difficult phoneme task proved quite impossible for younger children who had not yet learned to read.

The second example is the subtraction task invented by Bruce (1964). Here children had to work out what a series of words would sound like if particular sounds were subtracted from them (e.g. 'sand' without the 'n' sound). Again this apparently simple phoneme task proved enormously difficult for young children, and it was only by the age of 8 years or so that they began to have any successes at all. Together, these tasks seemed to establish that children are not aware of phonemes before they learn to read and, the argument went, since the phoneme is the crucial phonological unit in the learning of letter–sound relationships, other, cruder, forms of phonological sensitivity which children acquire in the preschool period are quite irrelevant to learning to read. This view was given considerable support by the results of studies of the phonological skills of illiterate people. Morais and his colleagues (Morais *et al.*, 1979; Morais *et al.*, 1986) carried out two important studies in Portugal in which a group of people who had never learned to read were compared with another group who had once been illiterate but had recently taken part in a literacy programme and now could read. In both studies the illiterate group did a great deal worse than the ex-illiterate group in tasks which involved judgements about phonemes—subtraction and addition tasks which resembled Bruce's test. The authors' conclusion was a radical one. It is that we only become aware of the way that words and syllables can be broken up into phonemes as a result of being taught to read. If we do not learn to read we remain unaware of phonemes. Analysing words in terms of their phonemes is, therefore, an unnatural act, and Morais and his colleagues' conclusion is the clearest argument that we have for discontinuity. The early phono-logical skills that children build up in the preschool period are, they hold, quite irrelevant. What matters is grapheme–phoneme correspondences, and awareness of phonemes is definitely not a natural product of development. We have to be taught about phonemes.

One might ask, then, how alphabetic languages were devised in the first place, but an answer is easy to find. It seems likely (Gelb, 1963) that the alphabet may only have been invented once, and so the original idea of the alphabet may have been the product of one brilliant, and entirely unrepresentative, Phoenician mind. But the question about the origins of alphabetic scripts is a useful reminder that these were preceded by other scripts such as syllabaries and logographic scripts and that these still exist and are used by a considerable number of people. The traditional Chinese script is mainly logographic (although Chinese symbols include phonetic radicals) and the Japanese read and write with two kinds of script, one a syllabary and the other a logographic script. Since the symbols in these scripts do not represent phonemes, the hypothesis that people only become aware of phonemes as a result of learning an alphabetic script would have to predict that Chinese and Japanese people should be as insensitive to phonemes as young English children and illiterate Portuguese people apparently are.

There is some evidence to support this claim. Charles Read and his colleagues (Read et al., 1986) gave Chinese people versions of the tasks that Morais and his colleagues had used; these people had either learned just the traditional Chinese script which, as we have remarked, is logographic, or they had learned both the traditional script and an alphabetic rendering of Chinese which is called Pinyin. The Pinyin group managed the phoneme tasks a great deal better than the non-Pinyin group did. This certainly supports the idea that people only become aware of phonemes as a result of learning to read an alphabetic script. A study by Mann (1986) provided further support for this idea. She compared 6-year-old American and Japanese children on the syllable and phoneme tapping task. The two groups were at much the same level as each other in the syllable tapping task, but the American children were much better than the Japanese in the phoneme task. Once again, the people who have had to learn something about the alphabet had the edge.

However, the extraordinary consistency of the results that I have described so far was disturbed by another finding of Mann's in the same study. She also tested a group of Japanese 9- and 10-year-olds who she claimed had no experience with English or any other alphabetic language. Yet, she found, at this older age level the Japanese children were as good at the phoneme task as American children of the same age, and she concluded that, though learning to read an alphabet speeds up the development of sensitivity to phonemes, children nevertheless acquire this sensitivity naturally without the help of instruction in reading. Of course, this conclusion conflicts with Charles Read's results and those of Morais and his colleagues. Why do Japanese children get there when Chinese adults and Portuguese illiterates do not? Fortunately there is another way of explaining this particular outcome of Mann's study. When Japanese children are taught to read the syllabaries (rather confusingly there are two Japanese syllabaries), they learn to group these syllables by their opening phonemes ('ka' 'ko') and by their end phonemes ('ta' 'na'). So the experience of being taught a syllabary entails explicit instructions about phonemes. That could be the reason why Japanese children eventually do quite well in the phoneme tapping task.

The evidence that we have dealt with so far seems to add up to a strong case for the discontinuity position. If the phonological skill that is crucial to reading is the analysis of phonemes and if awareness of phonemes comes only as a result of being taught to read, then our attention should be on the process of teaching reading and not on natural development. We should in effect reject children's pre-school phonological skills as being quite irrelevant to reading, and that indeed is what Content and his colleagues (Content et al., 1982) advise us to do. But before we abandon the much maligned early skills, we should perhaps consider what form these skills take.

Young children seem unable to break a word up into its constituent phonemes, as we have remarked, but they are quite good at producing (Dowker, 1989) and detecting rhymes and alliteration (Bryant et al., 1989, 1990). That means that they can judge that words and syllables, which are clearly different from each other, nevertheless have phonological segments in common. These common segments, at any rate in rhyming tasks, are usually larger than the phoneme in that they typically contain more than one phoneme. The rhyming sound in 'cat' and 'hat' is '-at', which is two phonemes. So the ability to detect rhyme is probably a great deal less refined than the ability to detect phonemes. The developmental relation between judgements about rhyme, alliteration and phonemes and the acquisition of reading is an intriguing one. One of the best measures of rhyme detection and also of phoneme detection is an oddity task. Children hear three of four words at a time and are told that all but one rhyme or that all but one begin with the same phoneme or end with the same phoneme. It is no surprise that young children can manage the rhyming oddity task quite well long before they learn to read, but it is rather more interesting to note (Kirtley *et al.*, 1989) that 5-year-old non-readers also do quite well (and well above chance level) when asked to detect the word which begins with a different phoneme from the rest (an alliteration task). The difficult task for them is to judge which word ends with the same phoneme. Five-year-old children who have not yet learned to read are at chance level in a task like this, while those who have learned to read do better than this.

So, even pre-readers detect rhyme and alliteration quite well and sometimes this even means that they rise above chance level in phoneme detection tasks, but other phoneme detection tasks flummox them and they are plainly unable to analyse the phonemes of most words fully. This leaves us with the question of whether these early rhyme and alliteration skills have anything to do with reading.

If you accept, as a lot of people do, the idea that the important phonological link in reading is the grapheme–phoneme correspondence, then it is quite reasonable to suggest that rhyme at any rate should be quite trivial as far as reading is concerned. Rhyme is too gross, too 'global', as Content *et al.* (1982) put it. But there is another possibility, which is that children learn not just about relations between single letters and phonemes but also between sequences of letters and strings of phonemes. Take, for example, the letter sequence '-ight'. It represents, in a relatively invariant way, a sound which contains more than one phoneme. What is to stop the child learning an association at this level?

The answer, it seems, is 'nothing at all'. This certainly is the conclusion to be drawn from some interesting experiments by Goswami (1986, 1988a, 1988b) which show that beginner readers are often quite eager to associate sounds with letter sequences of this sort. She gave children of 6, 7 and 8 years a set of words to read which were mostly too difficult for them. Then she told them what one of these written words, such as 'peak', meant. The result of her telling them how to read this word was that it helped them to read other rhyming words with similar spelling patterns like 'leak' and 'weak', but it had little effect on their ability to read other words, such as 'bake', which did not share the same spelling sequence or rhyming sound. Later, Goswami repeated this striking finding with a task in which children had to read passages of prose, and she also demonstrated the same kind of inference about rhyming words in a spelling task.

If children are ready right at the start of learning to read to infer that two words which end with the same spelling sequence also share a rhyming sound, it is quite likely that their ability to group words by rhyme should help them to learn to read and to spell. In fact there is ample evidence for this connection. Children's early (preschool) sensitivity to rhyme and alliteration are extremely powerful predictors of their eventual success in learning to read. It is also the case, as we have already seen, that training in rhyme helps children learn to read.

So, one's view on the continuity/discontinuity question about the links between phonological skills and reading depends on the phonological unit that one thinks of as important. If you hold the view that the crucial unit is the phoneme and the crucial link the grapheme–phoneme correspondence, then you will probably hold to a discontinuity position. If, on the other hand, you agree that children probably also learn that words which rhyme also have sequences of letters in common, the idea of continuity is bound to seem the more plausible one.

In fact, the evidence for the importance of rhyme and for its links with later success in reading seems so compelling that some version of the continuity position seems inescapable. Children's sensitivity to rhyme certainly feeds into the process of learning to read, but the experience of reading probably leads to the acquisition of entirely new skills. Attention to phonemes is one.

SYNTAX AND CONTEXT

The two groups of people who argue for developmental continuity in reading have, in every other respect, radically different views of the nature of learning to read. Those who argue for the link between early phonological skills and reading later on are in serious disagreement with the people who claim that children's linguistic knowledge is the crucial factor.

This latter position, originally developed by Frank Smith (1978) and Kenneth Goodman (1967, 1982), is extremely well known and easy to describe. They argue that when children learn to read they go far beyond the simple deciphering of single words on the basis of letter–sound relationships. They are, according to Smith, engaged in a 'psycholinguistic guessing game'. When they come to a word in a sentence which they cannot read they use their knowledge of the meaning of the sentence and the likely grammatical status of the difficult word to guess what it is. Thus their mistakes are far from random, and the systematic nature of these mistakes is one of Goodman's main points. He argues that such mistakes, which he calls 'miscues', provide us with an insight into the way children read. He proposes that children use three kinds of cues, which are: 'grapho-phonic', 'syntactic' and 'semantic'. One of Goodman's (1982) examples of a miscue, which probably involved all three kinds of cues, is: Text 'Wait a moment'; Reader 'Wait a minute'. The evidence that Goodman marshals to show that children rarely make mistakes which are inappropriate from the point of view both of syntax and of meaning is certainly convincing. There is no doubt that children do pay considerable attention to the linguistic context when they read and use it as far as they can when they get into difficulty. But that does not mean, of course, that their sensitivity to the syntax and to the meaning of the passages that they read necessarily helps them learn to read. Several attempts have been made recently to fill that gap.

The most significant was made by Tunmer and his colleagues. Tunmer (1989) made the claim that children employ their considerable syntactic and semantic knowledge to help them when their phonological and ortho-graphic knowledge fails them. According to Tunmer, children readily combine the two kinds of knowledge. So if a child cannot read the word 'milk' but can work out that it begins with an 'm' sound and ends with a 'k' sound, he will use this knowledge to help with the sentence, 'John got home and drank a glass of milk'. The rest of the sentence will tell him that the last word represents a drink, and the fact that he has deciphered the beginning and end sounds of the word will help him work out which drink it is. Tunmer goes further and makes the claim that this kind of successful inference will help the child read the word correctly next time, even without the help of context.

The main evidence for this second claim comes from the experiment by Tunmer, Nesdale & Wright (1987) in which a group of children whose progress in reading had been relatively slow (they were nearly 9 years old but their reading age was 2 years below their actual age) was compared with another group of children who were much younger but whose reading levels were roughly the same as those of the older group. Thus these two groups of children had arrived at the same level of reading but one group had got there a great deal slower than the other. Tunmer and his colleagues wanted to know whether this difference could be explained in terms of differences in sensitivity to the syntactic context. To test this idea they gave the children a sentence correction task in which children were read sentences which were wrong either because of a missing morpheme ('Tom strangled two kitten') or because the words were in the wrong order ('clapped his hands Mark'). They also gave the children a 'cloze' task—a task in which they were given sentences with missing words and had to fill in the gaps. Both tasks, they argued, were measures of the children's sensitivity to linguistic context.

The experiment showed quite clearly that the older children were worse than the younger ones at these two tasks, and from this the authors concluded that one of the reasons why the poor readers had been slow to learn to read may have been that they were not particularly good at taking advantage of their syntactic and semantic knowledge.

This last claim is a suitable reminder that there are two hypotheses here. One, which is actually indisputable, is that children use the syntactic and semantic context to help them decipher words which they would not be able to read in isolation. The other is that this sensitivity to context is a powerful factor in learning to read. It is this second claim which brings us back to the question of continuity and discontinuity. For children are certainly sensitive to the linguistic context of spoken language long before they learn to read. So, the hypothesis that children's sensitivity to the linguistic context is a powerful determinant of how well they learn to read amounts to a claim that a naturally occurring preschool skill plays a critical part in children's reading.

So it comes as something of a surprise to see that there have been very few attempts to link children's early linguistic awareness to their later success in learning to read. Research on phonological skills and reading bristles with longitudinal studies; in contrast, the empirical evidence that we have on the importance of syntactic and semantic skills comes mainly in the form of cross-sectional experiments.

One of the main attempts to fill this gap was made by Tunmer, Herriman & Nesdale (1988). Theirs was a 2-year longitudinal study which began when the children in the study were 5 years old. At that time, and also a year later, the children were given three tests of linguistic awareness: one was of phonological awareness (phoneme tapping), one of syntactic awareness (sentence correction) and the third of 'pragmatic' awareness (the children had to detect inter-sentence inconsistencies in a prose passage). They were also given some Piagetian test of 'operativity' and two tests devised by Marie Clay, one of which is called the 'Concepts about Print' test. The authors used path analysis to work out the relationships between these measures and the progress that the children made in reading during the project. They actually combined the three awareness measures— phonological, syntactic and pragmatic—as one 'metalinguistic' measure, which is a pity from the point of view being developed in this chapter since it is clear that these different forms of awareness might be quite independent of each other. This metalinguistic measure did not make an independent contribution to the children's reading according to Tunmer et al.'s path analyses, but was related to the children's concepts of print and through that made an indirect contribution to reading.

There is no clear answer to the question that we have asked about the contribution of children's early syntactic and semantic sensitivity to their later progress in reading. By combining the awareness measures, Tunmer et al. failed to tell us enough about the independent contribution of each, and another serious problem is that the authors took their first measures after the children had been in school for nearly a year and had already had a considerable amount of instruction in reading. So the connections that were picked up could have been a product of the experiences the children had already had while being taught to read and write.

This obvious gap has, to a large extent, been filled by a longitudinal study carried out recently at Oxford by Rego (1991). She worked with the same group of children from the age of 4 years 11 months through to 6 years 11 months. During the first year of the project she assessed the children's phonological skills with a phoneme tapping task and versions of the oddity tasks that we have already described; in addition their syntactic and semantic sensitivity was tested with sentence correction tasks (anagram: Ate Bill apples; completion: Sam [ ] his milk) and with a cloze task which was a story in which the child also had to fill in missing words (the difference between the sentence completion tasks and the cloze task was that the former consisted of a series of separate sentences, while the latter involved one complete and consecutive story). The children's progress in reading was monitored, mainly in the second year of the project, but these measures were not blanket ones. Great care was taken by Rego to introduce varied measures of reading in order to pick up specific connections that might exist between the two main different predictive measures (phonological sensitivity and semantic and syntactic sensitivity).

Rego's ingenious argument was that if children's efforts to learn to read are helped by their awareness of syntactic and semantic constraints, then the link between early phonological sensitivity and reading should be particularly strong in reading tasks which depend on their using context to help them learn to read. So she devised as one of her tests a 'word reading task primed by oral context'. In this, she took the first 10 words that individual children had not been able to read in a standardised single-word reading test (Schonell) and presented each of these words in a meaningful sentence. The measure of 'contextual facilitation' was the number of these words that the child was now able to read.

Rego also looked for a measure of reading which might be specifically connected to children's early phonological skills, and, not surprisingly, selected non-words on the argument that these can only be read with the help of knowledge of letter sound rules.

She also gave children more familiar measures of reading which were the Neale Analysis of Reading, in which children have to read and understand prose passages, and the Schonell tests of reading and spelling, which are single-word tests, and she also monitored the children's 'invented spelling', i.e. their use of letter–sound relationships, in working out how to write relatively unfamiliar words. On balance, the child's syntactic and semantic skills should, if they play any role at all, affect performance in the prose reading test rather than in the single-word tests.

The results of this study are intriguing. First it should be said that both sets of predictors, phonological and linguistic (semantic and syntactic), tended to predict both the prose and the single-word reading scores rather well even after stringent controls for differences in intelligence, verbal memory and vocabulary. This is impressive evidence that both kinds of preschool linguistic skill eventually play a considerable part in children's reading. But the general success of both measures as predictors does not answer the question about specific connections. We still need to know whether children's early phonological skills affect one aspect while their semantic and syntactic skills affect another aspect of reading.

Rego's other reading tests—her measure of non-word reading and contextual facilitation in reading—provide a plausible answer. The specific connections that she had predicted did emerge. The sentence correction tests predicted the amount of 'contextual facilitation' in the children's later reading extremely well, even after stringent control for differences in intelligence, vocabulary and verbal memory. As well as this, the phonological tests turned out to be extremely good predictors of the children's later ability to read non-words.

These connections were genuinely specific because there was no crossover. The children's performance in the sentence correction tests did not predict how well they read non-words later. Nor were their scores in the phonological tasks related to any significant degree to the extent to which they used context to help them read unfamiliar words (the degree of contextual facilitation) in the following year.

In a way this last result—no connection between children's early phonological skills and the extent to which they later took advantage of the context in reading—is a surprise. Tunmer and his colleagues, as we have shown, had the plausible hypothesis that there is an interaction between children's phonological skills and their use of context. They thought, as we have noted, that children use the context to fill in gaps left by the incomplete phonological analysis of unfamiliar words ('m_k' for 'milk'). This would mean that children use their phonological and contextual skills in concert, and thus that children's phonological skills should determine to some extent the degree to which they can take advantage of context. The analyses just described do not support this idea, but Rego reported one other result which suggests that the degree of contextual facilitation may, after all, be affected by children's phonological skills. In her analysis of children's spelling errors, Rego was able to show a developmental progression. Children began by producing spellings which bore no relation at all to the words that they were trying to write, then began to get the first letter right, then began to represent the end sound as well, and finally, though often incorrectly, began to represent all the sounds in the word. At the same time Rego was also monitoring the children's reading, and she was able to show a close connection between the stage that each child had reached in the pattern of spelling and the degree of contextual facilitation. The more comprehensive the phonological analysis of the words in the child's spelling, the greater the degree of contextual facilitation in reading. The relationship is a simultaneous one, but it provides strong support for Tunmer's idea of an interaction between children's phonological proficiency and their ability to take advantage of context to help them to read unfamiliar words.

DEVELOPMENTAL THEORY AND LEARNING TO READ

There can be no doubt from the evidence reviewed so far that reading 'develops' in the sense that children go through an ordered series of stages on the way to learning to read and write. So, one surely needs an adequate developmental theory of reading—a theory about changes both before and after children begin to learn to read. But there are few such theories and these few tend to deal with some specific aspects of reading and to ignore others.

I have already mentioned Ferreiro's developmental analysis, which is by far the most comprehensive theory about the ideas that children hold about reading and writing before they learn to read. This was based on Piagetian theory, and there has been one other attempt to use Piagetian theory as a basis for a developmental hypothesis about learning to read. This was produced by George Marsh and his colleagues (Marsh *et al.*, 1980; 1981; Marsh & Desberg, 1983) and it takes up the process of reading at roughly the point where Ferreiro's analysis stops. Marsh and his colleagues argued that children who have not reached the concrete operations stage will, as a consequence, be unable to learn what he called 'combinatorial rules', and this at first will stop them from being able to read words on the basis of putting together the sounds represented by the individual letters in a word. That skill comes with concrete operations, but even then there are cognitive constraints on children's reading. Children, according to Marsh, do not begin to master higher order, conditional rules, such as the pronunciation of 'c' when followed by the letter 'e' or 'y'.

Marsh's ideas about the initial difficulty of combinatorial rules have not stood up well to subsequent work on spelling (Marsh himself concentrated on reading) and it is now abundantly clear that children use such rules very early on when they begin to write words. But his claim for enduring difficulties with conditional rules remains largely untested; few people have worked directly on these more complex aspects of reading and it is to Marsh's credit to have pointed out their interest.

So far as I know, Ferreiro and Marsh are the only ones to have tried to bring the subject of learning to read into the mainstream of developmental psychology. It is interesting to note that Uta Frith's theory (1985) about learning to read, which is probably the best known of all current theories, is not a developmental one in the sense that I have used the word. Her theory is about changes in the way that children learn to read and spell, and she argues for three successive stages: logographic, alphabetic and orthographic. But Frith's ideas are only about reading and spelling. She does not link her stages to prior experiences or abilities, and, in as far as she does account for the change from one stage to the next, her explanations are internal to reading and spelling. Children, she argues, adopt a logographic approach to reading first and then, as a result, adopt the same approach to spelling; they come to the alphabetic code in spelling first and the experience of doing so eventually leads them to reading alphabetically as well. So, reading experiences affect the way that children spell and vice versa. But neither reading nor spelling are connected to anything else in Uta Frith's theory.

The upshot is that there are two genuinely developmental theories about learning to read, which happen to be Piagetian ones and which for different reasons are rather limited theories. They also share another typically Piagetian problem which is that they are decidedly negative. Both Ferreiro and Marsh concentrate on the intense difficulties that children have, either in the pre-reading period or in the years after children go to school. Such difficulties clearly exist, but surely the data reviewed in this chapter suggest that an adequate theory would have to deal with positive aspects as well. I have argued that children's phonological and other linguistic experiences prepare them for reading and are the basis for much of what happens when they are taught to read. If that is so, we also need a theoretical account of these connections and of how they work. We need a theory about what helps children to surmount the considerable hurdles that they face in reading, and not just a theory about the hurdles. That, surely, is how we will understand how reading develops.

REFERENCES

Bradley, L. and Bryant, P.E. (1983). Categorising sounds and learning to read—a causal connection, *Nature*, **301**, 419–421.
Bruce, D.J. (1964). The analysis of word sounds, *British Journal of Educational Psychology*, **34**, 158–170.
Bryant, P.E. and Goswami, U. (1987). Beyond grapheme-phoneme correspondence, *Cahiers de Psychologie Cognitive*, **7**, 439–443.
Bryant, P.E., Bradley, L., MacLean, M. and Crossland, J. (1989). Nursery rhymes, phonological skills and reading, *Journal of Child Language*, **16**, 407–428.
Bryant, P.E., MacLean, M., Bradley, L.L. and Crossland, J. (1990). Rhyme, alliteration, phoneme detection and learning to read, *Developmental Psychology*, **26**, 429–438.
Content, A., Morais, J., Alegria, J. and Bertelson, P. (1982). Accelerating the development of phonetic segmentation skills in kindergartners, *Cahiers de Psychologie Cognitive*, **2**, 259–269.
Dowker, A. (1989). Rhymes and alliteration in poems elicited from young children, *Journal of Child Language*, **16**, 181–202.
Ferreiro, E. and Palacio, M. (1982). Analisis de las perturbaciones en el processo de aprendizaje escolar de la lectura. Mexico: Direccion General de Educacion (cited in Rego, 1991).
Ferreiro, E. and Teberosky, A. (1982). *Literacy Before Schooling*. Exeter, New Hampshire: Heinemann Educational Books.
Frith, U. (1985). Beneath the surface of developmental dyslexia. In K. Patterson, M. Coltheart and J. Marshall (eds), *Surface Dyslexia*. London: Lawrence Erlbaum.
Gelb, I.J. (1963). *A Study of Writing*. Chicago: University of Chicago Press.

Goodman, K. (1967). Reading: a psycholinguistic guessing game, *Journal of the Reading Specialist*, **6**, 126–135.

Goodman, K. (1982). Miscue analysis: theory and reality in reading. In F.K. Gollasch (ed.), *Language and Literacy: The Selected Writings of Kenneth S. Goodman*. Boston: Routledge and Kegan Paul.

Goswami, U. (1986). Children's use of analogy in learning to read: a developmental study, *Journal of Experimental Child Psychology*, **42**, 73–83.

Goswami, U. (1988a). Orthographic analogies and reading development, *Quarterly Journal of Experimental Psychology*, **40A**, 239–268.

Goswami, U. (1988b). Children's use of analogy in learning to spell, *British Journal of Developmental Psychology*, **6**, 21–33.

Goswami, U. and Bryant, P. (1990). *Phonological Skills and Learning to Read*. London: Lawrence Erlbaum.

Gough, P.B. and Hillinger, M.L. (1980). Learning to read: an unnatural act, *Bulletin of the Orton Society*, **30**, 179–196.

Kirtley, C., Bryant, P., MacLean, M. and Bradley, L. (1989). Rhyme, rime and the onset of reading, *Journal of Experimental Child Psychology*, **48**, 224–245.

Liberman, I.Y., Shankweiler, D., Fischer, F.W. and Carter, B. (1974). Explicit syllable and phoneme segmentation in the young child, *Journal of Experimental Child Psychology*, **18**, 201–212.

Liberman, I.Y., Shankweiler, D. and Liberman, A. (1989). The alphabetic principle and learning to read. In D. Shankweiler and I.Y. Liberman (eds), *Phonology and Reading Disability* (pp. 1–34). Ann Arbor: University of Michigan Press.

Lundberg, I., Frost, J. and Petersen, O. (1988). Effects of an extensive program for stimulating phonological awareness in preschool children, *Reading Research Quarterly*, **23**, 263–284.

Mann, V.A. (1986). Phonological awareness: the role of reading experience, *Cognition*, **24**, 65–92.

Marsh, G. and Desberg, P. (1983). The development of strategies in the acquisition of symbolic skills. In D.R. Rogers and J.A. Sloboda (eds), *The Acquisition of Symbolic Skills* (pp. 149–154). New York: Plenum Press.

Marsh, G., Friedman, M.P., Welch, V. and Desberg, P. (1980). A cognitive-developmental approach to reading acquisition. In G.E. MacKinnon and T.G. Waller (eds), *Advances in Theory and Practice of Research in Reading*. New York: Academic Press.

Marsh, G., Friedman, M.P., Desberg, P. and Saterdahl, K. (1981). Comparison of reading and spelling strategies in normal and reading disabled children. In M. Friedman, J.P. Das and N. O'Connor, *Intelligence and Learning* (pp. 363–367). New York: Plenum Press.

Morais, J., Cary, L., Alegria, J. and Bertelson, P. (1979). Does awareness of speech as a sequence of phones arise spontaneously? *Cognition*, **7**, 323–331.

Morais, J., Bertelson, P., Cary, L. and Alegria, J. (1986). Literacy training and speech segmentation, *Cognition*, **24**, 45–64.

Read, C., Zhang, Y., Nie, H. and Ding, B. (1986). The ability to manipulate speech sounds depends on knowing alphabetic spelling, *Cognition*, **24**, 31–44.

Rego, L. (1991). The role of early linguistic awareness in children's reading and spelling. Unpublished DPhil thesis, Oxford University.

Smith, F. (1978). *Understanding Reading*. London: Holt, Rinehart and Winston.

Stanovich, K.E., Cunningham, A.E. and Cramer, B.R. (1984). Assessing phonological awareness in kindergarten children: issues of task comparability, *Journal of Experimental Child Psychology*, **38**, 175–190.

Tunmer, W. (1989). The role of language-related factors in reading disability. In
   D. Shankweiler and I.Y. Liberman (eds), *Phonology and Reading Disability*
   (pp. 91–132). Ann Arbor: University of Michigan Press.
Tunmer, W.E., Nesdale, A.R. and Wright, A.D. (1987). Syntactic awareness and
   reading acquisition, *British Journal of Developmental Psychology*, **5**, 25–34.
Tunmer, W.E., Herriman, M.L. and Nesdale, A.R. (1988). Metalinguistic abilities
   and beginning reading, *Reading Research Quarterly*, **23**, 134–158.

13 Representation in Problem Solving

ALISON F. GARTON
Health Department of Western Australia

How young children solve problems is a research issue that is arguably the core question in developmental psychology. Any form of human learning necessitates the successful solution of a particular cognitive task or problem, in the broadest sense. According to Karmiloff-Smith (1984), problem solving can be studied in all representational systems, including linguistic, spatial and physical ones. What distinguishes problem solving from other forms of behaviour is its applicability to a large range of domains, to macro- and micro-developmental changes within and between these domains, and to theoretical explanations for such changes.

The study of problem solving considers the role of both the external environment and internal, representational, mechanisms, and how the two aspects combine to initiate and facilitate developmental change. Change may occur because of failure or because of success, by conflict resolution or by collaboration. Change arises on both the behavioural level and the representational level and it is on the latter that I wish to concentrate in this chapter. The focus is on *change*, and on the way representational systems can assist developmental change in children's capacity to solve problems. Undeniably, behavioural change will occur too, but I wish mainly to address the issue of how representational activity expedites the achievement of successful problem solving, including both the process and the goal.

Firstly, however, I will present some examples of problem solving to illustrate the broad range of tasks, domains and mechanisms for change that fall under the rubric of 'problem solving'. Problem-solving research falls into two broad categories—that where children's learning and development are conceptualised as problem solving and that where the focus is on children's ability to solve particular problems. The former research seeks to explain development in some domain in terms of children becoming increasingly sophisticated at working out the challenges posed by normal developmental accomplishments. Thus, language and cognition, viewed as problem domains, are popular developmental foci for research efforts.

Systems of Representation in Children: Development and Use. Edited by C. Pratt and A.F. Garton
© 1993 John Wiley & Sons Ltd

LEARNING AND DEVELOPMENT AS PROBLEM SOLVING

Research on learning and development as problem solving has been conducted by a number of investigators. The illustrative research presented here has been undertaken by Bremner (for example Chapter 5) and Karmiloff-Smith (1984). Learning to search for a hidden object now displaced in location involves infants overcoming initial errors. These errors have been hypothesised to occur as a result of either something to do with the location, and the displacement, involved in hiding the object, or they reflect the infant's spatial ineptitude. Either way, both visual and motor solutions, either separately or together, permit successful searching (and location) behaviour. Indeed, Bremner refers to the infant as a 'spatial problem-solver'. That is, in order to succeed, developing infants construct new representations of their spatial environment. While Bremner explicitly recognises the infant as a spatial problem-solver, other researchers, also contributing to this book, acknowledge that the developing child must solve problems. Bremner further speculates that these early spatial representations are enhanced by the infant's increased locomotor activities such as sitting, standing up, rolling over, then crawling and finally walking. Whatever the means, the increased representations permit more flexible spatial problem solving and Bremner argues that representation and action are constantly determining one another, leading to more complex problem solving.

Karmiloff-Smith (for example, 1984) discusses the child's development of language as involving problem solving. In her analysis, the linguistic system is regarded as a 'problem space' in its own right. Karmiloff-Smith has presented a well-articulated theory of developmental change (a theory that itself is constantly being refined, see for example, Karmiloff-Smith & Inhelder, 1974; Karmiloff-Smith, 1986). I will discuss it here in relation to one aspect of language development. There are two fundamental principles in this theory. Behavioural changes result from *failure* to achieve the desired result in a problem-solving task. Representational changes occur in the light of problem-solving *success*. In the case of language, the child's task is to learn (conventional) rules and usage, requiring access to internal representations of language as well as socially determined representations. Language development can be described at the phonological level, the syntactic level, the pragmatic level and so on, but, in Karmiloff-Smith's model, the processes necessary for developmental change are identical. Specifically for language, children constantly need to map linguistic terms onto external referents, they need to construct grammatical sentences and they need to link ideas via language. The processes required to solve these 'problems' have been described in Karmiloff-Smith's three-phase model.

In her model of 1984, Karmiloff-Smith describes three recurrent macro- and micro-developmental phases in problem solving. The first phase, the *procedural* phase is exemplified by behaviour being dominated by 'data-driven' processes. That is, young children (in whatever domain) are so wrapped up with success on the task, they regard each instance individually. They lack any cohesive or integrative strategy for solving problems. Isolated behavioural units become increasingly automated but overt behaviour is still largely generated by the problem at hand.

In the next phase, the *metaprocedural* phase, the earlier procedures are rewritten as representations. Thus children become 'organisation-oriented', focusing on the integration of problem-solving behaviours *per se*, often at the expense of success on the task. That is, behaviour becomes less flexible and less responsive to external information and variation in environmental stimulation. Continued procedural successes result in the unification of strategies and the behaviour becomes top-down driven. Children are more concerned with storing appropriate and useful representations of successful procedures.

Karmiloff-Smith illustrates the difference between children at the procedural phase and those at the metaprocedural phase with reference to the production (in French) of the indefinite article (among other linguistic forms studied). At the procedural phase, children correctly use the indefinite article 'un/une' to cover both non-specific reference (= 'any') and the numerical function (one, two, three). There is no apparent realisation that the word is one and the same. At the metaprocedural phase, children show their increased awareness that a distinction between the two forms is necessary (somehow) by *incorrectly* elaborating their language. Karmiloff-Smith found instances of children marking the numerical function of 'un' as 'un de...' ('one of the...'). Their sensitivity to the dual function of a single word forces them to try to maintain a distinction in meaning via the use of different terms. During the metaprocedural phase, whilst the language forms are undergoing a process of representational change, children often manifest linguistic errors.

In the final, *conceptual* phase, errors of the previous type are no longer noted and children use the correct, adult-like forms of language, with no external embellishments. The child at the procedural phase, although apparently using, for example, the indefinite article correctly, has in fact a number of separate procedures for the different functions of 'a'. At the metaprocedural level, higher-order organisational processes unify these different uses in one representation, although the child attempts to maintain the distinctions explicitly. It is only at the conceptual level that children permit one language form to carry several meanings.

The model is not confined to the indefinite article, nor only to those other areas of language that Karmiloff-Smith studied, viz. gender marking, modifiers, possessive adjectives, postdeterminers, cohesion in story-telling. It is purportedly at a sufficiently wide level of generality to encompass a range of problem-solving domains while permitting specificity of particular details when necessary. The theoretical model explains changing representations and is a qualitative rather than a quantitative analysis of problem-solving behaviours.

PROBLEM-SOLVING TASKS

The second approach, that of setting children tasks or problems that require completing or solving, is guided by cognitive psychology. Some of the range of problems that have been investigated often involve examination of strategy use by children. For example, researchers have studied planning, i.e. the use of mental representations of strategies to solve problems (e.g. Hayes-Roth & Hayes-Roth, 1979), information processing approaches to problem solving (Siegler, 1983), studies of hypothesis generation and testing (e.g. Karmiloff-Smith & Inhelder, 1974) and the study of analogical reasoning (Goswami, 1991). Other problem-solving domains include the use of memory strategies in problem solving (Kail, 1984) and the acquisition of knowledge and cognitive skills, often using computer modelling (e.g. Chi, 1978; Klahr & Wallace, 1976). One other question that has puzzled researchers has been concerned with the conditions that facilitate the acquisition of problem-solving skills, including the acquisition of representational systems, and I shall return to this in a later section.

Problems, while being of many different types, can be described in terms of a discrepancy between the present state, or initial situation, and the desired state, or goal (Small, 1990). Whether or not a problem exists depends very much on the resources, experience and expertise of the individual perceiving the discrepancy. Once a problem has been identified and acknowledged, then the individual must operate on the initial situation to produce the desired outcome. The operations may be implicit or explicit but there are typically constraints on the available strategies (including physical, social and resource limitations).

The study of how children and adults solve specific problems has fascinated psychologists for many years. The range of activities studied and the theoretical models advanced are enormous although all seek ultimately to describe and explain children's learning and development. The study of how children solve particular problems is of intrinsic interest as it provides insights into the strategies, skills and knowledge brought to bear on different tasks.

Garton & Renshaw (1988) discuss how children determine the most efficacious way of resolving a specific problem-solving task. The problem concerned a block-matching task which required the children to form a line (or a 'train') of blocks such that each one was different from the previous one along only one dimension. The blocks were plastic shapes that varied along the dimensions of colour (red, yellow, blue, green), size (large, small), shape (square, triangle, circle, rectangle) and thickness (thick, thin). As many or as few dimensions (and resultant blocks) could be selected for the task as necessary, permitting graded tasks for children of different ages.

Success on the tasks was largely determined by the extent to which the children jointly participated in forming the line of blocks. In working together, children were encouraged to verbalise the rule(s) they were following. The nature of the different ways that children represented the task was fascinating. For example, in one pair of 7-year-old boys, the more domineering character perceived the task as one of making a train. He therefore chose blocks that best suited his idea of a train—with an engine, a tender, carriages and wheels. While he clearly did not fulfil the task requirements (as conceptualised by the experimenter), he did present an overt expression of: (a) his representation of the experimenter's instructions '...make a train', and (b) his representation of a train. In another example, two 7-year-old girls resolved their dilemma of how to select a block that was different from the previous one along one dimension by adopting a rule suggested by one of them. She suggested that they proceed 'red, white, blue' ('white' describing yellow) until all the shapes of different sizes and widths were exhausted. Again, success as defined by the experimenter was not achieved, but an interesting overt expression of a representation of the task was obtained.

Children, therefore, when working on cognitive tasks such as the one described above, may attempt to provide some external 'handle' to their solutions. Such an overt verbalisation facilitates the process of the task but does not necessarily (in the cases described above) lead to the correct strategy or eventual solution. There were other examples where children did represent the experimenter's intentions correctly, then verbalised the 'rule' and adhered to it throughout the formation of the line of blocks. On further investigation, however, measures of task success were not good indicators of the extent of collaboration between pairs of children. Subsequent analyses of the interactions focused exclusively on the language used by the children and how they communicated during the problem-solving interactions. From these analyses, there is reasonable evidence to suggest that the ways in which the children represent the task influence the communication patterns between children, the problem-solving strategies adopted and the eventual goal or outcome.

EXPERT AND NOVICE PROBLEM SOLVERS

This illustrative study of problem solving has approached the issue from a developmental perspective. There are other ways of studying problem solving which have implications for both children and adults. The contrast between *novices* and *experts* provides a useful basis for comparison on different types of problem-solving task. Again, any domain could be characterised as problem solving, including language, traditional problem-solving areas such as space or physics, or even social situations. Novices are those persons with lesser competence at the tasks under investigation; experts are those individuals with the necessary competence, experience or expertise to solve the problem in an efficient and economical manner. The characteristics of novices and experts can thus remain similar across all ages, all domains and all tasks.

There are therefore *domain-specific* experts and novices. In the study of problem solving, domain-specific knowledge is typically under investigation. That is, the problems selected for experimental study are characteristic of knowledge-rich domains (Small, 1990). For example, physics problems require for their solution not general world knowledge; rather they require very specific and intricate knowledge of the domain of physics. Domain-specific knowledge is acquired during development, often as a result of schooling. Mathematics, physics and other sciences are all examples of knowledge-rich domains. Because domain-specific knowledge exists, it can, theoretically at least, be described. While much of the knowledge of experts remains implicit, defying description, the actual domains can be described. In trying to ascertain the implicit knowledge of experts, the characteristics of those equipped with domain-specific expertise can be contrasted with individuals without the knowledge, or novices. Researchers can therefore investigate how both experts and novices approach and solve different problems, plus chart a developmental progression from novice to expert.

This distinction between expert and novice has been exploited by a number of researchers investigating a range of different problem-solving domains. Some general observations can be made regarding the differences between experts and novices. For example, in solving physics problems, experts have recourse to general physical laws or principles that guide their solutions; novices adopt a more piecemeal approach and solve problems on the basis of the information given (Wood, 1988; Small, 1990).

In addition, experts represent problems differently to novices. The former again bring principles or domain-specific laws to bear on their consideration of particular problems while the latter are possibly more concrete. Experts, by virtue of additional exposure to and experience with problem situations, have accumulated knowledge. Novices, characterised by having less knowledge, are disadvantaged through lack of experience, not because of age *per se* (Brown & DeLoache, 1978). Experts have more abstract representations which can be activated by specific information in a problem. Novices have less abstract representations and each representation can only be activated by a specific piece of information. There is little integration of representations. Each one remains fragmented. Individuals have different extents of knowledge or mental representations in different contexts. In one domain or context any individual can be regarded as a novice, whilst in another, an expert.

However, in many of the domains investigated by developmental psychologists, the mother (or adult) is regarded as the expert (by virtue of having the knowledge—it may or may not be represented abstractly) and the child as the novice. Adults and children can be viewed as having different levels of expertise (Wood, 1988) in their ability to problem solve, learn, think and communicate. Thus, an instructional component becomes evident and the study of problem solving also becomes pertinent to the study of children's learning and development. Adults (or mothers) are able to bring to bear expertise to such problems (be it a particular task or a broad domain), not only in an enhanced knowledge base but also in terms of greater skill and experience in all cognitive functions—language, memory and perception.

Studies of the way(s) in which experts might assist novices are fraught with difficulties since most teachers and learners have idiosyncrasies and individualities in the way they tackle the learning process. Wood, Wood & Middleton (1978) studied a specific instructional process to answer the question of what aspects of the teaching process facilitate learning in the novice. Mothers were asked to teach their 4- to 5-year-old children a construction task. Different demands are inherent in the task, involving correct sequencing and assembly of blocks. Success is not achieved until around the age of 7 or 8 years. Younger children, once instructed, can complete the construction. The form of the instruction was perceived as being critical to the child's ultimate level of success, and by analysing the components of the teaching delivered by the mother, Wood et al. identified optimal instructional 'styles'. Mothers whose children learned most about the task used instructional methods that combined explicit demonstrations with less direct verbal instruction and encouragement. Any help given was determined by the previous assistance offered and the child's under-standing and successful use of the proffered advice. This was termed 'contingent instruction' or scaffolding.

Contingent instruction involves such everyday activities as pointing out, prompting and assisting, all of which serve to direct the child towards the accomplishment of the goal at hand. There is thus a pervasive social element to problem solving, which assists the child to achieve success. The metaphor of a scaffold highlights the support necessary for the child to achieve small steps and is a very good description of the local, task-focused processes involved in problem solving. The emphasis is on the interactive nature of the instructional process at the heart of learning and characterises adult–child problem solving.

Not only can adult–child pairs be investigated while they solve problems, but children can be studied as they work jointly towards the solution of problems. These children may have different levels of skill and expertise when approaching the problem. An example of a developmental task comparing novice and expert children can be seen in the study by Azmitia (1988). Five-year-old children's competence on a task requiring the copying of a Lego structure was assessed, and, based on their performance, they were classified as novice (< 20% correct) or expert (> 80% correct). Children falling between the two extremes did not participate further. Dyads were formed of same-ability or mixed-ability children, and compared with children who worked alone. Another Lego copying task was used in the interaction sessions, requiring complex spatial representation and the achievement of a solution to the task, together with an active construction component, permitting easy engagement in the problem by the children. A post-test generalisation task was completed individually by all the children.

Basically, the results confirmed the well-documented superiority of collaboration for learning in the interaction sessions. Unfortunately, the abilities of the experts reached ceiling accuracy, but for novices, greater accuracy and task success were noted when they were working with an expert partner. Successful generalisation, hypothesised to be mediated either by the amount of progress made during the interaction or by the relation between levels of expertise within a dyad, was found only in the performances of novices who had previously worked with an expert.

A closer examination of the mediating mechanisms that facilitated and enhanced the copying accuracy of novices revealed that, during interaction, novices acquired useful task strategies. The quality of the verbal interaction, namely the use of explanation, demonstration and argument by the expert, also helped the novice. Novices were further observed *watching* the successful task solutions adopted and used by the experts. While novices clearly benefited from the interaction with the more competent expert in terms of interactive task behaviour and subsequent generalisation accuracy, Azmitia also observed that the novices were beginning to take responsibility for their own task-related behaviour. Observation, imitation and questioning are all task strategies used by novices that facilitate subsequent self-regulatory behaviours. An understanding of task strategies and their rationales permits an awareness of the need for self-regulation and planning. Thus, an expert can effect a shift from task-specific solutions to a more generalised awareness of the need for self-monitoring and regulation as effective means for learning.

Simple novice-to-expert transitions as explanations of development have been criticised (see Brown & Reeve, 1987), but the account offered by Azmitia is in accordance with a more socially mediated form of development such as proposed by Vygotsky (1978). Indeed, it is Vygotsky's theoretical framework that Azmitia (1988) and Wood (1988) adopt to accommodate their results. The novice-to-expert shift is thus explained as occurring not just as the transmission of specific skills or expertise but as a facilitation towards greater autonomy and self-regulation. An ability to monitor and guide one's own behaviour is clearly a far-reaching skill, applicable to any particular domain. The teaching of task-related heuristics or strategies is accompanied by the increased awareness on the part of the novice of the importance and relevance of self-regulatory abilities and the need for careful planning and monitoring. It is precisely the widespread use of self-regulatory behaviours that facilitates the accomplishment of specific goals and the solution to problems in particular domains. In the jargon of cognitive psychology, experts have both declarative knowledge and procedural knowledge. They know when to deploy specific knowledge to achieve a particular goal. They have procedures that are activated to solve problems. A degree of self-regulation permits the appropriate activation and use of procedural knowledge.

The preceding sections of the chapter have attempted to highlight the pervasiveness of problem solving both empirically and theoretically as a developmental research topic. It basically covers all manner of issues, with little commonality. There are a few general points worth noting in relation to the motivating mechanism for developmental change that require elaboration. Developmental change depends on the growth of representations at increasingly higher levels of abstraction, the growth of procedural knowledge, and the networking of isolated, fragmented representations via the compilation of increasing amounts of declarative knowledge. In any domain, thinking and problem solving become more flexible and abstract, less tied to the concrete. Nonetheless, fundamentally it still needs to be established whether developmental change is provoked by external, largely social, circumstances, or whether change is a result of internal, possibly innate, cognitive changes. The latter could either be wholly innate or could themselves be the results of behavioural changes, as Karmiloff-Smith has argued and as was described earlier in the chapter. I believe that social processes are fundamental to developmental change in problem-solving abilities. Social interaction facilitates the development of representation, particularly in children, and this then mediates future problem-solving developments and accomplishments.

PROBLEM SOLVING AS INDUCTION

It is imperative to remember that problem solving, however conceived, has a large social component. Children's developing understanding of the world and their attempts to find successful strategies and solutions to problems require exogenous social processes (see Garton, 1992, for a fuller discussion of this issue). Nonetheless, there is also an endogenous component, either genetically driven or dependent on initial external impetus. This view is characterised by the child as the little scientist (e.g. see Karmiloff-Smith, 1988) but has in recent times been developed along more sophisticated theoretical lines (e.g. Carey, 1985; Markman, 1989). A debate now exists regarding the extent to which the developing child should be regarded as an hypothesis-testing, theory-building scientist or as an inductivist, constrained by under-defined innate mechanisms (or parameters) that check progress until sufficient positive exemplars (of a concept, of word meaning or of a grammatical rule, for example) have been recorded to permit their specification. The under-specified rules are completed and 'fixed' according to whatever concepts, language(s) or contexts the child is exposed. It may be that the two are not really opposing hypotheses.

Induction of rules is regarded as a powerful developmental mechanism for cognitive growth. In the case of language development, induction can operate to capture relational, perceptual and conceptual similarities across objects. Induction presupposes the existence of categories that conceptualise the world and also that these categories are learned on the basis of implicit theories (Carey, 1985). Constraints oversee the developmental process by imposing limitations on the potential hypotheses that can be entertained, for example, during word learning. The constraints are structural (Keil, 1979; Carey, 1985) and both facilitate and restrict conceptual and language development. Natural kind categories (e.g. Gelman & Markman, 1986) capture categories based on intuitive similarities rather than perceptual appearances. Young children appear to base inductions on natural kinds (Markman, 1989). These natural kinds include thematic grouping, taxonomic groupings and family resemblances. A top-down processing mechanism, conceptually driven, forces category membership based initially on implicit knowledge (or constraints). Perceptual similarity may well be overlooked in favour of categories that support inductions. A highly developed and honed induction system would allow for rapid and probably accurate categorisation, which itself could be regarded as a problem-solving activity or which could advance other cognitive skills.

The processes involved in induction are regarded as different to those when we consider the child as a young scientist, testing, falsifying and confirming hypotheses in the real world. From these processes are derived internal representations that underlie subsequent behaviour. The inductivist child builds theories via endogenously provoked mechanisms; they are not socially mediated. To encompass these two views of how the child develops, Karmiloff-Smith (1988) expands the notion of the child as a problem solver. The child can also be viewed as a problem generator. Whilst initial learning might be determined by the environment, including the social environment, subsequent developmental change stems from exploitation of existing representations.

We must, however, not lose sight of the fact that social mediation is a vital element in cognitive development, the development of representation and in problem solving in particular. I wish to illustrate this claim with a range of experimental data which will show that the social mediation of representational activity is an important explanatory and possibly facilitatory mechanism.

PROBLEM SOLVING AS A SOCIAL ACTIVITY

The argument for adherence to a social basis for all developmental change has largely been driven by Vygotsky's theory (1962, 1978, 1986). In Vygotsky's opinion, *all* change—historical, economic, socio-political and developmental (linguistic and cognitive)—results from a dialectic between the prevailing (members of a) culture and the less knowledgeable. The latter gain knowledge (skill, expertise) through interacting with those persons responsible for teaching, defending or disseminating the beliefs and traditions of the existing socio-historical-cultural group. While Bruner (1962; see also 1984) believes the parallel between the developing child and the culture is perhaps erroneous, there are clear implications for developmental theory. And these implications have in recent years been driving developmental research, both practically and theoretically (Wood, 1988; Garton & Pratt, 1989).

An example of how Vygotskian theory has influenced research on problem solving is the study by Wertsch *et al.* (1980). Unlike the studies by Azmitia (1988) and Wood *et al.* (1978) already described, where Vygotsky's theory was invoked to explain patterns of results, the series of studies conducted by Wertsch and his colleagues has been driven by Vygotsky's theory rather than by the studies of novice-to-expert transitions (although the two are not wholly unconnected). In the study by Wertsch *et al.* (1980), mothers and their preschool children were observed whilst carrying out a jigsaw-puzzle problem. The main aim of the study was to examine the shift in *strategic responsibility*, rather than of expertise, from the mother to the child, both within the experimental session and across different ages ($2\frac{1}{2}$, $3\frac{1}{2}$ and $4\frac{1}{2}$ year olds were involved). Examination was made of the regulatory devices used by the mothers such as eye gazes and communicative language to guide and monitor their children's behaviour and how these strategies were adopted by the children once their significance was realised. The child's gaze to the model (from which to copy the jigsaw-puzzle) was taken as the best measure of the effectiveness of maternal strategic behaviour.

It was found that with increasing age, there was an increase in self-regulated gazes to the model and a concomitant decrease in maternal-regulated gazes. The success of these child-regulated gazes was measured in subsequent correct selection of a puzzle piece and its insertion in the jigsaw. In contrast, the younger children, once directed to the copy, required additional guidance for puzzle piece selection and insertion. It was concluded that the older children, unlike the younger children, could adopt behaviours of strategic significance and understand their utility in solving the problem. Studies such as this one indicate that adult–child interaction provides opportunities on the interpersonal plane for cognitive processes to have strategic and regulatory significance. Adoption of the relevant activities permits their use on the intrapersonal plane, enabling self-regulation and monitoring of successful problem-solving behaviours.

Notwithstanding the potential for dual mechanisms (endogenous and/or exogenous) being prerequisite for cognitive growth, an adherence to more socially governed (if not determined) processes of problem solving is advocated. Adoption of such a perspective influences a number of other important things, as Bruner & Haste (1987) remind us. These are discussed in relation to methodology, self-regulation, social representation, and language and discourse.

The *methodology* regarded as appropriate for examining the influence of social processes on children's developing problem-solving skills is usually a naturalistic (or quasi-naturalistic) one. Adults, usually mothers, and their children are watched or video-taped as they solve whatever problem comes either spontaneously or at the behest of the investigator. So for example, mothers and their children have been observed constructing jigsaw-puzzles (Wertsch *et al.*, 1980), reading books together (e.g. DeLoache & DeMendoza, 1987), and engaging in sorting tasks (Freund, 1990). For a review of some of the relevant research, see Rogoff & Gardner (1984).

Regarding problem solving as a social process necessitates a perception of a young child as competent and *self-regulatory*. The child must be able to deal with the social and environmental input in meaningful ways. The child's competencies must also be regarded as increasing, permitting greater flexibility in the range and type of problem that can be tackled. This view retains some sympathy with the inductivist position expounded by Karmiloff-Smith and discussed earlier. It also engenders favour from a social psychological perspective, including the work of Vygotsky and his emphasis on the relationship between individual development and the socio-historical development of the culture, and the work of sociologists Berger & Luckman (1966) with their 'social construction of reality'. Bruner & Haste (1987) forefront language as the creator and circumscriber of meaning and interpretation of experience. Echoing Vygotsky, they stress how language must be used in the company of another person to permit its meaningful expression, and through a process of language use and understanding, of hearing language and of having meanings unravelled, does both the child's language and its cognition develop. The research reported by Lloyd & Duveen (Chapter 9) illustrates how gender is a socially defined entity, culturally determined both linguistically and non-linguistically (such as via the assignment of 'gender-appropriate' toys and clothes to young children).

Social representations, which include such things as gender, are also important in problem solving. A child does not develop in a vacuum but is part of an ever-increasing and more complex social network. Children can benefit from working with others, especially adults or more competent peers (Vygotsky, 1978), and collaboration with others has a proven beneficial effect on a child's individual problem-solving capabilities. It is this latter aspect that I will dwell on in greater detail during the remainder of this chapter, but for some of the more traditional research and theoretical interpretations, see Garton (1992). Through language, there is facilitation of the solution of the current problem via scaffolding, the hypothetical supportive mechanism provided by an adult to a less able child (in whatever domain). In addition, there is the negotiation and co-construction of meaning by the participants and there is the transmission of cultural values, interpretations and meanings from the more experienced member of the culture to the less experienced. This transfer of cultural representations is at the heart of interactive communication and enables children to enter and remain part of the prevailing culture. The confluence of facilitation and cultural interpretations is unique to language and permits children to 'solve' all manner of tricky problems as they encounter them.

Obviously, *language* has a fundamental role in the development of successful problem solving—not just language in the sense of correct words and grammar, but in the sense of communication. Language is the means by which information is conveyed during interaction problem-solving sessions or sequences and must have a role, whether to control the speed or direction of the actual interchange, to specify the content of the way to solve the problem, to regulate the behaviour of the other participant, or to comment on ongoing success or failure. There is a myriad of uses of language in interaction that prevail upon the outcome of the particular form of problem solving under scrutiny. These will also be discussed in relation to the illustrative research examples presented.

STUDIES OF REPRESENTATION IN PROBLEM SOLVING

In the previous discussion on problem solving, reference was made to representation, but it was then undefined. Bearing in mind some of the definitional issues raised above, it is pertinent to consider some illustrative research integrating representation and problem solving. Typical research studies have examined potential representational mechanisms that facilitate successful problem solving. Such representational mechanisms can be externally (i.e. socially) mediated props, characterised as scaffolding (Wood, 1988), or mental models. Amongst the latter would be included such concepts as *metacognition, reflexive abstraction* and notions of *self-regulation, planning* and *monitoring*.

The study of external props, or scaffolding or 'contingent teaching', has focused on how sensitive, graded instruction provided by a more competent teacher can facilitate learning. The problem solving domains in which scaffolding has been studied have ranged from early language (Bruner, 1977, 1983) through to problem solving *per se* (Wood *et al.*, 1978; Wood, Bruner & Ross, 1976), or 'everyday activities' (Wood, 1988). What characterises adult assistance to children solving problems is the provision of regular and structured experiences from which children can learn. Adults point out the relevant details of the problem and ensure that children pay attention to these aspects. Adults remind children of the need to recall and remember past experiences and knowledge that they can bring to bear to the current situation. Adults provide a broader perspective on problem solving, focusing on the overall outcome or goal, not simply on the accomplishment of the immediate sub-task. Adults offer reassurance, praise and confirmation that results are being achieved. As Wood (1988) states, 'Pointing out, reminding, suggesting and praising, all serve to orchestrate and structure the child's activities...' (p. 76). These social props are then internalised by the child, permitting mental self-regulation. Learning thus involves not only the accomplishment of a particular goal but also the child learning how to structure her own knowledge and experience.

Internal representational systems have also been shown to have value in problem-solving situations. Cocking & Copple (1987) argue that the ability to form mental representations is at the root of all planning activities. Planning, as has been discussed, is one of the components of self-regulatory behaviour, essential for problem solving. In addition, Cocking & Copple believe that planning and metacognition share many common abilities and processes, e.g. representation, reflectiveness and awareness. They argue for the importance of representation in communication, memory and thinking, in particular about non-present objects and events. Representation and concept formation are regarded as fundamental to mental organisation and systematisation of what would otherwise be a chaotic state. Experiences need to be structured somehow to permit ordered reflection and anticipation. In addition, representation is accorded a central role in intellectual growth.

Many research studies lend credence to the view that the creation of mental models of experience assist in learning, specifically problem solving (Cocking & Copple, 1987; Small, 1990). However, some research has shown that the adoption of a mental model may constrain or hinder problem solving through the persistence of a mental 'set'. Planning skills apparently become obvious (recorded via successful use) around the age of $3\frac{1}{2}$ years (Wellman, Fabricus & Sophian, 1985), but this finding does not mitigate against planning occurring at a younger age. However, it seems as though mental representation, as a form of internal 'scaffolding', does benefit problem solving through the improved deployment of relevant and flexible strategies based on effective self-regulation.

HOW REPRESENTATIONAL ACTIVITY CHANGES

In this final section, the impact of social influences on representational activity and how this facilitates successful problem solving will be considered. Integrating some of the notions discussed so far will permit the postulation of a model to show how representation influences problem-solving activity, in particular problem-solving success. I have argued that social processes are fundamental both to problem solving and to representation, and the important social processes are the shift of regulation from more to less competent and the use of language to communicate. Language can be considered as a representational activity *per se* or it can be viewed as a representational activity within a communicative system. While the two are not mutually exclusive, it is this latter definition that will be used here in accordance with previous discussion (Garton & Pratt, 1989; Garton, 1992).

Language is regarded as the channel of communication between at least two active participants in interaction. Language is used to convey culturally conventionalised meanings to young children, who then internalise these whilst becoming competent social and linguistic beings. Language is thus also a representational system, which is actively used by children in the course of development. According to Vygotsky (1978), in problem-solving contexts, language used in the presence of others during interaction qualitatively changes what would be termed 'metacognitive skills'. *How* are planning, monitoring and evaluation influenced by socially mediated speech?

Metarepresentation is a term used to describe a level of representation and representational activity that permits more efficient functioning, in particular success on problem-solving tasks. Social interaction activates metarepresentational changes (Garton, 1992). Metarepresentation incorporates knowledge of and understanding of systems and uses of representation and how awareness contributes to even greater cognitive flexibility, permitting even more efficacious problem solving. Such higher order representations are essential aspects of the representational changes that occur as a result of social interaction. Language is the medium that ensures metarepresentations are culturally conventional and appropriate, permitting insight and awareness into the value of both external and internal cognitive and social support.

In terms of problem solving, communication is the means by which successful solutions are achieved. To adopt a term used by Strayer & Moss (1989), during social interaction there is the *co-construction of representational activity*. Although I do not intend to embrace the transactional framework advocated by Strayer & Moss, some of their ideas connect well with concepts discussed in this chapter. Strayer & Moss discuss the social construction of representation in relation to joint problem solving. Their distinction between *elaborative* tactics and *metacognitive* tactics has a direct parallel with adult attention-focusing and directing activities and child self-regulatory behaviours respectively. It has been mentioned in this chapter that the role of the adult in an instructional or problem-solving interaction is to focus and maintain the child's attention and to shift the onus for task regulation. Although the distinction between elaborative and meta-cognitive tactics may be an arbitrary one, both activities occur in problem-solving sequences and both activities may be considered to achieve representational change. A responsive adult in a problem-solving dyad will facilitate the development of self-regulatory activities as well as ensuring success on the immediate task.

Other aspects of adult support not discussed here include the adult's role in facilitating language development (Garton & Pratt, 1989; Garton, 1992) both in terms of scaffolded assistance and specific linguistic input. In addition, it is important that the child participates in the collaborative process and accepts and acts on the support and advice offered by the adult. Adult assistance facilitates representational change, particularly in Vygotsky's 'zone of proximal development' (1978), since there is aware-ness of children's actual cognitive level as well as their potential level. Accurate monitoring by an adult of a child's progress as well as regulation of representational abilities can influence cognitive growth in the long term as well as ensuring short-term problem-solving success. Diagrammatically, this process is shown in Figure 13.1.

The final aspect involved in this developmental sequence is the role played by language. Language is a critical element in the social interaction

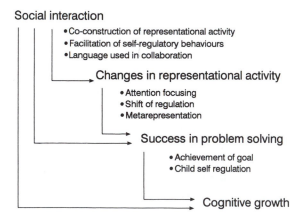

Figure 13.1 Progress in problem-solving success (the bulleted concepts are the processes involved)

sequence since language permits the achievement of a social and communicative framework within which representational models can be negotiated, maintained and established. Representational activity is co-constructed via language during social interaction. It is not assumed that this is all a one-way process, with the child adopting the adult's representational model unquestioningly. Rather there is negotiation between participants, and language is the vehicle whereby this can take place.

Representational activity can be triggered, negotiated, constructed or consolidated via discussion, questioning or criticism in either collaboration or in conflict during interaction. Both participants can use language (sometimes to a greater or lesser extent) and both come to the problem-solving context with some level of understanding of what has to be achieved. This is true whatever the domain of the problem—language, jigsaw-puzzles or mathematics. Joint negotiation of both the procedural and declarative aspects of the problem needs to take place, since this facilitates subsequent progress (Forman & Cazden, 1985; Renshaw & Garton, 1986). In so doing, representations, both procedural and declarative, are altered, engendering a successful short-term goal of solving the task (learning the language or completing the jigsaw) as well as the longer-term outcome of a shift from adult to child regulation. Cognitive growth is the beneficial outcome of social interaction, the development of representational abilities and successful problem solving.

REFERENCES

Azmitia, M. (1988). Peer interaction and problem solving: when are two heads better than one? *Child Development*, **59**, 87–96.

Berger, P. and Luckman, T. (1966). *The Social Construction of Reality*. Harmondsworth: Penguin.

Brown, A.L. and DeLoache, J. (1978). Skills, plans and self-regulation. In R.S. Siegler (ed.), *Children's Thinking: What Develops?* Hillsdale, New Jersey: Lawrence Erlbaum.

Brown, A.L. and Reeve, R. (1987). Bandwidths of competence: the role of supportive contexts in learning and development. In L.S. Liben (ed.), *Development or Learning: Conflict or Congruence?* Hillsdale, New Jersey: Lawrence Erlbaum.

Bruner, J.S. (1962). Introduction. In L. Vygotsky, *Thought and Language*. Cambridge, Massachusetts: MIT Press.

Bruner, J.S. (1977). Early social interaction and language development. In H.R. Schaffer (ed.), *Studies in Mother–Child Interaction*. London: Academic Press.

Bruner, J.S. (1983). *Child's Talk*. New York: Norton.

Bruner, J.S. (1984). Vygotsky's zone of proximal development: the hidden agenda. In B. Rogoff and J.V. Wertsch (eds), *Children's Learning in the 'Zone of Proximal Development'*. San Francisco: Jossey Bass.

Bruner, J.S. and Haste, H. (1987). Introduction. In J.S. Bruner & H. Haste (eds), *Making Sense: The Child's Construction of the World*. London: Methuen.

Carey, S. (1985). *Conceptual Change in Childhood*. Cambridge, Massachusetts: MIT Press/Bradford Books.

Chi, M.T.H. (1978). Knowledge structures and memory development. In R. Siegler (ed.), *Children's Thinking: What Develops?* Hillsdale, New Jersey: Lawrence Erlbaum.

Cocking, R.R. and Copple, C.E. (1987). Social influences on representational awareness: plans for representing and plans as representation. In S.L. Friedman, E.K. Scholnick and R.R. Cocking (eds), *Blueprints for Thinking: The Role of Planning in Cognitive Development*. Cambridge: Cambridge University Press.

DeLoache, J. and DeMendoza, O. (1987). Joint picturebook interactions of mothers and 1-year-old children, *British Journal of Developmental Psychology*, **5**, 111–123.

Forman, E. and Cazden, C. (1985). Exploring Vygotskian perspectives in education: the cognitive value of peer interaction. In J.V. Wertsch (ed.), *Culture, Communication and Cognition: Vygotskian Perspectives*. Cambridge: Cambridge University Press.

Freund, L. (1990). Maternal regulation of children's problem-solving behaviour and its impact on children's performance, *Child Development*, **61**, 113–126.

Garton, A.F. (1992). *Social Interaction and the Development of Language and Cognition*. Hove: Lawrence Erlbaum.

Garton, A.F. and Pratt, C. (1989). *Learning to be Literate: The Development of Spoken and Written Language*. Oxford: Basil Blackwell.

Garton, A.F. and Renshaw, P.D. (1988). Linguistic processes occurring in disagreements in young children's dyadic problem solving, *British Journal of Developmental Psychology*, **6**, 275–284.

Gelman, S. and Markman, E. (1986). Categories and induction in young children, *Cognition*, **23**, 183–209.

Goswami, U. (1991). Analogical reasoning: what develops? A review of research and theory, *Child Development*, **62**, 1–22.

Hayes-Roth, B. and Hayes-Roth, F. (1979). A cognitive model of planning, *Cognitive Science*, **3**, 275–310.

Kail, R.V. (1984). *The Development of Memory in Children*, 2nd edn. New York: Freeman.

Karmiloff-Smith, A. (1984). Children's problem solving. In M.E. Lamb, A.L. Brown and B. Rogoff (eds), *Advances in Developmental Psychology, Vol. 3*. Hillsdale, New Jersey: Lawrence Erlbaum.

Karmiloff-Smith, A. (1986). From meta-processes to conscious repair: evidence from children's metalinguistic and repair data, *Cognition*, **23**, 95–147.

Karmiloff-Smith, A. (1988). The child is a theoretician, not an inductivist, *Mind and Language*, **3**, 1–13.

Karmiloff-Smith, A. and Inhelder, B. (1974). If you want to get ahead, get a theory, *Cognition*, **3**, 195–212.

Keil, F. (1979). *Semantic and Conceptual Development: An Ontological Perspective*. Cambridge, Massachusetts: Harvard University Press.

Klahr, D. and Wallace, J.G. (1976). *Cognitive Development: An Information Processing View*. Hillsdale, New Jersey: Lawrence Erlbaum.

Markman, E. (1989). *Naming and Categorization: Problems of Induction*. Cambridge, Massachusetts: MIT Press/Bradford Books.

Renshaw, P.D. and Garton, A.F. (1986). Children's collaboration and conflict in dyadic problem solving. In C. Pratt, A.F. Garton, W.E. Tunmer and A.R. Nesdale (eds), *Research Issues in Child Development*. Sydney: Allen and Unwin Australia.

Rogoff, B. and Gardner, W. (1984). Adult guidance of cognitive development. In B. Rogoff and J. Lave (eds), *Everyday Cognition: Its Development in Social Context*. Cambridge, Massachusetts: Harvard University Press.

Siegler, R.S. (1983). Information processing approaches to development. In P.H. Mussen (ed.), *Handbook of Child Psychology, Vol. 1*: W. Kessen (ed.), *History, Theory and Methods*. New York: Wiley.

Small, M. (1990). *Cognitive Development*. New York: Harcourt Brace Jovanovich.

Strayer, F.F. and Moss, E. (1989). The co-construction of representational activity during social interaction. In M. Bornstein and J.S. Bruner (eds), *Interaction in Human Development*. Hillsdale, New Jersey: Lawrence Erlbaum.

Vygotsky, L. (1962). *Thought and Language*. Cambridge, Massachusetts: MIT Press.

Vygotsky, L. (1978). *Mind in Society: The Development of Higher Mental Processes*. Cambridge, Massachusetts: Harvard University Press.

Vygotsky, L. (1986). *Thought and Language, New edn*. Cambridge, Massachusetts: MIT Press.

Wellman, H.M., Fabricus, W.V. and Sophian, C. (1985). The early development of planning. In H.M. Wellman (ed.), *Children's Searching and the Development of Search Skill and Spatial Representation*. Hillsdale, New Jersey: Lawrence Erlbaum.

Wertsch, J.V., McNamee, G.D., McLane, J.B. and Budwig, N.A. (1980). The adult–child dyad as a problem-solving system, *Child Development*, **51**, 1215–1221.

Wood, D. (1988). *How Children Think and Learn*. Oxford: Basil Blackwell.

Wood, D., Bruner, J.S. and Ross, G. (1976). The role of tutoring in problem solving, *Journal of Child Psychology and Psychiatry*, **17**, 89–100.

Wood, D., Wood, H. and Middleton, D.J. (1978). An experimental evaluation of four face-to-face teaching strategies, *International Journal of Behavioural Development*, **1**, 131–147.

Author Index

Subject Index